THE BAPTISTS

WILLIAM H. BRACKNEY

Foreword by Henry Warner Bowden

Westport, Connecticut
London

For Mildred Pointer Brackney,
my Mother

The Library of Congress has cataloged the hardcover edition as follows:

Brackney, William H.
The Baptists.

(Denominations in America, ISSN 0193–6883 ; no. 2)
Bibliography: p.
Includes index.
1. Baptists—United States. I. Title. II. Series.
BX6235.B628 1988 286 87–15047
ISBN 0–313–23822–7 (lib. bdg. : alk. paper)

British Library Cataloguing in Publication Data is available.

An expanded, hardcover edition of *The Baptists* is available
from the Greenwood Press imprint of Greenwood Publishing
Group, Inc. (Denominations in America, Number 2; ISBN: 0–313–23822–7).

Library of Congress Catalog Card Number: 87–15047
ISBN: 0–275–94859–5 (pbk.)

First published in 1994

Praeger Publishers, 88 Post Road West, Westport, CT 06881
An imprint of Greenwood Publishing Group, Inc.

Printed in the United States of America

The paper used in this book complies with the
Permanent Paper Standard issued by the National
Information Standards Organization (Z39.48–1984).

P

CONTENTS

FOREWORD

The Praeger series of denominational studies follows a distinguished precedent. These current volumes improve on earlier works by including more churches than before and by looking at all of them in a wider cultural context. The prototype for this series appeared almost a century ago. Between 1893 and 1897, twenty-four scholars collaborated in publishing thirteen volumes known popularly as the American Church History Series. That shelf of books found twenty religious groups to be worthy of separate treatment, either as major sections of a volume or as whole books to themselves. Scholars in this current series have found that outline to be unrealistic, with regional subgroups no longer warranting separate status and others having sunk to marginality. Twenty organizations in the earlier series survive as nine in this collection, while two churches and an interdenominational bureau have been omitted. The old series also excluded some important churches of that time; others have risen to great strength since then. So today a new list of denominations, rectifying imbalance and recognizing modern significance, features many groups not included a century ago. The solid core of the old series remains in this new one, and in the present case a wider range of topics makes the study of denominational life in America more inclusive.

Some recent denominational histories have improved with greater attention to primary sources and more rigorous scholarly standards, but they have too frequently pursued themes for internal consumption alone. Their solipsistic priorities focus on developments interesting to insiders who assume that their group constitutes everything necessary for true religious expression. Volumes in the Praeger series strive to surmount parochialism while remaining grounded in the specific materials of concrete ecclesiastical traditions. They avoid placing a single denomination above others in its distinctive truth claims, ethical norms, and liturgical patterns. Instead, they set the history of each church in the larger religious and social context that shaped the emergence of notable denominational features.

In this way the authors in this series help us understand the interaction that has occurred between different churches and the broader aspects of American culture.

Each of the historical studies in this current series has a strong biographical focus, utilizing the real-life experiences of men and women in church life to highlight significant elements of an unfolding sequence. Every volume singles out important watershed issues that affected each particular denomination's outlook and discusses the roles of those who influenced the flow of events. This format allows authors to emphasize the distinctive features of their chosen subject and at the same time to recognize the sharp particularities of individual attributes in the cumulative richness that their denomination possesses.

This book by William H. Brackney brings together the central threads of a denomination known for ideological squabbling and institutional splintering. Its thoughtful consideration of shared characteristics allows room for idiosyncratic forms as developed over the past three centuries. Brackney identifies an emphasis on religious experience, a particular mode of baptism, and a conception of church autonomy as the only durable traits to which Baptists have adhered in various times and places. While unifying principles are few, he points out that their persistence nevertheless suffices to incorporate a host of different movements under this denominational canopy. Under such broad conceptions he also shows how environmental and cultural influences have determined the direction of local Baptist life. Members have responded variously to every important question regarding intellectual issues, moral behavior (collective as well as personal), and questions involving social change. This subtheme of variability helps explain how some members could be liberal theologians and others fundamentalists, some ethical relativists and others authoritarian, some advocates of cultural reform and others defenders of the status quo. Baptists have been, and are, all these and more. This seminal study clarifies their origins and charts their many vigorous expressions that still represent a spectrum of options at the present time.

HENRY WARNER BOWDEN

PREFACE

Those who cautiously presume to interpret Baptist history will find early in their investigations a formidable obstacle in their path: Baptists are a denominational family with a common heritage, while at the same time they have done everything imaginable to atomize their respective identities as local churches, associations, and individual fellowships, with few external relationships. Often, it is only the historian who sees the broader patterns, similarities and linkages with a common tradition. Baptists struggle with their history and with historians, and no one can hope to blend all of the ingredients into a recipe which is palatable to all family members. However, the historians heroically pursue their quest.

Happily, there are those within and without the Baptist fold who welcome a general perspective on Baptist life as a part of the greater American religious mosaic, people who emphasize commonality and consensus over differentiation. That is what this book is all about. As I have read and observed Baptist history and behavior there are five vertices which are important to all Baptists: the Bible, the Church, the ordinances/sacraments, voluntarism, and religious liberty. My focus has been upon Baptists in North America, with references to English and European Baptists where appropriate.

Following the main text, there is a bibliographic essay with suggestions for further study. Readers will also find a chronology of Baptist history relevant to North America, and a listing of major Baptist groups (this is the *only* volume in which this last information appears in one place, updated through 1992).

ACKNOWLEDGMENTS

John Bunyan, a nonconformist minister of the Restoration period in English history, envisioned the Christian life as a pilgrimage, and later Baptists have been fond of his metaphor. My own pilgrimage involves over four decades among the Baptists in a family, various congregations, denominational service, and theological education in five institutions internationally. I have had the privilege of sharing in the ministry of Baptists of several kinds and regions; most broadening has been my recent involvement in Canadian Baptist life which has created a North American perspective for me.

This edition is a revision of an earlier work, *The Baptists* (1988), in which I expressed appreciation to a number of people and institutions. In the preparation of this work, several others have been generous and helpful. They include James Lynch of the American Baptist Historical Society, Judith Coldwell of the Canadian Baptist Archives, and Ruby Burke of the Baptist World Alliance, who assisted in my research. Trustee chair, John Irwin and the Executive Committee of McMaster Divinity College, allowed me the time to complete the project. Norman Maring, J. K. Zeman, George Peck, Walter Shurden, Edwin S. Gaustad, Robert Handy, Reinhold Kerstan, and Clark Pinnock all offered helpful insights or historical suggestions. Student responses in my classes have been challenging and provocative. Terri Galan, administrative secretary to the principal, provided much-needed technical advice with the new manuscript. Peter Coveney of Greenwood Press, who suggested the revised edition, has been an affirmation of the value of my earlier work. Any infelicities or inadequacies in this edition are entirely my own.

Note: Asterisks next to various names throughout the text indicate that these individuals are the subjects of entries that make up the Biographical Dictionary which appears in the expanded hardcover edition.

INTRODUCTION:
THE PROBLEM OF BAPTIST IDENTITY

The issue of identity constitutes a major problem for the Baptists. Over the past three and one-half centuries Baptists have differed widely about their origins and their composition. Some have the notion that an unbroken line of "Baptistic" churches may be traced back to Jesus and the Apostles (or even John the Baptist!). Others find significant affinities between the Continental Anabaptists of the sixteenth century and the Baptists, so-called, of the 1600s. Still another interpretation is that Baptists arose out of the greater family of English Puritans/Separatists and are traceable to definite ecclesiological roots in that tradition. Finally, there are some modern Baptists who would argue that Baptists originate wherever and whenever the Holy Spirit calls forth a congregation which conforms to literal Biblical revelation, regardless of historical antecedents or relationships with any other groups. There will never be an answer which satisfies all or even most Baptists since there is no date, no place, and no person to whom all can look with complete confidence as the locus classicus of the movement.

If Baptists disagree about their origins, they are equally disagreeable about what constitutes a Baptist. Modern Baptists are sometimes described as "Bible-believing Christians" who "preach the book, the blood, and the blessed hope." Yet there are others who stress broad principles such as the priesthood of all believers, believers' baptism, regenerate church membership, the primacy of Scriptures, and congregational autonomy. And there are some who would call attention to religious liberty and the associational principle as the appropriate emphases. None would agree that Baptists are merely sacramentarians—insisting upon a particular mode of baptism—yet there is something to the suggestion that what all Baptists have in common is a visible sign of their faith in believers' baptism by immersion and the Christian experience that practice suggests.

The reason for disintegration among the people called Baptists often outweigh what Baptists hold in common. From the beginning of the seventeenth century when Baptists were historically identifiable by name, there were deep theological differences which rose out of differing socio-political and hermeneutical contexts. The English General Baptists favored a liberal interpretation of Christ's atonement while the Particular Baptists held to a more conventional Calvinistic viewpoint. Within four decades of the establishment of the first Baptist church on English soil in 1611, a third stream emerged which adopted sabbatarian views. These same basic differences characterized Baptists in America in the seventeenth and eighteenth centuries, where their numbers indicated measurable success in propagating their views. In the nineteenth century, Baptists differed over organizational styles, the nature of the church, moral issues, and regionalism. In the twentieth century, their differences are focused on ecumenism, the sacraments, organizations, and hermeneutics. In many ways Baptists resemble the primitive Church; both the Baptists and the early Church were forced to deal with similar theological and social issues, both recognizing only one source of authority, the biblical tradition. Since Scripture is lent to so many interpretations and styles, it is no wonder that Christians, then and now, who predicate their identity upon such a foundation, should be so diverse.

The Baptist self-understanding begins with Scripture. Early Baptists argued solely from Scripture in contrast to the Anglicans, Presbyterians, and Catholics, who built upon Scripture, tradition, and at times, reason. Collectively, modern Baptists continue to maintain a very high view of Scripture and, in some cases, come close to bibliolatry in their attempts to purify theology of human and historical inventions. For most, the Bible is a manual of specific guidelines and principles for the Christian believer and the corporate fellowship. All hypotheses must be validated by being tested against the Old and New Testaments. Biblical language, metaphors, and illustrations dominate Baptist sermons, literature, and organizational life. Long before biblical theology was fashionable, Baptists were crudely practicing its techniques.

Next in importance is the Baptist view of the Church. For all Baptists the most vivid expression of the Christian community is the local congregation. Each congregation most closely resembles the New Testament church when it includes those who have claimed Jesus Christ as Lord and Savior and have covenanted to practice their Christian faith diligently. Each church represents the whole Church and is sufficiently spiritually endowed to govern its own affairs and determine its own identity. Baptists believe that in an imperfect world, such churches together constitute the visible Body of Christ, to use the biblical motif.

Third, Baptists share a common concern for a witness to their religious experience. Some give evidence of this by energetically sharing their convictions with others; this trend has produced countless missionaries and self-styled evangelists in the movement. In contrast, other Baptists, a bit more quiescent, choose to illustrate their faith in the act of believers' baptism, where their ritual depicts the death, burial, and resurrection of Jesus Christ, each time that it is practiced publicly. It is common to all Baptists to assert that believers' baptism by immersion suggests ultimate obedience to Christ as evidenced in the biblical accounts of his ministry.

Scripture, the Church, and Christian witness, then, comprise the core of the Baptist character, when understood in relation to each other and with an undiminished sense of fidelity and commitment. More often than not, Baptists arrive at their self-understanding after much struggle and persecution. One cannot, then, fully understand Baptists out of their socio-political and religious contexts.

More often than not, opponents of the Baptist persuasion have set the agenda in Baptist identity. Historically, when Baptists have met with opposition, they have bristled and redoubled their efforts. Their views have never been easily accepted among other Christian groups, in part because of the manner in which Baptists advocate them. Consider, for instance, the case which Baptists made in the seventeenth century for religious liberty. Beyond the reasoned calls for toleration of all religious views, Baptists slandered the parish churches as unscriptural, false systems usurping the Christian gospel. In the nineteenth century, when Baptists experimented with inter-evangelical organized missionary endeavor, they soon broke fellowship with "pedo-baptists" because infant baptism was "vain and superstitious"! In the twentieth century, Baptists have been known to scathingly rebuke each other for toleration of modernistic interpretations of biblical passages or the mores of popular culture. It matters not whether the foe is the truly pagan or a different form of Christian expression; most Baptists are not by nature given to compromise. As one early writer put it, "We would rather be stript of all outward comforts . . . than act against the light of our own consciences."[1]

Negatively, then, Baptists may be characterized as biblicists who build their sense of the Church and its mission upon New Testament models and the visibility of the local congregation. Because of the sharp delineations in their ecclesiology and the vehemence with which they express their views, Baptists have also been seen as theologically reactionary. To no one's surprise, Baptist identity has often become a function of misunderstanding and non-Baptistic representations.

HISTORY AND IDENTITY

The history of the denomination thus serves as an important corrective. When the entire three centuries of Baptist evolution are laid out, significant patterns emerge and continuity of basic tenets is evident. Indeed, there are three critical points in documented Baptist history which serve to shape an evolving Baptist identity. These are the issuance of the London Confession in 1644, the establishment of the Baptist Missionary Society in 1792, and the formation of the Baptist Bible Union in 1923. Each signals a new departure in Baptist identity.

A little over three decades after the first congregation in England was started, seven churches primarily from the London area published what has come to be called the first London Confession of Faith. Although relative freedom for many dissenters was temporarily secured by the parliamentary government takeover in the 1640s, Baptists soon became the target of at least literary persecution which sought to identify them with the radical wing of Continental Anabaptists or Pelagianism and anarchy, or all three. In response, the Particular Baptists in London issued the Confession which sought above all else to link Baptists with the mainstream of English Protestant life.

Beyond its theological pronouncements and often infelicitous wording, the Confession represents an important departure for Baptists. As described earlier, the Baptist view of Scripture and the Church tended to favor independent, autonomous congregations which freely interpreted the Bible without reference to acceptable theological principles recognized in other, possibly similar churches. But the Baptist leaders soon determined that consultation with each other was helpful and regular informal meetings led to an agreement which produced a joint doctrinal statement or confession in 1644. In this statement from the several churches it was agreed that every single church is "a compact and knit city in itself" but also, significantly, "by all means convenient to have the counsel and help one of another in all needful affairs of the Church." These were not merely enthusiastic sectarians who were willing to "die a thousand deaths rather than to do anything against the least tittle of the truth of God." Here was the root of a genuine denominational spirit which sought its place in the recognized expressions of the Christian church.

While early Baptists carefully defined their doctrinal and practical differences with other groups, there is indisputable evidence that the two main divisions, General and Particular, desired voluntary relations within their confessions and at times with other groups, notably the Presbyterians and Congregationalists. This irenic attitude was confirmed in other English Baptist confessions and in the earliest American confessions and local church statements of faith. It was this posture which later allowed Baptists to agree on forms of missionary cooperation which helped to foster permanent national and international organizational unity. Only the early-nineteenth-century individualism expressed in the work of Francis Wayland and the Landmarkist Movement seriously threatened Baptist associationalism.

A second critical point occurred with the creation, in 1792, of the English Particular Baptist Society for the Propagation of the Gospel Among the Heathen. This organization, later known as the Baptist Missionary Society, was a response to William Carey's plea for world evangelistic outreach. The society was the first of the many voluntary associations which Baptists in Britain and America would create to fulfill the extra-congregational vision of their leadership. Singular in purpose, these organizations permitted involvement in education, home and foreign missions, literature distribution, and welfare efforts that were clearly beyond the scope of any single congregation and not in the agenda for associational life.

From the one initial society, Baptists responded quickly to form hundreds of these groups, often with interlocking directorates which allowed missions to give a cohesion to Baptist church life which otherwise autonomous sentiments militated against. This is especially relevant since virtually all of the major twentieth-century Baptist organizations have their origin in organized missionary endeavor.

By the establishment of the first missionary society Baptists became pro-active in world evangelization and denominational expansion.

Such organizational evolution also had its drawbacks for Baptists. Small groups in both Britain and the United States recoiled at the thought of "societies" which were not under the control of local congregations and which performed some tasks associated with congregational life. A combination of hyper-Calvinistic theology, Baptist distrust of structures, and regional individualism, led to large numbers of protesters variously called "antimissionists," "hardshells," or Primitive Baptists who refused to cooperate in such ventures. This disinclination continues into the twentieth century in the rise of independent Baptist churches which are highly critical of organized efforts and maintain missionary endeavors by direct sponsorship.

The third watershed event in the making of Baptist identity was the establishment of the Baptist Bible Union in 1923. This fundamentalist reaction to modernization forces in polity and the intellectual life of the denomination was the catalyst for disintegration along theological lines and set the pattern for Baptist life in the twentieth century. The Union was the coalescence of several streams of theological conservatism in Great Britain and the United States, including the legacy of Charles Haddon Spurgeon,* local church protectionism and the personal crusade of several young jeremiads in the Northern, Southern, and Canadian Conventions. By placing stress upon the autonomy of local congregations, leaders of the fundamentalist movement sought to redefine Baptist identity according to their own specifications, thus legitimating fragmentation.

For many Baptists caught in the uproar of the 1920s, the easiest and most comfortable solution to this dilemma of relationships (mainstream conventions or one of the fundamentalist groups) was to resort to traditional patterns of biblical authority and a simple, unadulterated New Testament faith. The more conservative Baptist leaders were aware of the popularity of their position and the simplicity of their solutions. For most Baptists it was an entirely acceptable premise to affirm complete loyalty to Scripture and the autonomy of the Church, even at the cost of mission, fellowship, and unity as a denomination. What was not clearly perceived at the time is that the Baptist penchant for Christian primitivism became confused with cultural anti-modernism and anti-progressivism; most Baptists found themselves identified with an archaic world view which was inextricably attached to a viable theological self-understanding. No longer could all Baptists agree on how Scripture is authoritative, what the nature of the Church to the churches is, or what constitutes Christian mission. Most Baptists chose to affirm the old formulae; the oldest unions and more affluent memberships opting for more flexible and progressive interpretations. The distance between many Baptists increased, therefore, and became greater than between some Baptists and non-Baptists, as a result of the formation of the Baptist Bible Union.

With all of the disintegrative forces which militate against pan-Baptist unity, the movement has still become a major force in the advance of global Christianity. Part of the generic believers' church tradition, Baptists emerged in definite socio-theological circumstances in early sixteenth-century England. Their principles quickly gained acceptance in the American colonies and thrived in an unusual way. The colonial revivals, plus a frontier experience which fostered individualism, allowed Baptists to overtake the older forms of evangelicalism in America by 1800. In less than three decades, American and British Baptists were exporting their faith to every continent in the inhabited world. While missionary expansion occurred overseas, expansion of another kind took place in the United States. Political and regional divisions among Baptists again dominated their development but did not diminish their numbers: By 1970 Southern Baptists were the largest non-Catholic group in U.S. religious statistics, and "independent" Baptists claimed the largest single congregations in the world. Presently, the Baptist World Alliance reports over 35 million Baptists worldwide with a regional breakdown as follows: Africa, 1 million; Asia, 1.5 million; Central America, 200,000; Europe, 1.2 million; North America, 30 million; South America, 600,000; Oceania, 100,000.

The story of that development follows.

THE BAPTISTS

1
AN OVERVIEW OF BAPTIST HISTORY

IN THE PURITAN-SEPARATIST TRADITION

John Smyth* of Cambridge rebaptized himself in early 1609, probably at his exiled home in Amsterdam and in the company of several who agreed with his action. With his baptism the modern Baptist movement is said to have begun. According to Smyth the reasoning behind this supremely audacious act was, "There is good warrant for a man churching himself. For two men singly are no church; so may two men put baptism upon themselves." He reasoned that as people who are unchurched can constitute a church with each other, so could they also assume the right to baptize themselves.[1]

Smyth had studied for the Anglican priesthood at Cambridge. However, in 1606 after lengthy consultation with Separatists and Brownists, he separated to gather a wholly new church of "saints" irrespective of parochial or diocesan boundaries. He and a group of like-minded folk formed a congregation at Gainsborough in Nottinghamshire, and Smyth assumed the role of a pastor. Modestly, the group decided to reconstitute the Church by entering into a convenant—a pledge between themselves and God "to walk in all His ways, made known or to be made known unto them . . . whatever it might cost them." This covenant among consenting adults was at the heart of the blossoming Free Church tradition and represented an absolute break with what the covenanters referred to as "the Church of Antichrist." Bypassing tradition altogether, it was a compact with God Himself: He had given the "whole Christ" to the faithful, and the faithful agreed to be God's people, to wholly deny themselves, and to obey every one of God's precepts.[2] The true Christian Church thus was reduced to single groups of professing believers.

Smyth's pilgrimage was not over. Once the Anglican authorities found out about the Gainsborough Church, persecution set in and the group voted to em-

*See Preface, p. viii, for explanation.

igrate to Amsterdam in late 1607. The Act of 1593, which had been renewed in the first year of King James (1603), declared that absence from one's parish church for a month, with intent to exercise religion in an unauthorized assembly, carried the penalty of imprisonment and possible perpetual banishment. Without a license, Smyth and his company of less than fifty members travelled by way of Trent and the Humber River to the open sea and the Dutch mainland. There they expected to worship and perfect their faith in freedom in consultation with other exiled English Christians.

In Smyth's attempts to reconstitute the Church on a literal New Testament model, he ran into one controversy after another. Smyth differed from Francis Johnson's exiled London congregation on the matter of Scripture in worship. Smyth would not tolerate the use of English translations because "it savoured of formality." He also opposed psalm-singing, sermon-reading, and collection of financial offerings from non-believers. Against John Robinson and others, Smyth contended that the officers of a true visible church were rightly confined to bishops (also called elders or presbyters) and deacons. These two offices were to be elected by members of a congregation and ordained only after fasting and prayer. For Smyth, church leaders were altogether accountable to the congregational body and for this reason, Smyth is rightly remembered as the first egalitarian among the Separatists.[3]

To no one's surprise, Smyth continued to search the Scriptures and came to the question of baptism. Perhaps under the influence of Dutch Waterlander Mennonites, perhaps from his own reading of Scripture, he concluded that a new baptism of believers was called for. His logic was impeccable: If the Church of England were really a false church then her baptism must be false. In organizing a new church on the New Testament model, there must be a new beginning with a valid baptism. Other Separatists had also earlier reached this conclusion but demured because "re-baptism" was associated with the dreaded radical continental Anabaptist movement. Not so John Smyth, who feared his covenant with God more than an ill reputation, and he made history when in 1609 he confessed his own faith, baptized himself and then Thomas Helwys* and several others present, thus constituting the first English Baptist Church in Amsterdam on the primitive Apostolic model.

In order to bring his congregation and doctrines into a broader circle of co-religionists or to be truly ecumenical in spirit, Smyth opened conversations with the Waterlander Mennonites, hoping that they would recognize his confession and baptism. He moved faster and farther than his English friends desired in this regard and by 1611 a small segment of the church led by Thomas Helwys withdrew to form a separate body. Although Helwys revered Smyth in most matters, he could not accept the Mennonite doctrine of Christ nor their principle of ministerial succession. When Smyth actually made application for Menonnite church membership, the Helwys group excommunicated him and proclaimed themselves another "true church." In failing health, Smyth continued to defend his views, and ultimately his following did join the Mennonite movement. He died in Holland in August 1616 and is justly revered as the fountainhead of consecutive Baptist history, as the English historian A. C. Underwood eloquently put it.

If John Smyth's baptismal audacity gave birth to the Baptist movement, Thomas Helwys followed in his train. Helwys was better born than Smyth and gave generously of his funds and hospitality at Broxtowe Hall in Nottinghamshire to support the original Separatist cause in Gainsborough. Probably it was he who provided funds for the journey to Holland and it was Helwys who experienced the most marked sense of alienation among the emigrés. After their arrival in Amsterdam, Helwys learned that his wife had been imprisoned at York as a matter of guilt by association. About the same time that Smyth embraced a Mennonite relationship, Helwys and his congregation made plans to return to England because "thousands of ignorant souls in our own country were perishing for lack of instruction." When Helwys made his dauntless return to England in 1612, he found "a general departing from the faith and an utter desolation of all true religion." Moreover, in the true strength of seventeenth-century enthusiasm, he felt a deep concern for the salvation of King James I.[4]

The congregation that Helwys established at Spitalfields near London in 1612 was so small in number that John Robinson quipped that he had gained more to the Lord than Mr. Helwys' Church consisted of! Yet, what the congregation lacked in members it contained in quality. This first Baptist church on English soil was made up entirely of laypersons with the officers and pastors also laity. It adopted a general view of the Atonement (that Christ died for all) and preached heroically in the midst of a great metropolitan area. Although Helwys and others were imprisoned more often than not, neither Puritans nor the civil authorities silenced the witness. Helwys's great contribution after his insistence upon a regenerate baptized church was his claim for complete religious liberty. As a libertarian, Thomas Helwys proclaimed a beginning of the end of the medieval synthesis of a Christian state. Although his words changed little in their immediate context, they resounded in the later writings of all those who held that God alone is Lord of the conscience.

Thomas Helwys was dead by 1616, and the leadership of the first Baptist Church in England shifted to Helwys's friend and protege, John Murton. Murton who issued a sequel to Helwys's call for religious liberty and was probably imprisoned for his remarks. In spite of a continuing leadership crisis, the church apparently thrived and was the catalyst for at least four other congregations about London, which by 1626 claimed to be General Baptists. These congregations were so theologically isolated because of their opposition to predestinarianism and their lack of trained clergy that their chief correspondents were the Dutch Waterlander Mennonites, whom Helwys had earlier rebuked rather stoutly. This relationship, with a few scattered membership transfers, lasted until the end of the century when English General Baptists drew closer either to their more Calvinistic brethren or to English Unitarians.[5]

Until the time of the English Civil Wars (1640–50) Baptists were for the most part considered a radical sect in English church life and frequently endured intolerance and persecution. Separatists, Independents, and other Puritan sects eschewed the Arminian theology and the Anabaptist practices of these General Baptists. Anglicans considered them dangerous schismatics and used political and ecclesiastical machinery to silence their message. It would not be until after mid-century that these first English General Baptists began to grow numerically, and even then some historians argue that their influence upon main currents of Baptist life was slight. However, the relative obscurity of the General Baptists was soon to be overshadowed by another distinct body of Baptists which emerged from a different set of circumstances.

Particular Baptists were so-called because, like the Independents from whom they sprang, the churches understood the doctrine of the Atonement to be limited to an elect group of saints. The first Particular Church is said to have evolved from a London Separatist Congregation which enjoyed an especially gifted series of pastors, beginning in 1616 with Henry Jacob, John Lathrop, and Henry Jessey. Within this church, as early as the 1620s, certain of the members were studying the New Testament on the matter of baptism; apparently concluding that infant baptism was unscriptural, they sought a believer's baptism. A similar circumstance occurred again in 1633. In 1638 six members of Henry Jessey's congregation seeking rebaptism separated to form an "anti-pedobaptist" (literally, opposed to infant baptism) fellowship, with John Spilsbury as pastor. Within three years, and after consultation with the Dutch Collegiants, the question of the proper mode of baptism was answered with the practice of immersion. Here was an innovation which the earlier General Baptists had not achieved; the record shows that in the 1640s they too became immersionists.

Much more is known of the identity of early Particular Baptists, and there is great variety. John Spilsbury was a commoner, a cobbler by trade. Publishing several titles which reveal his Calvinistic theological perspective, he is known to have enjoyed the respect of political leaders. Henry Cromwell, for instance, wanted Spilsbury to go to Ireland to assuage the revolutionary sentiments of the Irish Baptists. Another outstanding leader in the movement was William Kiffin,* an artisan who progressed in the brewing industry to a point of great wealth. Kiffin, though self-taught in the Scriptures, had also imbibed much of the thinking of John Lilburne, a Puritan and Leveller. In a debate with Anglican divines at Southwark in 1642, Kiffin represented the Baptists quite capably.[6] Finally, Hanserd Knollys* was an important leader among the Particular Baptists. Knollys was originally an Anglican clergyman, then an Independent in the Lathrop congregation; finally he adopted Baptist sentiments. Following a stay in the American colonies, Knollys returned to London where he was an exceedingly popular Baptist pastor who preached boldly against the Established Church. The great majority of the early Particular Baptists were biblically literate, theologically astute, comparatively sophisticated—a diverse lot in all.

A third stream of the Baptist persuasion also demands attention. Smaller in numbers, more heavily persecuted, and no less adamant about their faith were the Seventh Day Baptists. In the biblicism of the age when the Scriptures were being constantly reexamined as a standard of Free Church doctrine and practice, it is not surprising that a person or church should conclude that keeping the Sabbath was an inescapable requirement of biblical Christianity. Along with believer's baptism and, for some who held that the thousand-year reign of Christ was near, sabbatarianism was the chief distinguishing mark of Seventh Day Baptists, born probably about the mid-seventeenth century. Seventh Day historians have attempted to locate the first congregation at Mill Yard in London as early as 1617 but no records exist before 1673. The consensus is that the first full-fledged congregations appeared about 1640 (Natton), 1654 (Mill Yard), and 1652 (Dorchester). It is likely that individual members of established Baptist and Independent congregations at first broke away to keep the Sabbath; thus the location of many Seventh Day churches was in the vicinity of the First Day congregations. Another possible source of Seventh Day Baptist principles may have been the Fifth Monarchy movement which predicted an imminent earthly kingdom with Christ as its head.[7]

By 1665, at least ten Seventh Day churches were known to exist from London to Northumberland. Like other Baptists, the sabbatarians included well-to-do middle class adherents such as Dr. Peter Chamberlen (1601–83) at Mill Yard and Theophilus Brabourne (d. 1656) who left part of his estate for the upkeep of the Church at Norwich, Norfolk. Francis Bampfield (1615–84), earlier an Oxford-trained Anglican vicar at Sherborne in 1657, was also a pioneer. When he declined to take the Oath of Allegiance in 1662, he was imprisoned for nine years; during this time he adopted Seventh Day Baptist views.

The Seventh Day Baptists provide a kaleidoscopic variety to the early Baptists, and for their views they seem to have sustained more intense persecution in troubled times and enjoyed less toleration in permissive periods than their General or Particular brethren. This was obviously due to their position on the Sabbath, which resulted in their being grouped with such extremists as the Fifth Monarchists, Ranters, Seekers, and Quakers, all of whom maintained some sort of obvious idiosyncrasy. There is little evidence of relationships between First- and Seventh-Day congregations other than an occasional visit by a First Day minister such as Henry Jessey, who visited the Dorchester sabbatarians in 1655. Seventh Day Baptists did not join other Baptists as signatories to any of the confessions nor did they participate in the associational life of other Baptists.

By the middle of the seventeenth century, Baptists of all persuasions in the British Isles could count a large measure of progress. After suffering through the persecutions by Anglicans and then Presbyterians, the Baptists were the foci of a brief expression of Parliamentary favor in March 1647:

For their opinion against the baptism of *infants* it is only a difference about a circumstance of time in the administration of an *ordinance*, wherein former ages, as well as this, learned men have differed both in opinion and practice.[8]

Thomas Crosby thought that this change of opinion about Baptists was the result of either the increased numbers of Baptists, their presence in the Army, or the prominent business leaders who espoused Baptist principles. In any case, Baptists enjoyed legal toleration until the Ordinance of 2 May 1648, "for Punishing Blasphemies and Heresies," was issued by Parliament.

The presence of Baptists in the New Model Army is a vivid illustration of the progress which Baptists had made. William T. Whitley has shown the extent to which Baptists populated, educated, and officered Cromwell's forces and the concomitant effect this had on the growth of the sect. One of the marked distinctions between Baptists and the true Anabaptists was the willingness of the Baptists to bear arms. Not only did Baptists answer the call to arms largely as their means to secure religious liberty, but the most widely used drill books for both Cavalry and infantry were written by Baptists. Several in the denomination won their way to high ranks: Richard Deane was comptroller of ordnance and then a naval officer; Thomas Harrison organized and commanded the detachment which delivered Charles I and his Scottish friends to Worcester. Many of the regimental chaplains were Baptists who took advantage of an encampment to occupy the pulpit in a local parish church. In 1647, in the face of the Westminster Assembly's production of new service books, hymnals, and catechisms according to the principle of uniformity, Baptist officers in the Army organized a council to agitate on matters from pay arrears to religious liberty. When in the same year the army occupied London to quell the mob violence which had broken out, the members of Parliament were obliged to take seriously the proposals to repeal those statutes and customs which might lead to punishment for nonconformity. The Army was pleased when in November 1647 it was announced that while all persons were required to worship on the Lord's Day, "dissenters would enjoy the liberty to meet in any fit and convenient place."[9]

The obverse side of the Baptist presence in the military suggests more relevance to this connection. The Baptist soldiers and officers were effective evangelists. John Wigan planted the first Baptist congregation in Manchester while in service there; Colonel Rede captured the last rebellious infantry at Warrington where a Baptist church appeared within three years. In Ireland, similar circumstances obtained where Army officers were paid off in land grants wherein they settled in military colonies with their chaplains as pastors. Whitley estimated that in the fourteen precincts which formed the new divisions, nine of the governors were Baptists and that the church leadership was of a quality to be found nowhere else. While some question the thesis that Baptist associational life grew up as a function of military organization, there can be little doubt that these churches had mutual doctrinal and political concerns and maintained cordial relations through the clergy.[10]

The New Model Army was not the only place where Baptists gained significant power and influence. In defiance of an old Baptist disinclination to accept ecclesiastical appointments for ministry, many Baptists accepted preaching assignments to fill vacant pulpits where "unfit" priests had formerly worked. One of those selected was Thomas Tillam, a Jew–turned–Roman Catholic who lectured on Baptist doctrines in Hexham Abbey, while he was a member of Hanserd Knollys's church in London. In 1652 Parliament designed a clever scheme for the subjugation and indoctrination of Wales, which also proved to be a Baptist opportunity. Two hundred seventy-eight ministers had to be replaced by "Approvers" who certified the fitness of new clergy for activities as diverse as open-air preaching, school teaching, and settled pastorates. Among the Approvers were two Baptists from Oxford, Jenkin Jones and John Myles,* who laid a strong foundation for the Baptist faith in Wales. Vavasor Powell, another Baptist Approver, allowed Hugh Evans and Thomas Lamb, General Baptists, to itinerate in Wales, the location of many new churches. During the subsequent program which Cromwell devised where "Triers" invited clergy to London to evaluate their competence, eminent Baptists like John Toombes, Daniel Dyke, and Henry Jessey served as Triers and, in Joseph Ivimey's assessment, "saved many a congregation from ignorant, ungodly, and drunken teachers."[11] Of course this did not escape the notice of Presbyterians who, like Thomas Edwards, complained that Baptists were violating the parish system by claiming members who lived twenty miles from the meetingplace, which allowed for non-resident members and infrequent attendance at worship. Edwards caustically prodded the Baptists that they were undermining the very essence of their church fellowship by engaging in such practices![12] So it was, when the former outcasts seized the ecclesiastical machinery.

On the eve of the Restoration in 1660, the Baptists had become a major force in Great Britain and their numbers had increased far beyond the handful of churches in 1625. One historian estimated that there were Baptist churches in thirty English counties, five substantial congregations in Ireland, and small churches scattered throughout Wales. A perusal of the extant records suggests that by 1655 there were about seventy-nine General Baptist churches, ninety-six Particular Baptist churches, and fewer than ten congregations holding sabbatarian views. Amid periods of renewed persecution (1660–88) in England, a new door of opportunity would open for the Baptists in the American colonies. There, Baptists struggled with the same identity issues and followed basically the same patterns of evolution. Ironically, the antagonists of the group bore the same character as those in the old country and, because history repeats itself, Baptists fought the old battles on new ground.

During the seventeenth century, individuals often played a more heroic role than congregations in Baptist history. In part this was true because the laws persecuting Baptists were focused on individual misconduct and punishment, and the English Civil Code history is replete with Baptist violations from 1620 to 1689. But it is equally true that singular voices crying out for the religious liberty and articulating a new vision of the church constituted the primary recollection of the first half century on native soil. Only with permanent toleration after 1689 did the English congregation emerge as the visible shape of the Baptist principle; even then most congregations were identified by their significant leadership, usually that of the pastor.

NEW BEGINNINGS IN THE COLONIES

In the American colonies, Baptists emerged first as individual believers with a vision for the church (and often contrary to the prevailing Puritan spirit) and then more quickly than their English counterparts, as visible congregational units. For instance, what is known about the first Baptist church in America at Providence, Rhode Island, which Roger Williams* and Ezekiel Holliman founded, is that it was a seminal congregation for General Six Principle Baptist development. In fact, Williams was a Baptist for only a short time and later pastoral leaders were not as well known. Evidence suggests, rather, that the origins and growth of Baptists in America more appropriately were a function of the congregations at Newport, Swansea, and Boston. While the contributions of John Clarke,* John Myles, and Henry Dunster* are important chapters in the story, it is the presence and influence of the chain of developing congregations which left its imprint on the broader stream of American religious evolution in the seventeenth century.

The history of Baptists in Newport, Rhode Island, actually began in the midst of an earlier congregation, probably of Puritan/Separatist leaning in Portsmouth, New Hampshire. John Clarke arrived in 1637, and accounts external to the situation indicate that by 1644 he and the church evolved doctrinally, relocating to Newport, Rhode Island, a safe distance from Massachusetts for dissenters. Clarke and friends emerged with Baptist principles by 1648 and during Clarke's long history in the community and colony, the church survived amidst controversies over the Sabbath and the application of Six Principle theology. Clarke served as pastor 1640–51 and 1644–76, while also giving important leadership as attorney, schoolteacher, and physician. The congregation was the catalyst for Baptist expansion into Connecticut, Massachusetts, and the middle colonies.

About 1663 another landmark in American Baptist history was established. When John Myles of Ilston, Wales, immigrated with members of his congregation to Rehoboth, Massachusetts, he met others sympathetic to his views (or at least attracted by his preaching). A church was formed which espoused religious liberty and practiced believer's baptism. The congregation at Swansea in Massachusetts under Myles's leadership proved to dubious religious authorities in the colony that Baptists could provide stable leadership and could serve the spiritual needs of a community without schismatic disruptions. This Welsh pastor had learned his lessons well in the old country, where he had often worked closely with Presbyterians and had managed the interests of the Cromwell party without incident.

An evangelistic visit to Boston by Obadiah Holmes,* John Clarke, and John Crandall, all of Newport, Rhode Island, provided the impetus for the establishment of the most influential Baptist congregation in New England. While the three intruders were imprisoned and fined for their visit (Holmes was publicly whipped), they served permanent notice at their trial that Baptists were not easily dissuaded. Just three years later, Henry Dunster, the first president of Harvard College, by refusing to have his child baptized in the Puritan church, brought more public attention to the Baptist vision. While Dunster was forced to leave Boston in 1655, he influenced his close friend, Thomas Goold, a landowner, to adopt similar convictions. Goold and others gathered the first Baptist church in their homes, and it became a reminder of the permanence of dissent in the Puritan Commonwealth. From this beginning would emerge the first congregations in Maine and New Hampshire, a substantial community of churches encircling Boston, and an informal ecclesiastical peace between the Baptists and Congregationalists in 1718.

Who were the early Baptists in the American colonies? The first to arrive varied from middle class entrepreneurs to poorer folk. The little data about the first churches in New England suggests that the American opportunity improved the status of some, though not dramatically; most in the first congregations appear to have been landowners or merchant farmers. In the second decade, Obadiah Holmes was typical: an English farmer-craftsman whose skills were useful in a frontier community and who soon rose to the rank of "Freeman" though his religious views kept him in constant social turmoil. This was certainly the case with Thomas Goold of Boston, who appears on several lists of landowners and selectmen. The clergy cannot be neglected, as illustrated by Roger Williams, John Myles, and Henry Dunster. Among this class was the venerable John Clarke, who brought a truly professional identity to Baptists in America. As Puritans-becoming-Baptists, several of the American leaders did enjoy university training, particularly of the Cambridge tradition. Later in the seventeenth century, as new Baptist converts emerged from the Standing Order, a few distinguished and propertied persons joined the ranks, though not without the loss of social standing. On the whole, the early Baptists in the Colonies improved on the lot of their "hole-in-the-wall" brethren in England, while still carrying a stigma of dissent in their new world communities.

Baptists of the seventeenth century struggled valiantly to plant new congregations in the face of opposition from both Congregationalist and Anglican church leaders. In some cases this led to the geographical expansion of the group into the southern and middle colonies. A coastal merchant of some means, William Screven,* refused to heed the admonitions of the Maine authorities to have his children baptized and after a prolonged battle in the Kittery courts, Screven with his family emigrated in 1681 to the Ashley and Cooper Rivers in the vicinity of present Charleston, South Carolina. There he organized the first congregation in the South. Members of the Dungan family provided the impetus for the first Baptist congregation in the middle colonies. Thomas, the Irish paternal immigrant, had originally located at Newport, Rhode Island, and was active in the church there. When William Penn offered liberal land grants to new settlers for

Pennsylvania, Dungan again moved and obtained property near Penn's own manor on the Delaware River. The Dungan family formed there the first Baptist church at Cold Spring, which survived until the turn of the eighteenth century.

Along the way, Seventh Day Baptists added to the variety of the denomination in the New World. Partly in conflict with the General and Particular strains in Newport, Rhode Island, Stephen Mumford started in 1671 the first congregation of sabbatarians. These sentiments spread directly to seven other groups in New England and New York by 1790. The Newport group also served as a catalyst for John Rogers* of New London, Connecticut, who formed in 1674 a radical group of libertarian, sabbatarian, Baptistic enthusiasts known as the Rogerenes. The Rogers family drew the wrath of Governor Saltonstall more than once, because of publicly offensive acts such as working on Sundays at the Congregationalist meetinghouse and openly travelling on the Sabbath in violation of Puritan laws. Members of the Rogerenes were accused of indecency (because of public baptisms) and subjected to fines, imprisonment, and loss of property.

Far from being the isolationists they have been accused of, colonial Baptists early associated with each other, this cooperation leading to further growth. The first association meeting was held in 1670 among the General Six Principle Baptists in Rhode Island which numbered five congregations. Another cluster of churches in the Delaware Valley of Pennsylvania formed the Philadelphia Association, which held its first meeting in 1707 and was originally composed of ten churches. Not surprisingly the Charleston, South Carolina, congregations agreed to meet regularly in 1751, and thereafter associations were organized in New England, the South, and the Piedmont frontier. The purpose of these associations was to provide Baptists with theological and political advice, financial support, and a sense of cooperative endeavor. The Rhode Islanders consulted on church discipline and doctrine; the Philadelphia churches debated issues as diverse as the laying on of hands and membership qualifications, and they agreed to sponsor educational projects and itinerant evangelists. When the problem of unfair taxation and infringement upon religious liberties grew acute in the 1740s and again in the 1770s, the Warren Association in New England led the way in building a case for complete religious liberty.[13]

Contacts between English and American Baptists were frequent and significant during the colonial period. As early as 1702 General Baptists in Carolina requested assistance from their English friends, in books if not money. When the College of Rhode Island opened in 1764, its Baptist leadership sought the counsel of well-known distant pastors such as John Rippon, John Gill,* and the faculty at Bristol College in England. Principal James Manning* even requested a list of prominent English Baptists who might be considered for honorary doctorates. And, when colonial pastorates opened, English Baptist clergy recommended candidates to fill the posts; Morgan Edwards* of Pembrokeshire, Wales, carried the affirmation of Dr. John Gill to the pulpit at First Baptist Philadelphia in 1761. In the later eighteenth century, Samuel Jones of the Great Valley (Pa.) Church carried on an extensive transatlantic correspondence with Morgan John

Rhys of Pontypool, Wales. Discussions of polity, piety, and politics were frequent and detailed between British and American Baptists.

At the local church level of Baptist life, the Great Awakening had a profound influence on the denomination. Large numbers of Congregational churches in Massachusetts and Connecticut responded to the impulses of revivalism by restricting membership and tightening their disciplinary standards. These so-called "Separates" found themselves at cross purposes with the Congregationalist leadership and, in many cases, adopted relationships with the Baptists. Isaac Backus,* a pastor at Middleborough, Massachusetts, from 1748 to 1806, illustrated this trend most vividly as he moved from Congregationalist to Separate, to New Light or the more revivalistic style among Baptists. Other Baptists also participated in the evangelical outreach of the Awakening, as evidenced in the ministry of Hezekiah Smith* of Haverhill, Massachusetts, who made a number of extensive evangelistic preaching tours of Maine and New Hampshire and started thirteen new churches from the parent Haverhill ministry. In New England and the middle colonies, it has been estimated that 191 organizations moved into the Baptist fold during the Great Awakening.[14]

Elsewhere in New England, another ripple of the Awakening was felt by a young sailmaker and tailor. In the 1770s Benjamin Randall* of Portsmouth, New Hampshire, having heard George Whitefield preach, experienced the new birth. He subsequently studied his Bible and concluded that he would not baptize his children in his familial Congregational faith. Further, he felt called to preach and enjoyed modest success. In 1778 the church in New Durham, New Hampshire, offered the young itinerant its unoccupied pulpit and his long association with the village began. Randall openly declared himself a Baptist, though both Baptists and Congregationalists eschewed his theological emphases of "free grace, free will, and free communion" as undesirable Arminianism. Undaunted, Randall organized his following as the Freewill Baptist Connexion, later adopting a quasi-Quaker system of meetings and a structural connectionalism unique among Baptists. The Freewillers did much to revive the sagging religiosity of northern New England and the New York frontier.[15]

Shubal Stearns,* a native Connecticut Baptist, helped to export the revival far beyond his region. Converted in 1745, Stearns journeyed south and with his sister, Martha, and brother-in-law, Daniel Marshall, produced a major awakening in the Piedmont area of North Carolina between 1746 and 1760. Stearns was an enthusiastic preacher who drew large crowds to his impassioned rhetoric and flamboyant gestures; he is credited with organizing the Sandy Creek Association of churches (1758) which became a powerful force in the development of a Baptist separatism in the American South.[16]

As the eighteenth century closed, Baptists in America of several kinds could claim legitimately about 750 churches and 80,000 members. Congregations existed in the major cities and Baptist preachers were found across a frontier which stretched from western New York to Kentucky and Alabama. The first church founded west of the Appalachians was at Duck Creek (now Cincinnati) in 1790 by a group of peripatetic New Englanders. Assisting in the denominational advance were associational missionaries who journeyed far into the interior to develop new churches and preach to the Indians. Baptists were not always sectarian about such enterprises in the late 1700s, as illustrated in the case of Rev. Elkanah Holmes,* who carried the support of several denominations to the Six Nations Indians on the Niagara Frontier. There was indeed a maturity which was mixed with a sense that America was God's kingdom, causing most Baptists to look far beyond local congregations to define the borders of the Church.

ORGANIZING FOR MISSION

For Baptists the nineteenth century really began in 1792. That year a little-known cobbler-turned-missionary embarked for India with the support of the first voluntary society for foreign missions in modern Christian history. William Carey* of Moulton, England, was the first appointee of the Baptist Missionary Society, which was organized in 1792. His experience and vision, as reported to both English and American Baptists, radically altered the development of the denomination on both sides of the Atlantic. In England, the combination of evangelical theology and vision breathed new life into a fragmented and sagging Baptist body. Dan Taylor's* New Connection of General Baptists, plus the modified Calvinism of Robert Hall and Andrew Fuller,* were hints of the new spiritual waves among British Baptists. In America, Carey's work was the catalyst for a benevolent empire in which Baptists participated just after the turn of the century; this gave the denomination a new sense of purpose and solidarity.

While Baptists did not organize a "sending agency" for overseas missions until their Congregational brethren had set the pace, many expressed an interest in missions as early as 1800. Mary Webb,* a disabled Baptist laywoman in Boston's Second Baptist Church, organized that year the first voluntary society among Baptists in the United States in support of missionary projects. At first, Webb raised money for the Carey Mission; later she developed her own projects among Boston's black community and among the city's prostitutes. Her example and the vision of her pastor, Thomas Baldwin,* led in 1802 to the formation of a larger group, the Massachusetts Baptist Missionary Society (MBMS), which had as its stated purpose, "to furnish occasional preaching and to promote the knowledge of evangelical truth in new settlements within these United States or farther if circumstances should render it proper."[17] The Massachusetts plan was to follow Yankee emigrants to the West with a chain of churches and pastors to maintain Christian morality and social cohesion. Noteworthy also in this venture was the conflict between Massachusetts and New York over the suzerainty of western New York and New England's desire to plan for its own cultural expansion. The MBMS was successful beyond its most extravagant expectations: By 1825 the Society had administered over 2,300 weeks of service for over forty missionaries at an expense exceeding $12,750.00.[18]

Another chapter in Baptist advance was written by three Congregationalists.

Ann Hasseltine (Judson),* Adoniram Judson,* and Luther Rice* determined for separate reasons to follow the example of William Carey and, with two other married couples and one single man, they presented their plan, and themselves, to a group of Congregational clergy in 1810 for support as America's first foreign missionaries. Judson and Rice completed their preparation at the newly opened Andover Theological Seminary while Hasseltine read widely and eventually married Judson. When they departed Salem's port in 1812 they did so as Congregationalists and with the support of the American Board of Commissioners for Foreign Missions; when they arrived in India seven months later their sentiments had shifted to the Baptist position and each was baptized at William Carey's Lall Bazaar Chapel. With plenty of personal vision but no domestic support, the American Baptist missionary enterprise got underway when the Judsons fled to Burma, and Rice returned home to construct a support system.

Luther Rice may rightly be called the parent of an American Baptist denomination. In his career are the dovetailing talents of organizational genius, fundraising, new church development, and leadership recruitment. Upon his arrival in the United States in 1813, Rice travelled widely among the churches and associations, calling for the creation of a Baptist foreign society with affiliate chapters in each of the states. Once this organization was a reality, Rice served as its agent in raising money and circulating Baptist statistical data. He was particularly useful in the South in assisting with the establishment of new churches, associations, and state conventions. He helped to recruit new missionaries (John Mason Peck* and Isaac McCoy* were his proteges) and he almost single-handedly founded a university at Washington, DC, for the training of a new generation of learned Baptist missionaries and ministers. Rice, with the help of Richard Furman* of South Carolina and William Staughton* of Philadelphia, brought a national vision to the Baptists and drew the strands of a Free Church polity together into a formidable rope.

The birth of a truly united Baptist denomination in America occurred when Richard Furman called to order the opening session of the General Missionary Convention of the Baptist Denomination in the United States for Foreign Missions on 18 May 1814 at Philadelphia's historic First Baptist Church. Based on the single purpose voluntary society model, this meeting of thirty-six delegates from eleven states and the District of Columbia laid the plans for overseas missions and new church development in the United States. Within its first six years, the "Triennial Convention" took responsibility for work with Indians and blacks, for a college and seminary, for the publication of a major religious periodical, as well as for the Judson mission in Burma and a similar project in Africa.[19] If a set of unpredictable factors had not intervened to spoil the grand design, Luther Rice's full vision might well have been achieved three decades before it actually was.

Almost immediately after the formation of the General Missionary Convention, there were currents of dissent about the idea. In places as diverse as Boston, Maryland, North Carolina, western Pennsylvania, and the Ohio Valley, some local churches expressed dismay at fundraising strategies and the extra-church societies which were not directly accountable to the congregations. Luther Rice was denounced as a sycophant, and tracts were printed in protest of the entire missionary enterprise. These "antimission Baptists," as they were first called, posited theological and political argumentation from a devout predestinarian Calvinism and frontier localism in support of their opposition; later, their tenacity earned them appellations such as "hard-shells," "Old School," or Primitive Baptists.[20]

The General Missionary Convention also suffered from downturns in the national economy. At the core of the antimission movement were a paucity of specie in the West and real antagonism to centralization of capital and administration in the East. To make matters worse, the Panic of 1819 caused scores of financial pledges to default, and Luther Rice was hard-pressed to maintain a cash flow large enough to support all of the Convention's projects. In fact, his scheme to speculate in real estate and mix the accounts of the Washington college with missions backfired, and a committee of investigation was convened in 1824 to determine both Rice's and the Convention's future. The result was that Rice was released from his role as agent, and the General Missionary Convention reverted to a single-purpose foreign mission society. New Englanders, who had opposed both the university and domestic missions, were happily in control after reorganization.

Baptists in America had learned a hard lesson in the proliferation of projects under the aegis of one voluntary society. Already before the reorganization other societies were springing up to assume important functions. In 1824 a Washington-based coterie organized the Baptist General Tract Society to assist the missionary movement with the printed word; elsewhere, regional education societies were formed to provide ministerial training. Some of the latter became colleges or seminaries like Colby (1813), Colgate (1819), Newton (1825), and Furman (1827). In 1832 a major force was unleashed in the formation of the American Baptist Home Mission Society to marshal the efforts of all Baptists to evangelize North America. At mid-century, the Baptist benevolent empire included work in Sunday Schools, Bible translation, schools, colleges, evangelism, social welfare, foreign and domestic missions, printing, and historical preservation.

Another area of Baptist organizational evolution was at the regional or state level. Luther Rice had suggested that the associations and churches within a given state should band together at least annually to promote fellowship and raise missionary funds. In New England and New York, voluntary societies which had served this purpose were reorganized in the 1830s as state convention bodies. In the middle states, the South, and the West, new structures evolved, beginning with South Carolina in 1821, which played an important role for cooperating churches. In its simplest form, the state convention was an assembly of delegates who represented local churches and met once a year to review the status of Baptist affairs and agree on priorities for missions and an accompanying budget. Officers were elected to collect and disburse funds and statistical information. However, with the rise of the states' rights movement in Jacksonian America, these assemblies became natural forums for discussion and debate of matters ranging from slavery to war to western settlement. Gradually, state conventions in a given region, particularly the South, represented a peculiar ethos which strengthened bonds of a socio-political type more than those ties which had originally given birth to the idea. Thus when the Alabama Baptist State Convention expressed its disinclination to participate in a national Baptist organization which frowned upon slaveholding, eleven others followed its lead. The conventions became the popular voices of the churches and the embodiment of regionalism.[21]

The ethos of the South led in 1845 to the formation of the first comprehensive Baptist organization, the Southern Baptist Convention. The desire to protect the "peculiar institution" was the ostensible reason for the action of 293 delegates at Augusta, Georgia, but there was really much more involved. As a region, the South had peculiar social needs and expectations. Southerners in general preferred more centralized organizational styles that promoted a variety of programs but that were also popularly accountable to a broad constituency. There was also in the South a long tradition of revivalism and separatist attitudes; some historians have found a greater ideological cohesion than among northern or western Baptists. Following the opening of the southwestern frontier, Baptist numbers rapidly advanced in the overall southern population. At first the Southern Convention struggled for credibility among its church constituency as its boards rebuilt a sense of mission from a regional ethos. Later, in the rising sectionalism of the 1850s and 1860s the Convention drew positive support as an advocate of Southern states' rights and economic solidarity.[22]

As the Southern Baptists pursued a separate course, Baptists in the North and West redoubled their efforts to reach a variety of new constituencies. In 1834, as the Foreign Mission Society began its work in Europe, the Home Mission Society inaugurated efforts among American immigrant groups, particularly the Germans and Scandinavians. Leaders of the Home Society believed that their evangelical task involved Americanization and they started numerous programs in education and new church development, which had as their unifying purpose the transformation of old world culture. While immigrant leaders appreciated the funds and opportunities made possible by these efforts, the response was more often a reaction which led to separate, but cooperating, ethnically diverse conferences.[23] By 1865 these conferences together constituted 130 congregations of discrete German, Danish, Norwegian, Swedish, and Welsh styles. Significantly, the original languages were retained as unifying cultural forces among local constituencies.

A PAINFUL MATURING PROCESS

A noteworthy development in the family of Baptists during the mid-nineteenth century was the emergence of separate black Baptist churches and organizations.

Although forbidden by law in many states, black churches had been organized as early as 1778 in Georgia; in Boston, New York, and Philadelphia, similar churches were started in the early 1800s. In the South such congregations were free-standing before emancipation; in the North and West the black churches were invited to attend associational meetings and other society gatherings as cooperating members. The first black association was created among eight churches in Ohio in 1834. Like other Christian groups, white Baptists were not prepared for racial integration, even in the associational context, and black Baptists were thus forced to seek fellowship and mission involvement within their own organizational patterns. During the Reconstruction this segregation became acute and black Baptist leaders formed first their own national mission societies and later a national convention in 1886.[24]

While the last three decades of the nineteenth century witnessed the maturation of the Baptist movement, severe tensions developed which created an ominous future for Baptist solidarity in the United States. On the one hand, everywhere could be seen evidence of Baptist advance. Fifteen new state conventions were formed in the western territories between 1865 and 1912. Eighty-five new schools, colleges, and seminaries attested to a renewed interest in church-related education. Churches like Russell Conwell's* Baptist Temple in Philadelphia (seating capacity, 3,000) and San Francisco's First Baptist Church missionary programs to seamen and Chinese immigrants were a constant reminder of Baptist sophistication. Baptist theologians Augustus H. Strong,* William Newton Clarke,* and Edgar Y. Mullins* won respect far beyond their denominational constituencies and prominent laymen like John P. Crozer,* William Colgate* and his family, and John D. Rockefeller ensured the Baptists of enough endowment and capital funding to perpetuate their institutional life.

In contrast, both white Anglo-Baptist groups (North and South) began to absorb troublesome tendencies in part borne out of anti-modern responses to industrialization, extreme localism, and importantly, forces unleashed in British Baptist life. With the establishment of schools like the University of Chicago (1886) and curriculum changes at Brown University, some Baptist leaders imbibed the new thought of German educators and theologians and espoused new scientific perspectives on the Bible and the nature of human society. In some circles concern for social service gradually supplanted individualistic evangelism. Among Baptists in the South a persistent localism called the Landmarkist Movement permeated churches, periodicals, and some state conventions with an extreme emphasis upon sectarian doctrines and practices and a dominant sense of local church autonomy. The Landmarkers refused any sort of cooperative endeavor with other Christian groups and espoused a theory of Baptist origins that reached back to John the Baptist. A third disintegrative force was the influence of the illustrious British Baptist preacher, Charles Haddon Spurgeon.* During the later years of his ministry in London, Spurgeon, after accusing British Baptist Union leaders of liberal theological directions, broke fellowship with the mainstream of Baptist life. Spurgeon's vast following in the United States noted his criticisms with interest and regarded their own institutions and leadership with suspicion.

At the onset of the twentieth century, Baptists in the United States together presented a formidable religious force of over four million members.[25] In reality, there were major divisions along regional, racial/ethnic, and theological lines. Although important overtures to cooperation were made, the divisions nonetheless deepened. In the late nineteenth century progressive Southern Baptist leaders considered reunion with the northern societies, and some of the northern leadership discussed merger with the Disciples of Christ. Aside from the actual union of the Freewill Baptists with the Northern Baptists in 1911, U.S. Baptists would have to be content with quinquennial meetings of the Baptist World Alliance (formed in 1905) to exercise their denominational unity. With increasing intensity the Northern leaders and the Southern Convention accused each other's emphases in hyperbolic polarities; ''Northerners were slipping into the social gospel movement and were compromising their essential Baptistic principles,'' while ''Southern Baptists were exercising aggressive new church development in traditionally Northern geographical areas.''

While the two principally white Baptist conventions nurtured their respective institutional and regional networks, disaffected elements and the older separate groups proliferated the variety within the Baptist witness. Between 1920 and 1950 the major ethnically diverse groups made permanent their distinctiveness by severing most ties with the Northern Baptist Convention. In 1915 a split within the black National Baptist Convention led to a second large predominantly black convention. The fundamentalist movement, focussing on liberal policies in educational institutions and the lack of a doctrinal position in the Northern Convention, produced a new association in the 1920s (the General Association of Regular Baptist Churches) and a second in the late 1940s (the Conservative Baptist Association). The second schism was a response to a permissive appointment policy in the Foreign Mission Society. In the Southern Convention, fundamentalism focused on personal power struggles and local versus national relationships; beginning in the 1930s, three distinct groups, the American Baptist Association, the Baptist Missionary Association, and the Baptist Bible Fellowship, emerged to oppose the direction of the Southern Convention phalanx. Most of the early-twentieth-century splinter groups reluctantly recognized their historic pilgrimages out of the mainstream traditions, the leading exceptions being those pockets of Primitive Baptist life which claimed their origins in the antimission movement of the early nineteenth century.

After World War II, when American society became more mobile and individualistic, a new style of Baptist life arose which had no necessary relationship to the earlier evolutionary patterns. Highly gifted preachers, for the most part quite conservative theologically, organized aggressive local churches which they claimed were entirely independent of conventions, societies, or associations. Baptist to the extent that the Church was defined as local and the practice of believer's baptism was strictly required of new converts, these "superchurches" were strengthened by splits in regular Baptist congregations or flagrant disregard for existing Baptist work by proselytizing techniques and house-to-house "soul-winning." Because such churches required a constant supply of new clergy and mission outlets free of modernistic tendencies, a spate of new "faith-mission" enterprises were created to identify appropriate benevolent projects and Baptist bible colleges were started to train the leadership. Although the leadership has been highly critical of mainstream Baptists, they have emulated the associational patterns of conventions and coalitions and have produced fellowships of "Bible-believing independent Baptists." Outnumbered overall by the older Baptist groups, the super-pastors have had a profound influence upon American religiosity and have done more to create a stereotype for Baptists than their more moderate coreligionists in the larger Baptist family.[26]

Baptists in both Great Britain and North America have actively pursued international missions, with United States Baptists very much in the vanguard. As noted earlier, it was the missionary task around which Baptists organized and their progress in the nineteenth century was remarkable indeed. The northern society for foreign missions developed stations on six continents by 1900; so also did the southern board in the second half of the twentieth century. Less well known were the efforts of the Freewill and National (black) Baptists who pioneered in India and Africa, respectively. As more resources became available in the twentieth century, all major groups increased their efforts. Following concerted financial campaigns in 1963 and 1973 respectively, Northern and Southern U.S. Baptists spent a total of over $120 million in a decade on overseas missions. The various "come-outer" groups have followed this pattern; in 1985 there were more than fifty Baptist-related foreign missionary agencies in the U.S. alone.[27]

The result of all of this outreach effort has been to place an indelibly American stamp on most Baptists worldwide, regardless of national identity. Uncontextual and anachronistic as it may appear, Northern and Southern Baptists both serve in India and "independent" Baptists have churches in Argentina and Chile, predominantly Roman Catholic countries. Because of the steady flow of U.S. dollars and personnel, there is slow divestiture as northern (ABC) Baptists report more affiliate members overseas through their Baptist Council on World Mission than they register at home. Likewise, the Southern Baptists have created English-speaking, U.S. influenced conventions within the territories of discrete international Baptist bodies. This pattern ensures that the worldwide advance of the Baptist tradition will continue to be rooted in the original General or Particular traditions of English/American heritage.

It might appear to the non-Baptist that in the late twentieth century the Baptist tradition is hopelessly disintegrated and self-destructive. It is true that the more theologically conservative and "independent" Baptists consider the two U.S. conventions anathema, and that the more liberal northern (American) Baptists are perhaps closer in spirit to other Protestant groups than to many fellow Baptists.

Even with the recent theological strife, Southern Baptist growth and financial resources have created a solidarity and purpose which has insulated Convention churches from a need to cooperate with any other group, thus perpetuating an overall lack of unity for the denominational family. But, there are identification factors that all Baptists still share in common and that disclose their common heritage. Foremost among these characteristics is the sense of biblical authority, which causes all Baptists to be disinclined to trust other sources of faith and practice, even though there is a wide variety of opinions about the interpretation and use of the Bible. At a popular level, there is not much difference in terminology from one Baptist group to another when biblical language is used.

Baptists also share a stubbornness about the self-governance of their local congregations. From their inception, Baptists have resisted ecclesiastical or political control external to the congregation. When associations, societies, and conventions posed a threat to congregational autonomy, local congregations criticized the presumption of authority or discipline and if necessary, withdrew. The spirit of individual religious liberty has been easily transferred to congregations, and given a controversial issue or uncomfortable leadership in an association or society, churches often affirm their autonomy above all else. This proclivity makes denominational unity a function of voluntary decision even at the cost of good stewardship and effective mission.

Finally, as their name implies, all Baptists do have in common the orthopraxis of believer's baptism by immersion. Since the 1640s when the English Particular Baptists prescribed both the ordinance and the mode of administration, the vast majority of Baptist congregations have adopted the practice as a symbolic act of initiation into the Church and the theology of the new birth. Historically, Baptists have refused to compromise on the relevance or technique of baptism as they understand it and this has certainly differentiated them from the rest of Christendom. Within the denomination there is, of course, great variety of baptismal opinion and practices, ranging from a requirement that each new member be baptized within a given local church (regardless of previous baptisms), to open air baptisms in "living waters," to triune immersion of each candidate. Whatever the diversity in specifying the practice, believer's baptism by immersion is essentially Baptist.

Understood thus against their unique history, Baptists as a whole continue to divide and conquer, sometimes even each other.

2
THE BIBLE: AUTHORITY OR BATTLEGROUND?

BELIEVING THE BIBLE

"God said it, we believe it, and that settles it" is a phrase coined among Baptists and which fairly describes how the popular Baptist mentality understands the role of the bible in the Christian life. Reacting against creeds and episcopal and conciliar pronouncements, early Baptists affirmed Scripture alone as authoritative in matters of faith and practice. In a twofold sense, Baptists "believe in the Bible and they believe the Bible"; that is, the Baptist position on Scripture is both ontological and ethical.

To comprehend the hyperbole among early Baptists about the importance of Scripture, one has to appreciate the climate of religious authority in which the Baptist movement was born. In Elizabethan England a theological compromise was achieved which was summarized in 1560. Concerning Scripture, it said, "Holy Scripture containeth all things necessary to salvation; so that whatsoever is not read therein, nor may be proved thereby, is not to be required of any man."[1] Increasingly, the Puritan party became disconcerted with the trappings of Anglicanism and the theology of compromise, and a new interest in biblical tradition gradually emerged. By 1590 clusters of Separatists were noticeably moving away from the Puritan fold. These Separatists were intense students of the Bible and organized their theology around key passages which has been negatively referred to as a "proof-texting" methodology in contrast with later, more analytical approaches. On balance, their intent was to recover a form of the Church that was consistent with their understanding of the biblical covenants and a genuine Christian lifestyle and ministry. In their use of Scripture, Separatists frequently spiritualized or harmonized difficult passages and adhered to generally accepted views within the Reformed tradition, as, for instance, with the sacraments.

It is evident from their Gainsborough covenant that the followers of John

Smyth* had a primary commitment to biblical Christianity and secondarily to tradition. In 1606 they agreed "to be the Lord's free people . . . to walk in all His wayes made known or to be made known unto them according to their best endeavors, whatsoever it should cost them, the Lord assisting them."[2] Upon their arrival in Amsterdam, Smyth and this congregation continued to study the Bible and derive a new vision for the Church. Even opposition from trusted co-religionists such as Separatist Richard Clifton did not dissuade them from recovering a primitive, apostolic pattern. For them, it was a matter of approaching the Bible consistently.

To say that Baptists "believe in the Bible" is to identify a basic emphasis that the Bible is the sole authority for determining matters related to the Christian faith. All doctrines and practices, individual and corporate, are to be tested in light of Scripture, particularly the New Testament, because it is "an absolute and perfect rule of direction, for all persons, at all times, to bee observed."[3] In this first confessional document of the first congregation, a doctrine of Scripture emerged which illustrates intentional dependence upon the Reformed tradition. Trusting that God had predetermined what He "thought needful for us to know, believe and acknowledge," the written Word of God was God's special revelation to mankind, the New Testament particularly for the Church. A lesser known General Baptist confession from the mid-seventeenth century limited very strictly the idea of special revelation to those "doctrines which are contained in the record of God, which was given by inspiration of the Holy Ghost." In the Puritan tradition, the authority of the Scriptures for early Baptists was "divine, absolute, sovereign . . . the Bible was nothing less than God's own writing." Perhaps the most memorable statement in three hundred years of Baptist life in this regard is contained in the Second London Confession, "The Holy Scripture is the only sufficient, certain, and infallible rule of all saving Knowledge, Faith, and Obedience . . . the authority for which it ought to be believed, dependeth wholly upon God . . . because it is the Word of God."[4]

For Baptists, the written canonical literature replaced the writings of the Church Fathers, the creeds and early confessions, and, of course, the Book of Common Prayer. If a study of the Scriptures had led to the formation of the first congregations, the Bible was certainly the principal resource for reconstituting the visible church. Each of the confessional articles carried an added weight of five to ten passages of Scripture listed in the margins, which served as the bedrock of each pronouncement. Following a tradition honored by William Tyndale, Baptists tended toward literal interpretation methods. Allegory, typology, and medieval philosophical approaches were all irrelevent because "the Scripture hath but one sense, which is the literal sense. . . . the anchor that never faileth, whereunto if thou cleave, thou canst never err or go out of the way."[5] The new vision for the Church was based squarely upon the notion that the Bible contained the charter, constitution, and by-laws of the true Church.

If early Baptists took the bible seriously, they also took it specifically. Practically speaking, it was the Baptists who popularized the English Bible as a manual for the Christian life. As Baptist controversialists argued literalistically from the Genevan Version (1560) (and only much later from the King James version of 1611) other denominations and scholars were prompted to exegete the text and build a case for their respective positions as well. No other issue better illustrates this textual preoccupation than the case for immersion as the proper mode of baptism. William Kiffin noticed in his studies that the term " 'baptizo' signified to dip under water" and countless others followed with apologetic tracts which caused pedobaptists a serious methodological problem. Edward Barber (1641), Isaac Backus* (1760), John Dowling (1838), Anders Wiberg* (1852), and B. H. Carroll* (1912), all hammered away at this point of specific textual evidence well into the present century, all arguing that if the Bible is supremely authoritative and it teaches immersion, then no other form of baptism is valid.

Baptists took the Bible specifically in other ways as well. The visible manifestations of a believer were evident from a list of biblical marks: love, obedience to Christ's commands, sacrifice, and a declaration of Christian experience. Conversely, when a person was disciplined, clear injunctions from the Bible were listed as causes with penalties. The New Testament epistles contained lists of Christian virtues and duties; for Baptists these became commandments. Examples of drunkenness in the Old Testament provided a rationale for a prohibition against alcoholic grape wine being served at the Lord's Supper after 1865, and the example of the Apostles spoke loudly to early Baptists to share worldly goods with the poor.

Virtually every recorded debate in early associational records in England and America illustrates the Baptist preoccupation with biblical teachings. The role and function of officers in the church and of the proper role for women were cast against the Apostolic era. The description and purpose of a Christian family were discussed at the Warren, Rhode Island, Association in 1785, while at the Northampton, England meetings during the same period, Andrew Fuller* and William Carey* were making a biblical case for a new evangelism and a sense of world mission.[6] Political issues were likewise debated: in America between 1790 and 1860 Baptists north and south tried to marshal the Bible to support opposing views on human slavery.[7] And from Thomas Helwys* to Isaac Backus, Baptists found scriptural reasons for supporting a doctrine of religious liberty, although that idea was only a secondary concern for biblical theology. Indeed, after reading Acts 14, Thomas Helwys decided to return to England from exile and face stiff persecution for righteousness' sake.[8] The power of the specific written word was great indeed.

A SOURCE OF CONTROVERSY

The Bible also played an important part in the making of black Baptist identity. Unlike the literate white society where Bible reading and study were encouraged, the American slave population came to appreciate the power of the spoken Bible,

particularly its stories. Despite slaveholders' attempts to justify the peculiar
institution from biblical bases, blacks saw in the Old and New Testaments the
characters, names, and events of redemption, liberation, and individual values.
Children were given biblical names and the ever-present spiritual music attested
to an enduring love for the Bible. Black Baptist services of baptism and the
Lord's Supper were sacraments of cleansing, liberation and community building.
As several writers have shown, black Baptists created the only theology they
could before Emancipation and it was a biblical theology with "Sweet Jesus"
at the center. Jesus,

the Redeemer and Liberator, was the Lily of the Valley, the Rose of Sharon, the Bright
and Morning star. He was a Bridge over deep waters, a Ladder for high mountains, Water
in dry places, and Bread in a starving land.[9]

For the first 250 years of denominational history, the Bible was for Baptists
a certain authority. But, beginning in the 1840s, it proved to be a source of great
controversy. In three successive eras, the Bible Society controversy, the Down-
Grade Movement, and fundamentalism, Baptists have fought each other plus the
rest of the Christian world over the meaning and purpose of the Bible.

The first series of problems which Baptists faced concerning the Bible sur-
rounded the need for an authoritative text for missionary translation work. From
the origin of Baptist mission work under William Carey and, later, Adoniram
Judson* and Ann Hasseltine* translation of the Bible had been a primary task.
It afforded the missionaries a keener understanding of the native languages and
produced the first useful tool for the conversion of the non-Christian population.
In 1836 the American and Foreign Bible Society was founded by several groups
(including Baptists) "to promote a wider circulation of the Holy Scriptures in
the most faithful versions that can be procured." For over a decade the Society
prospered in making available copies of the King James Version and supporting
translation projects in overseas countries. However, in 1839 several Baptist
pastors and laymen pointed out to the Society's board that "there was not one
Baptist among the forty-seven translators appointed by King James and that we
have never acknowledged that this version of the Scriptures was in all respects
faithful."[10] In the next several years the Baptists pointed out the deficiencies of
an "Episcopal Bible" such as archaic language, inaccurate phrases, and most
important, an erroneous translation of the Greek word "baptizo."

The Baptists argued repeatedly that they did not want a new version, but
improvements made to the Authorized Version. In short, they said, "the word
'immerse' expresses the precise meaning of *baptizo* and is not equivocal . . . so
far then as the word baptize is concerned, the English version is not a faithful
translation and ought to be corrected."[11] However, in 1850, under pressure from
non-Baptist members, the Society resolved to restrict their work to "the commonly received version without note or comment" and further, that it was not

their duty to attempt to procure a revision of the commonly received English version. The Baptists maintained that such actions violated the original intention of the Society to provide "the most faithful version," and prominent Baptist businessmen and clergy in New York City convened on 10 June 1850 to organize a new Bible society, known as the American Bible Union (ABU). Their purpose was to spare no expense or exertion to procure "a correct English Bible" and "to encourage pure versions of God's word throughout the World." Men of the stature of William Colgate* spared no expense and scholars like Thomas Jefferson Conant of Hamilton Seminary spared no scholarly exertion. The splinter group expected first to revise the Authorized Version of 1611.[12]

Within a few months, auxiliary societies had been formed among Baptists in the south and west, and the approbation of leaders like Adoniram Judson* was given to the project. In the next several years, scores of translators worked over the text of both Testaments, exulting in the fact they were dealing with the original languages. Ultimately, in 1866 a first and only edition of the American Bible Union Version was issued and, to no one's surprise, its chief distinction was the substitution of "immerse" for "baptize" in the New Testament. Although the Union members had warned that "culpability is unavoidable when the fault is known and permitted," the ABU Work and version lagged far behind the original American and Foreign Bible Society version and resources.[13] In their attempt to prove their fidelity to Holy Scripture in its purest essence, the plot backfired and Baptists earned a reputation of subjecting even the Bible to their sectarian viewpoints. The Bible itself became a divisive force between Baptists and other Protestants in the world mission crusade.

A second controversy among Baptists over the authority and pursuit of the Bible began in 1887 in Great Britain. That year, Charles H. Spurgeon, "prince of preachers" at London's Metropolitan Tabernacle, declared that heresy was creeping insidiously into churches. In particular, Spurgeon noted a "downgrading" of the old Puritan godliness of life and an "inadequate faith in the divine inspiration of the sacred Scriptures." Spurgeon himself held that the Bible was an "infallible rule of faith and practice" and that denying this principle was the first step toward "leaving the King's Highway."[14] In a series of editorials entitled "The Down Grade," Spurgeon bitterly attacked his friends in the Baptist Union of Great Britain and particularly leaders like John Clifford* and Samuel Cox, who favored higher criticism and even universal restoration. Spurgeon saw the pace of declension ever-increasing: "We are going down hill at break-neck speed," he told his colleagues in the Baptist Union annual session of 1887.

To offset the problem, Spurgeon proposed a creed in place of the Declaration of Faith, a move which was soundly defeated. Spurgeon continued to contend for the old faith and a high view of Scriptural authority, though after his humiliation in the Union, he was largely uninvolved in its affairs. The college which he had created became a center for old-style evangelical Baptist training, and Spurgeon contented himself with an unparalleled personal library of Puritan classic literature. Because his paper, *The Sword and Trowel*, had an international reputation, the impact of the Down-Grade Controversy in galvanizing international Baptist opinion about the Bible cannot be overestimated.[15]

Ominous clouds also showed up on the American Baptist horizon. As more and more Baptists turned to an educated ministry, theological ideas and scholarship usually confined to universities and European circles gradually came to the attention of the Baptist public. Questions arose over the origin of books of the Bible and the authenticity of some of the Old Testament materials. Darwin's evolutionary theories had implications for ancient history, and the time-honored inspiration theories of an earlier century did not easily coincide with scientific-historical methods.

THE CHALLENGE OF MODERNISM

The central and most complex problem which Baptist Americans of the later nineteenth century faced concerning the Bible was its interpretation. As historical, archaeological, and natural science discoveries were made, plus comparative linguistic analyses from ancient languages, the integrity of the information in the Bible came into question. Baptist ministers who had been educated in colleges and seminaries predictably followed a progressive trend, usually trying to harmonize Scripture and science; most, however, mistrusted "modernism" and fought to retain the older, simpler understanding of the "revealed word."

Hermeneutical questions focussed on several classic concerns. For instance, in light of physical science, could the events described as miracles in the Bible actually have violated the laws of nature? The literal, bodily resurrection of Jesus Christ was an all-important miracle, most Baptists thought. Second, did the biblical figures have the ability to foretell specifically the events of the future, or was "prophecy" written after the events? From the Fifth Monarchy Movement to William Miller of Lowville, New York, who, as a Baptist, gave birth to the modern Adventist movement, most Baptists again thought prophets could foretell. Thirdly, there was a gnawing concern after 1860 for many scientists and educators over the credibility of the Genesis account of Creation. At the turn of the twentieth century most Baptist Christians accepted Archbishop Ussher's dating of Creation in Genesis, unaware that in their colleges and universities, students were routinely exposed to a new theory called "evolution."

Under pressure from the natural and social sciences and progressive education, interpretive styles changed from about 1880 to the 1920s.[16] Two distinct approaches warred against each other for credibility. One that included most pastors and chronologically older theology professors such as Henry G. Weston of Crozer Seminary, Alvah Hovey* of Newton Seminary, and Edgar Y. Mullins* of Southern Seminary could be called "orthodox." This was the approach of countless devotional works, popular theological books, and the official denominational presses.

The basic technique assumed a literary and theological unity of sixty-six books written across a span of about two and a half millennia. As Baptists have longed believed, "the author of the Bible is the Holy Spirit"; many pointed to the unity which the Bible claimed for itself. Practically, this meant that words, phrases, paragraphs, and ideas could be taken from one discrete context and blended with another, because "no scripture is of any private interpretation." One of the most widely read exponents of the orthodox school was Adoniram Judson Gordon,* pastor of Boston's Clarendon Street Baptist Church. He wrote of the importance of Christ's resurrection,

"But now is Christ risen from the dead." And since we are risen with Him, we are not dead in our sins. In his renewal from the dead, we are lifted forever from dark enfolding condemnation. They cannot bind a single fetter on us now. . . . Because the God of Peace has brought again from the dead our Lord Jesus Christ, the Great Shepherd of the Sheep, all the flock folded in Him by faith, are safe. "They shall never perish, neither shall any man pluck them out of his hands."[17]

In this remarkable passage, Gordon fused eight different pieces of Scripture from five different books and underscored seven different orthodox tenets. He presupposed that the Bible contained consistent propositional truths.

Others in the Baptist denomination, however, approached the Bible differently. The modernist approach was seen among younger scholars, educators, and pastors of the larger, urban churches. Men like Walter Rauschenbusch,* William N. Clarke,* William H. P. Faunce, George D. Boardman, Jr. and Milton Evans all exemplified the new thrusts. Clarke told the Yale Divinity School community in 1905 that "the vogue of biblical theology is the death of the doctrine of an equal bible."[18] He taught that the New Testament must have primacy over the Old if theology was to be Christian and that only that which was in accord with Jesus' teachings was to be prized. George D. Boardman, pastor of First Baptist Philadelphia and a stepson of Adoniram Judson, concluded after considering Charles Darwin's theories that "I do not believe that the Creation Record is to be taken literally. The words describing Creation are figurative or parabolic."[19] Perhaps most telling of all were the words of Dean Shailer Mathews* at the Divinity School of the University of Chicago, who saw the meaning of Christ's resurrection in a way which contrasted sharply with A. J. Gordon:

The sublime truth that stands out in the resurrection of Jesus is the emancipation of the spiritual life from the physical order as culminating in death, not information as to physiological details. . . . Immortality in the Christian sense does not mean that human life simply takes up its old interests. It means a new birth upward; a new advance, a new stage of human evolution, a freer and more complete spiritual personality.[20]

The issues surrounding biblical authority might never have troubled the Baptist family so, particularly in the northern United States, without the organizational centralization which took place after 1900. In little over a decade, the Northern Baptist Convention was founded (1907), a merger with Freewill Baptists was concluded (1911), the Convention became a charter member of the Federal Council of Churches of Christ in the U.S. (1908), a Board of Education was created in 1911, and the same year John D. Rockefeller gave a large sum to help found a pension board. Among Baptists in the South, the Southern Convention gradually moved toward modernization and centralization with the establishment in 1927 of an Executive Committee and a financial Cooperative Program. Opponents of this system argued from the Bible against organized missions and extra-congregational relationships.

In the Northern Baptist Convention, the response to all of the organizational development was to rally around the autonomy of local churches and to uphold the Bible as the sole legitimate authority for Baptists. Orthodox spokesmen saw in the events of 1907–13 a concerted program of progressives and modernists to engage Baptists in dialogues, missionary endeavors, and educational pursuits that were unattainable before the Convention and repugnant to many in any generation. Beginning in 1915, the orthodox advocates began to lobby heavily at the local church and associational levels in favor of an investigation of liberal teachings in church-related schools; their goal was to detect any denial of orthodox doctrines. Militant evangelists like William Bell Riley,* J. Frank Norris,* and John Roach Straton spoke at rallies of churches across the country to increase public awareness of the issues. Many of these leaders had already joined the World's Christian Fundamentals Association (organized in 1919) when the stormy Buffalo sessions of the Northern Baptist Convention opened in 1920.[21]

Under the leadership of Jasper C. Massee, the organization of fundamentalists succeeded in focusing their efforts in 1920 on a single issue, "false teaching in Baptist schools." By this they meant that evolution, destructive world religions, and socialist political theory was being taught in the classrooms of academies, colleges, and universities supported by faithful Baptist churches. The intention of the group was to establish a test of orthodoxy by which the schools could be judged, for instance the New Hampshire Baptist Confession of Faith which declared that the Scriptures were "divinely inspired . . . a perfect treasure . . . without any mixture of error." Such authority easily transcended mere theology and touched upon every philosophical and practical endeavor. The fundamentalists won the first round as the 1920 Northern Convention authorized a commission to investigate all denominational schools.[22]

Much rancor and misunderstanding ensued in the months following the 1920 meetings. The fundamentalists struggled to create a creedal statement for the evaluation process and the more progressive teachers and administrators attempted either to defend their right to free exchange of ideas or to make their educational processes appear to be orthodox. One of the most troubled administrators was President William H. P. Faunce of Brown University, who while he was sympathetic to a "Christian" education, declined even to respond to the official questionnaire on grounds that the college's charter forbade any sort of religious test whatsoever. Faunce went so far as to advise other schools to "stand fast in the soul liberty of Roger Williams."[23] Wisely, the special investigatory commission reported to the 1921 Convention a general approval for the institutions of the Northern Baptists. The damage had been done, however, as a steady decline in church relationship began in schools such as Colgate, Colby, Bates, and Rochester Universities, all of which would sever the ties by 1950.[24]

Believing that a creedal foundation must be established, the fundamentalists attempted in 1922 to have the NBC adopt the New Hampshire Confession and "take a stand ready to announce their faith both to the believing and unbelieving world." That year the fellowship leaders spoke of biblical inerrancy (akin to a dictation theory for the origin of the Bible), a literal virgin birth for Jesus Christ, and a literal return of Christ to set up a millennial kingdom.[25] All of their concerns reached to the authority of a Bible which declared specific data in an infallible formula. With all the force of biblical authority behind the cause, however, the campaign in the Northern Convention came to an abrupt standstill when, due to indecision among fundamentalist leaders and careful political maneuvering by the moderates, the delegates voted 1,264 to 637 to affirm the New Testament as the "all-sufficient ground of our faith and practice."[26] Such a statement, which was broad enough to include almost all churches in the Convention but not too broad for many fundamentalists, has remained the official doctrinal position of the Northern (now American) Baptists for over fifty years. More liberal Northern Baptists like Henry C. Vedder of Crozer Seminary rejoiced in his own definition of *fundamental* Christianity, namely, that "it has to do with verifiable facts of experience." As far as "fundamentalists" were concerned, Vedder wrote, "the essence of obscurantism is blind clinging to discredited facts and theories of religion."[27] Gradually, the more militant fundamentalist leaders like William Bell Riley, J. C. Massee, and Robert T. Ketcham* made plans in 1924–25 to organize anew with stricter formulations.

During the uproar over the Bible in the Northern Baptist Convention the issue was also agitated among Southern Baptists. For largely cultural reasons, Baptists in the South were not educationally or theologically as progressive as their northern counterparts, and by 1920 their general support for biblical infallibility was undiminished. With a deep sense of piety and a heavy dose of Southern masculinity, evangelist A. C. Dixon put the Bible on a pedestal with womanhood and dared anyone to impugn the integrity of either. For other Southern Baptists the Bible came alive and "bled" when under attack by modernists. While higher critics searched for the historical Jesus and applied the techniques of scientific modernism to biblical theology, Southern Baptist educators like E. Y. Mullins and A. T. Robertson* responded that critics had been unscientific in trying to rid the New Testament of its supernatural elements.[28] A few university men like William L. Poteat at Wake Forest and Edward B. Pollard at Crozer Seminary valiantly fought literalistic biblical interpretation but were drowned in the prevailing tide of Southern Baptist opinion of the 1920s.[29]

Part of the reason for the victory of fundamentalist bibliolatry was the crusade of J. Frank Norris. Within his own region, he launched diatribes against the Convention from the 1920s until his death in 1952. Norris thought the Bible was the only book worth studying and consequently, "every Baptist preacher ought to be imprisoned for forty days with nothing but his Bible and a diet of bread and water." Within his own church in Fort Worth, members confessed that "the Bible does not contain and convey the word of God, but *is* the very word of God."[30] The fiery and often erratic preacher went beyond mere affirmation of biblical infallibility though and singlehandedly wedded a particular interpretive style in Southern Baptist life. Norris used world events such as the Great Depression and the rise of dictators like Adolf Hitler to legitimate a dispensationalist hermeneutic far beyond graduates of his own Southwestern Premillennial Bible School. Leading Southern Baptist historians are convinced that Norris made premillennialism the trademark of Southern Baptist fundamentalism.[31] Little wonder, then, that in 1925 the Southern Baptist Convention actually adopted the New Hampshire Confession of Faith with ten additional sections, one of which focussed on the Second Coming and which established a level of comfort for the fundamentalist forces within the Convention.[32] Following this debate which eventuated in the "Baptist Faith and Message Statement," the majority of Southern Baptists were content to confess their faith in the bible using an oft-repeated credo:

> I pledge allegiance to the Bible—God's Holy Word
> A Lamp unto my feet and a light unto my path
> I will hide its words in my heart that I may not sin against God.[33]

IN THE WAKE OF DISINTEGRATION

While both of the mainstream Baptist conventions in the United States experienced disintegration over continuing perceptions of liberal policies within institutions and missionary programs, an entirely new type of Baptist emerged on the American scene after 1923. Leaders from the Northern, Southern, and Canadian Conventions met at Kansas City, Missouri, that year to create a permanent Baptist organization to combat modernism. At the outset, J. C. Massee, J. Frank Norris and T. T. Shields* designed a confessional framework for their respective conventions; over a thousand Baptist ministers in Kansas City adopted a modified New Hampshire Confession with more elaborate articles on the Holy Spirit, and "the return of Christ and related events."[34] The Union set up offices in the United States and Canada to provide copies of the new Confession, to maintain a list of approved pastors and schools, to produce periodicals, and to set up a campaign chest to continue the battle against modernism. Uniting all elements of the Baptist Bible Union was its stated purpose: "a union of all Baptists who believe the Bible to be the Word of God."[35]

While many fundamentalist leaders preferred to remain within the organized conventions and effect reform, men like J. Frank Norris and Robert Ketcham moved in a separatistic direction. One of the hallmarks of the Union was the strong affirmation of the autonomy of local churches (which the New Hampshire

Confession underscored) against other forms of associations and combinations. "The local church," the charter read, "must be allowed to be the final judge."[36] Union leaders appealed to the rank and file of Baptist congregations to express their Baptistic principles through the Union's channels. A bold step was taken when churches were advised not to cooperate with organized modernism:

> We believe it to be as wrong to give money where it may be used for the propagation of error as it would be by voice or pen to propagate error ourselves. . . . Members are encouraged absolutely to refuse longer to contribute money to any educational institution or missionary organization which refuses to avow this allegiance to the fundamentals of the faith.[37]

Moreover, all literature for Sunday School, Christian Colleges, or family circles was to be in full harmony with the Union's position on the Scriptures. The Bible was to be the chief textbook.

In the decade between 1925 and 1935 the younger leaders of the Baptist fundamentalists exhibited their own personal needs of organizational power and authority, and they led thousands of congregations into new categories of "non-alignment." Robert Ketcham, for instance, argued that a church could still proudly be a member of the Baptist "denomination" without being a member of the Northern Convention; likewise J. Frank Norris called upon his following to join a premillennial confederation and flee from the evil of "conventionism."[38] Organizationally the results were the General Association of Regular Baptists in the North (1932) and the World Baptist Fellowship (1949) and the Baptist Missionary Association (1950) in the South. The vast majority of subsequent fundamentalist Baptist groups and churches have sprung from one or more of these roots. As historians of fundamentalism have shown, these groups were hardly passing anachronisms associated with "monkey trials"; since 1960 the "non-convention" Baptists in the U.S. claim the largest congregations and Sunday Schools and the biggest share of media attention with their own networks of educational institutions and missionary organizations.[39] During the early decades of the twentieth century, then, the Bible was transformed among Baptists from a source of unquestioned authority to a battleground for scientists and theologians, and finally into a nursery of hybrid Baptists.

The disarray in which the fundamentalist "battle for the Bible" has left the Baptists since 1940 was greater among the Northern/American Baptists than in the Southern Convention. In the 1940s a new wave of theological controversy began among Northern loyalists who were yet concerned with establishing a confessional stance. The new leaders of the liberal tradition included voices like Albert W. Beaven, president of Colgate-Rochester Divinity School, and Harry Emerson Fosdick, the indomitable pastor of Riverside Church in New York City, a congregation dually aligned with the American Baptist Convention and the United Church of Christ. Beaven attempted to recover the spirit of Walter Rauschenbusch and was accused of being a Communist or Bolshevist.[40] Fosdick declared in his classic book, *The Modern Use of the Bible* (1924) that he had no desire "to harmonize the Bible with itself . . . or to resolve its conflicts and contradictions into a strained and artificial unity." Many Northern Baptists probably agreed with the New York pastor I. M. Haldeman, that Fosdick was a "pitiful example of a minister of the gospel, who couldn't defend that Bible which underwrites the church."[41] A new generation of wrangling occurred in which the Northern/American Convention held tenaciously to its position on affirming only the New Testament, while Bible college and interdenominational conservative seminary graduates persuaded continuing numbers of congregations to break fellowship with the Convention. Ultimately, both the Swedish and German conferences severed their ties with Northern Baptists, giving their reason as unchecked theological modernism.[42]

Southern Baptists have been more successful in retaining the more biblically conservative elements within their family. By skillfully adopting strong compromise terminology on Scriptural authority like "the Bible is a perfect treasure . . . without any mixture of error," conservative to fundamentalistic adherents have safeguarded their more restrictive definitions of inerrancy, while progressives have held that religious liberty in matters of biblical interpretation is a cherished Baptist principle. When, however, Convention delegates have become convinced that evidence exists of "liberal tendencies," particularly concerning biblical authority, their action has been swift and unsparing. In 1962, Dr. Ralph H. Elliott, a professor of Old Testament at Midwestern Baptist Theological Seminary, was fired for publishing a book in which he espoused more of a theological (rather than strictly historical) interpretation for the book of Genesis. In 1970 the Broadman Press commentary volume on Genesis, written by G. Henton Davies of Oxford University, in which he took account of historical-critical methods, was withdrawn and rewritten to be in harmony with the historic Southern Baptist positions.[43]

PRACTICAL DIMENSIONS OF BIBLICISM

Controversies about the Bible aside, Baptists have helped to produce a strong interest in the Scriptures within their own ranks and beyond. For instance, the early Baptists produced a number of bible study tools, including Vavasor Powell's *A New and Useful Concordance to the Holy Bible* (1671), Henry Jessey's *Scripture Motives for Calendar Reformation* (1650), and an important hermeneutical treatise, *Some Considerations Tending to the Asserting and Vindicating of the Use of Holy Scriptures and Christian Ordinances* (1649), by Henry Lawrence. In the eighteenth century, an important accomplishment was Benjamin Beddome's *Scriptural Exposition of the Baptist Catechism* (1752) and in America, Thomas Baldwin's* *Catechism* (1818).

By the late 1700s, Baptists began to produce expository works like John Gill's *Exposition of Scripture* (1780) and the collected works of Robert Hall. The first full commentaries were those written by W. N. Clarke (1850) and B. H. Carroll*

(1920), the latter of which was produced for a popular audience. In the twentieth century, the two major Baptist conventions in America have produced commentary series which presumably reflect Baptistic perspectives on the Bible.[44]

Modern Baptists have made their mark in the work of biblical exegesis and language study. Early in the twentieth century, Archibald T. Robertson, a long-time professor at Southern Baptist Seminary, produced the most comprehensive grammar of the Greek New Testament in his era, as well as a multivolume language study, *Word Pictures in the New Testament* (1930–33). Helen B. Montgomery* produced a centenary version of the New Testament from the original languages which still carries unique linguistic nuances. Perhaps the most impressive work of all was that of Edgar J. Goodspeed,* who was for forty years a professor at the University of Chicago.[45] Goodspeed approached biblical languages and literature from archaeological evidence and enriched the scholarly world with his new translation of the Bible, while also developing in fifty published works a reputation as a popular Bible teacher and preacher.

Because Baptists have spearheaded missionary work in non-English-speaking cultures, their contribution to Bible translation has been great. Beginning with William Carey's first edition in 1808 of portions of the New Testament and the Psalms, and continuing to the turn of the twentieth century, Baptists have produced well in excess of 150 foreign language translations of Scripture. Much of this work was done without prior training in the languages and involved the preparation of grammar books and dictionaries, which have remained major cultural contributions. To the credit of his denominational support and personal brilliance, William Carey, trained as a cobbler, was named in 1806 a professor of Sanskrit and Indian Languages at the British University in India, a high achievement for the first Baptist missionary. Challenged by his commitment to Scripture translation, Carey was proficient in 34 Indian dialects.[46] Carey's example was perpetuated in the later work of William Dean in China, who produced the first Scripture portions in a Chinese dialect, Jonathan Goble, who pioneered a Japanese translation in 1871, and Josiah and Ellen Cushing,* who completed the first language work in the Shan language.

Finally, the Bible has played a prominent role in the personal conversion narratives of some of the most prominent Baptists. John Smyth's biographers are clear that he altered his spiritual pilgrimage because of new insights in his personal studies of the New Testament.[47] Later in the seventeenth century, William Kiffin, unschooled insofar as the universities were concerned, took justifiable pride in his knowledge of the Greek and Hebrew languages that he used in Bible study. His saga could be multiplied many times over in the cases of John Gill, Isaac Backus, James R. Graves,* Helen Barrett Montgomery, and Billy Graham.* The freshness of their insights and the simplicity of their interpretation has frequently confounded and irritated those who have spent longer in the classrooms of higher education.

Even for those who do have formal theological training, the Bible has been a catalyst in change of sentiments to adopt Baptistic principles. Adoniram and

Ann Judson, in anticipation of a strong Baptistic case which William Carey would make upon their arrival in India, began to study "baptism" in the New Testament while at sea in 1812. Before they ever arrived, "after much laborious research and painful trial," they concluded that "the immersion of a professing believer is the only Christian baptism." Their colleague, Luther Rice,* on another ship, but facing the same circumstances, likewise found that the preponderance of Scripture evidence supported believer's baptism by immersion. So strong were their convictions that they were baptized in India and eventually severed their ties with the very organization which had provided their support for the mission endeavor![48]

Historically, then, Baptists have taken the Bible seriously and specifically. Whether it has been the exclamation of W. A. Criswell, pastor of First Baptist Church, Dallas, Texas, "I believe the Bible is literally true!" or the studied, quiet confidence of William Newton Clarke, "I saw the Bible in an entirely new light, free of proof-texts and scientific details,"[49] the Baptist commitment to Scripture's authority remains firm. For Baptists, the Bible is the sole font of revelation which speaks to both the intellect and the experience, the Church and the individual.

3
A NEW VISION FOR THE CHURCH

A CHURCH OF TRUE BELIEVERS

At the close of the nineteenth century, an insightful partisan wrote, "Baptists have always contended that the church is not worldly, but a spiritual body . . . organized on the basis of spiritual life."[1] The most fundamental contribution which Baptists made to Christian theology was a new vision for the visible Church. While it is certainly true that the first Baptists did make a significant break even with the Puritan/Separatist tradition, a more fully articulated Baptist doctrine of the Church has evolved over three centuries. From this vision of the Church has proceeded a particular view of the sacraments, church membership, denominational organization beyond the local congregation, and of the ministry.

Basic to the Baptist understanding of the Church is that the "true church is composed of true believers." Baptists followed the lead of Anabaptists, Puritans, Separatists, and others in Radical Protestantism in eschewing parish forms of Christianity or pedobaptist practices in providing opportunities for persons to be related to the Church who have never made an individual profession of faith. Further, Baptists have studiously avoided using the term "church" to describe buildings or ecclesiastical organizations; instead, preferring to apply "church" to individual persons or a congregation of people. This is hardly surprising since early Baptists lacked church buildings, and in both the English and American colonial contexts, non-Anglicans were frequently forbidden to refer to themselves or their property as "churches."

When John Smyth* wrote in 1607 that "the visible church is a visible communion of saints" he wrote as part of a great tradition of the believer's churches. Sixty years before Smyth, Peter Riedemann, a Moravian Anabaptist pastor, drew up a summary of doctrinal practices which read in part:

The true church is composed of true believers separated from the world and ruled over by the Holy Spirit, where righteousness dwells; existing church buildings, having been put to idolatrous uses, ought to be pulled down and utterly destroyed—Anabaptists never enter them.[2]

A generation later, the Dutch Mennonites, in a confession written about 1580, defined the Church as "believing and regenerated men, dispersed throughout the whole earth . . . the true people of god."[3] Most historians believe that Smyth, the Englishman, was aware of this tradition and was eventually influenced by it directly when he met the Mennonites during his exile in Holland 1608–12.

Thomas Helwys,* Smyth's colleague and successor, accepted Smyth's view of the Church and even embellished it: "A company of faithful people . . . separated from the world by the Word and Spirit of God . . . being knit unto the Lord, and one unto another, by baptism . . . upon their owne confession of the faith."[4] Similar to Helwys and the General Baptist view was the "church" of Particular Baptists: "a company of visible saints, called and separated from the world . . . to the visible profession of the faith, being baptized into that faith."[5]

For practical reasons, early Baptists laid aside the nagging question from the Reformation concerning the relationship between the "visible" and the "invisible" churches. Both Calvinistic and Arminian Baptists accepted Calvin's view of the invisible church as the elect of God, known ultimately to God. They chose, however, to focus upon the nature of that which was visible. Even after affirming the "visibility of saints" the Baptists of the late seventeenth century conceded that "the purest Churches under heaven are subject to mixture and error," the point being that members of true Churches will "consent to walk together according to the appointment of Christ, giving up themselves to the Lord and one another . . . in professed subjection to the ordinances of the Gospel" The idea of a believers' church was basic to the Baptist vision and predated them in the Anabaptist churches.[6]

The Baptists, however, moved a step further and so made their view of the Church distinctive. Smyth and his first congregation agreed with other Separatists that the churches of England and Rome were "antichrist"; Smyth disagreed that somehow true baptism had been preserved. He therefore envisioned a new church, based upon the "Ancient Church" with a new baptism to signify its reconstitution. Believer's baptism was not so much a requirement for church membership as a sign of the true church. "One holy baptism" was a vital bond among those who acknowledged "one faith, one spirit, one Lord and one body."

Helwys introduced in his 1611 Confession a nuance that would become a central concern in the Baptist doctrine of the Church. Admitting the oneness of the Church, his specific focus was on "divers particular congregations, even so many as there shall bee in the world." What was most visible to the original Baptists was a local congregation, which they presumed to have "all the means of their salvation" and the responsibility to celebrate the ordinances and exercise all the appropriate spiritual gifts. Helwys also argued that no single congregation has any prerogative over another, including the choice of pastors and members.[7] Each of the London Particular Baptist Confessions of Faith (1644, 1678) recognized individual congregations as having "all that power and authority, which is in any way needful" for a particular church, "compleatly Organized."[8] Only from such congregations would there be any legitimate para-church organizational life such as associations, unions, societies, and conventions.

After 1640 the majority of Baptist churches in England and the colonies practiced believer's baptism. Because the act was so vivid and the identification with church membership so strong, Baptists soon earned a reputation of having an exclusivist theology of the Church. Fiercely independent of any external authority and often opposed socially and politically to the establishment churches, Baptists had to work hard to overcome what appeared to be an atomized understanding of the Church. It was, therefore, through their joint creeds and confessions and also their need for concerted action in the face of persecution that they achieved a level of cooperative Christianity.

AUTONOMY AND INTERDEPENDENCE

Baptists were not originally local church protectionists. John Smyth's writings evince a support for the "Catholic Church" which he understood to be "the company of the elect," and which was invisible. Helwys thought that the "catholic" church was a combination of all the true particular churches and was less relevant than each congregation. In the Particular Baptist tradition, their last Confession of the seventeenth century unabashedly described the universal Church which the London churches held to be "invisible . . . the whole number of the Elect, that have been, are, or shall be gathered into one." Cogently, the Baptists were willing to admit that there were true Christians in other churches; they were reluctant, however, to admit that any other organization or ecclesiastical structure was scriptural and thus legitimate. In their view, the true universal church and the true particular churches were always composed only of the true believers. The Confession of 1677 put it well: "Each church and all the members of it are bound to pray continually for the good and prosperity of all the churches of Christ in all places. . . . The churches ought to hold communion amongst themselves."[9]

In the next century, Baptist concepts of the Church were profoundly influenced by two major theologians, John Gill* and Andrew Fuller.* Their preaching, writing, and personal influence affected generations of Baptists on both sides of the Atlantic, and in America led to two clearly delineated approaches among Baptists.

John Gill was the leading theologian among Baptists in the early 1700s. His adoption of extreme Calvinism led to a predictable doctrine of the Church, which was that body of individuals who were "the elect of God, the general assembly and the church of the first born, whose names are written in heaven." It was the task of the Lord of the Church "to convert daily God's elect." Fighting against perceived evils of rationalism and Pelagianism, Gill maintained that "it was not his practice to address unconverted sinners, not to enforce the invitations of the

Gospel."[10] The task of the Church, as a small local gospel church, was to receive the elect and nurture them in faith and holiness. Worship and nurture were paramount over service and outreach in Gill's system, and he allowed no interference or connectionalism outside the local congregation. As a pastor, Gill was indefatigable; but as a co-laborer with other pastors, Gill had great limitations.

In the last two decades of the eighteenth century, Andrew Fuller of Kettering challenged "Gillism." Fuller's new aggressive evangelism called into question the nature and purpose of the Church and provided the theological rationale for the great missionary movement. For the pastor at Kettering, the Church was universal: "True catholic zeal will have the good of the universal church of Christ for its grand object, and will rejoice in the prosperity of every denomination of Christians." Moreover, he held that the church had a mission: "In the New Testament Church all the gifts and graces by which Christians were distinguished was given them with the design of their communicating it to others." In another context, Fuller characterized the Church as "armies of the Lamb, the grand object of which is to extend the Redeemer's Kingdom." Unlike Gill, Fuller believed the work of the Church was primarily evangelism, which included the sermon, the study of Scripture, and Christian vocation: "The end of your existence is to hold forth the word of life," he said.[11] In both Gill and Fuller, the two great impulses of the Church can be seen from within a Baptist perspective, although, unfortunately, at counterpoint. Baptists in America reflected these same positions and, in many ways, they pressed each to its logical extreme.

In the American context, the vast majority of the Baptist congregations accepted the London Particular Baptist view and acted upon it creatively. Doctrinally, most people would have agreed with John Gill, but had little enthusiasm for wading through his "continent of mud," as Robert Hall called Gill's theological writings.[12] In 1670 General Baptist congregations in New England recognized the value of intrachurch relations for reasons of survival and formed the first American association: likewise, the Philadelphia Baptists organized in 1707 and formally adopted the Second London Confession in 1742. Seven years later in 1749 Philadelphia Baptists approved a definition of the Church and associational life which significantly asserted that "each Church hath a complete power and authority from Jesus Christ . . . and that several such independent churches . . . may and ought . . . to enter into an agreement and confederation."[13] The early experience of Baptists in America recognized both the spiritual independence of local congregations and the practical need for a larger vision of the Church.

But, beginning in the mid-eighteenth century in New England, some U.S. Baptists expressed chagrin at expressions of the Church existing beyond the local congregation. Isaac Backus, for instance, wrote in his diary concerning membership in the Warren, Rhode Island, Association: "I do not see my way clear to join now, if ever I do."[14] He was predictably wary of any organization of churches which might interfere with the affairs of a single congregation, as the Congregationalist Association had done in his case over the issue of "New-

Side'' theology. Although there was cooperation among the churches for matters of ordination and political advice, there was a growing local church protectionism among the Separate Baptists in New England following the Great Awakening.

Whatever the reasons—social, political and theological—local church protectionism reached a peak among Baptist in the nineteenth century and threatened some traditional Baptist ideas about the Church. In the antimission movement, a strange combination of antagonism to fund-raisers and far-flung benevolent projects, plus a hyper-Calvinist theology, placed severe limitations on the Baptist concept of the Church. Of God, the hyper-Calvinists queried, ''Shall we be employed in holding him up to view as a being not able to accomplish the good pleasure of his will?'' Likewise, the antimissionists exclaimed, ''We believe the gospel dispensation to embrace a system of faith and obedience . . . and the seasons of declension and of darkness . . . are for trying the faith of God's people in His wisdom, power, and faithfulness to sustain His Church.''[15] Such reasoning, usually associated with the early Primitive or Old School Baptists, was not limited to peripheral frontier churches.

Among well-educated Baptists, on the Eastern seaboard, it was President Francis Wayland of Brown University who said in 1856: ''The Baptists have ever believed in the entire and absolute independence of the churches . . . with the church all ecclesiastical relations of every member, are limited to the church to which he belongs.''[16] Wayland did not, however, as the antimission folk did, adopt a hyper-Calvinistic theology to accompany his local church protectionism. Indeed, he argued very strongly that the object of the visible church is ''the conversion of souls.'' For this reason he fits well in the company of the New School adherents of his era. Because most leadership in the primary urban churches and educational institutions was influenced by President Wayland, his impact upon the denomination was profound.

The New Hampshire Confession of Faith, issued in 1833 and enlarged and distributed broadly in 1853, infused a new authority to the Wayland doctrine of the Church. J. Newton Brown and a committee of three others in the New Hampshire Baptist State Convention wrote of a gospel church: ''that a visible Church of Christ is a congregation of baptized believers,'' thus omitting any reference to a universal church, time-honored Baptist associationalism, or any concern with the historic issue of the ''invisible church.'' Brown was later able to reproduce in the thousands the Confession as part of his *Baptist Church Manual* (1853), which, because he was an officer of the American Baptist Publication Society, carried great weight in Baptist circles.[17]

The legacy of J. Newton Brown and the New Hampshire Confession was far-reaching. J. M. Pendleton and Edward T. Hiscox wrote their Baptist manuals and directories around its articles. This enabled the Confession to survive well into the twentieth century. When doctrinal controversy erupted in the Northern Baptist Convention following World War I, the New Hampshire Confession was a rallying point for moderate Fundamentalists. Two of the schismatic groups in the North, the General Association of Regular Baptists and the Conservative

Baptist Association, adopted modified versions of the 1853 edition as their doctrinal basis. More significantly, in 1925, the Southern Baptist Convention had approved a statement on "Baptist Faith and Message" which was essentially the New Hampshire Confession with additional articles on peace, social service, and education.[18] The limited doctrine of the church as a single congregation, inherent in the ethos of nineteenth-century New Hampshire, thus became the authority for the majority of Baptists in the United States.

In addition to the official pronouncements in which a Baptist doctrine of the Church was articulated, there were other influential factors which shaped denominational ecclesiology. The reduction of the Church to a local congregation had found wide acceptance in the Landmark movement of the late nineteenth century. James R. Graves,* considered the progenitor of Landmarkers, had no doubts but that the scriptural form of a church was "a single congregation, complete in itself, independent of all other bodies . . . and the highest and only source of ecclesiastical authority on earth, amenable only to Christ." Another in this tradition went even further by writing that:

Every local congregation of baptized believers united in church worship and work is as complete a church as ever existed and is perfectly competent to do whatever a church can of right do. It is as complete as if it were the only church in the world.[19]

E. Y. Mullins,* a staunch Southern Baptist and no doubt aware of the Landmark influence in his own fellowship, was pointed in his recognition of congregational independence as a Baptist distinctive by the turn of the twentieth century. While he recognized the value of cooperation in Christian work, he also knew that

Jesus Christ is Lord of the church. It exists in obedience to His command and has no mission on earth save the carrying out of His will. It must not form alliances of any kind with the state so that it surrenders any of its own functions or assumes any of the functions of civil government. Its government is democratic and autonomous.[20]

Mullins thereby introduced in 1912 a new term—"autonomous"—to the Baptist vocabulary. It has been used to the present era as an accepted watermark of Baptist identity in both the mainstream and non-aligned Baptist groups. So pervasive has been the influence of local church protectionism in SBC churches, that persons who attend the annual Convention sessions are still referred to as "messengers" rather than delegates with full representational powers.

Among Baptists in the northern United States, Henry Vedder, a well-known Baptist church historian, observed the congregational tendency and even went so far as to suggest that even the Presbyterians, Episcopalians, and Methodists recognize the practical independence of the local church. Within his own communion, the Northern Baptist Convention, the 1907 founders were well aware of the need to reassure Baptists with respect to the new national body: "The

Northern Baptist Convention declares its belief in the independence of the local church and in the purely advisory nature of all denominational organizations composed of representatives of churches."[21]

While the legacy of local church protectionism characterized most Baptists in America who lived in rural and small town settings, the urban context also influenced the Baptist understanding of the Church. At about 1850 those old, first churches in the cities took on the accouterments of the other Protestant congregations and developed architecturally grand meeting houses and elaborate programs of outreach, the latter prompted by the Home Mission Society's interest in immigrants. David Benedict, premier Baptist historian at mid-century, noted the formidable church buildings among the Baptists, particularly those in Baltimore, Charleston, and New York— Baltimore's being designed by a prominent architect, Robert Mills.[22] All of this material advance was made possible by the new-found wealth and social mobility of families like William Colgate* and John D. Rockefeller.

With a good financial base and adequate facilities, several Baptist pastors inaugurated in the next several decades what came to be known as the institutional church. Such churches were typically downtown, wealthy, and socially directed. By 'institutional church' they meant organized efforts in pastoral visitation, Sunday School education, child care, food and shelter, athletics, choirs, hospitals, youth groups, fresh air for children, flower cultivation, and cool, fresh water. Additionally, there were standard forms adopted for worship, Bible study, music, evangelism, and church growth. Edward Judson,* pastor of the Memorial Church at Washington Square, New York City, who visited scores of people each week, called it simply "organized kindness"[23]—touching people in their physical, social and intellectual contexts to draw them within reach of the gospel.

Many of the institutional Baptist churches took on the name "temple" after Russell Conwell's* example in Philadelphia. By 1891 his small Grace Baptist Church in North Philadelphia had moved to its new magnificent home on Broad Street, which included a five-thousand seat auditorium, offices, classrooms, and eventually, a college and hospital. The building was designed in the form of a Greco-Roman temple. It quickly became a symbol, in the city and the denomination, of the institutional church, open seven days a week and all night. By 1920, the Baptist temple movement extended to Boston, Rochester, Akron, Charleston, Los Angeles, Cincinnati, Detroit, and Pittsburgh. In some cases, handsome theater-like auditoriums filled the cores of multistory office buildings which earned rental income for the church's all-missionary budget. Others featured imposing edifices characteristic of Charles Spurgeon's Metopolitan Tabernacle in London, where great throngs came to enjoy expository preaching.[24] No longer a small, closed-communion, intimate body of believers, the Baptist institutional churches were community focal points and sought to meet the needs of what has often been an adversarial, non-Christian social context in recent years.

Although for all practical purposes the vast majority of Baptists posit their ecclesiology squarely in individual congregations, there are exceptions where Baptists of the twentieth century have achieved a broader vision. Northern/ American Baptists, for instance, have risked membership in ecumenical organizations at the local, national and international levels. In fact, American Baptists have provided, in proportion to their size, more of the national ecumenical leadership than any other single Protestant body. Similarly, Baptists in Great Britain and Ireland are members of the British Council of Churches and are frequently invited to participate as ecclesiastical delegates in affairs of state. Something of the vision of the seventeenth-century Baptist community is thus recaptured in the British statement:

It is in membership of a local church in one place that the fellowship of the one, holy, catholic Church becomes significant. Indeed, such gathered companies of believers are the local manifestation of the one Church of God on earth and in heaven.

MEMBERSHIP AND THE COVENANTING COMMUNITY

Doctrines of the Church notwithstanding, Baptists have been more concerned with the outworking or practicality of church membership. Central to this concern was the church covenant, which among early Baptists was individually devised by congregations and later made standard by a common form. In the Free Church tradition, the church covenant serves the vital purpose of voluntarily creating Christian community, in the absence of creeds or episcopal structures.

Church covenants were not unique to the Baptist tradition in the early seventeenth century. As early as 1527 the idea of a covenant between believers was noticeable among Anabaptists. In a series of seven articles, Michael Satler was identified with a community which formed a brotherhood "to do the will of God" following baptism. Part of their agreement was to be separated both from the "devil's evil and wickedness" and from "papal church ways." Later, Melchior Hoffmann, another Anabaptist in Strasburg, wrote of the covenant that "it is a union similar to a marriage covenant and that in the Lord's Supper the Lord offers to his bride a piece of bread as a ring."[26] Though Hoffmann's own popularity waned after the fall of Muenster in 1535, Hoffmann's followers fled to England and Holland, presumably carrying their principle of the covenant with them.

The most likely immediate background for the use of covenants among Baptists is their use among the Brownists. Robert Browne, an Englishman, conceived of the covenant relationship in a two-fold way; first, that God has called His people together and has assured them of salvation, and second that God's people are expected to give themselves up to the Church, beginning as children and then submitting continually to God's laws and government. The seal of the covenant was baptism, and spiritual nurture was to be provided by God in Holy Communion. Critics of Browne thought that he had borrowed his ideas from the Anabaptists; he may also have been influenced by the Scottish national covenant, which was signed in 1580. Whatever the origins of Robert Browne's ideas, several Independent congregations, notably Francis Johnson's and John Robinson's churches, followed the pattern.[27] The classic example of the tradition in America was the ratification of the covenant among the so-called Mayflower Church, bound for the New World in 1620.

The earliest Baptists did not readily accept the idea of the covenant. In the first place, John Smyth desired a more purely Apostolic pattern than Robert Browne's polity afforded. By 1609, when Smyth published his book, *The Character of the Beast or the False Constitution of the Church*, he clearly thought that "baptisme is the visible forme of the Church (not the church covenant)." Baptism became the critical sign of the new order: first, repentance and confession of faith, then the true church gathered by baptism. John Robinson, formerly a colleague of Smyth and Helwys and later one of their critics, said that the Baptists "could not even pray together, before they had baptism."[28] Of key importance to Smyth, Helwys, and later their successor, John Murton, were the New Testament concepts that "except a man be born of water and the spirit he cannot enter into the Kingdom of God" (John 8:36) and the order of repentance, faith, and baptism taught in Hebrews 6:1–2. In fact, Murton wrote that the Separatists were wrong about baptism as the seal of any covenant, but that the biblical pattern was faith and baptism "and not by the one only." Among the Baptist pioneers, God had made an irrevocable covenant in the New Testament with his people, which could be enjoyed by any who would believe the gospel and be baptized.

Not all Baptists before 1650 agreed that covenants were of little or no use. Although the term covenant was not used among them, the Particular Baptists created descriptive agreements amongst themselves that summarized their theological and practical tenets. William Kiffin,* for example, spoke of baptism as "a pledge of entering into Covenant with God, and our giving up ourselves unto Him in the Solemn Bond of Religion." Benjamin Keach* likewise in 1693 asserted that true believers "consent to give themselves up to the Lord, and one to another, to walk in fellowship and communion in all the Ordinances of the Gospel," thus recognizing that it was appropriate for church members to have an obligation to each other. Finally, shortly after the issuance of the First London Confession in 1644, the critic of the Baptists, Daniel Featley, noted "the schismaticall covenants" of the group, by which he probably meant their theological agreements, were proliferating in number all too rapidly.[29]

In the early American colonies, Baptists wrote covenants almost from the beginning, perhaps because it was the recognized pattern of church organization in the Puritan Commonwealth or perhaps to avoid undue persecution for misunderstood "heretical" views. Neither the Providence nor Newport congregations created covenants which have survived; the church at Newport is said not to have adopted its first statement until 1727. The third church at Swansea, which John Myles* transferred from Wales to Massachusetts, did have a covenant, however, and it served as an important pattern for other congregations. In the document, the authors noted that because of the "exceeding Riches of God's

Infinite Grace,'' Christians have a ''Duty to walk in visible communion with Christ and each other according to the Prescript Rule of his most Holy Word.'' Specifically, the Swansea folk found it ''loathsome to their souls'' to create principles or practices which divide the people of God and they thus declared that ''Union in Christ is the sole ground of our Communion.''[30] The first known covenant among Baptist Americans was a compact between members to practice charitable feelings among themselves.

Similar to the Swansea agreement were those of Boston and Kittery, Maine (later removed to Charleston, South Carolina). At the organization meetings of the Boston church in the home of its founder Thomas Goold, there was a consensus ''to walk together in all the appointments of the Lord & Master,'' and they then were baptized. Key to their compact was the proper performance of the ordinances. When William Screven* gathered the Kittery church, he presented their covenant to the Baptist congregation at Boston, and a copy of their agreement was entered in the 1682 Boston records. The Maine group unabashedly called it a solemn covenant between themselves and purposed to observe faithfully the commandments, ordinances, institutions and appointments revealed in the Scriptures. All ten members of the new church signed the covenant.[31] Since Screven's congregation was forced to emigrate to the South about 1685 with their covenant, the implications of covenant use among the Southern churches is exceedingly important.

Baptist congregations in America continued to frame covenantal statements well into the eighteenth century. These intercongregational agreements followed the basic pattern of Swansea and Boston and used many of the time-honored phrases of the English Baptists from the previous century. Often accompanying the covenant, which focused upon membership obligations, was a confession of faith or articles of belief, which listed typical theological assertions about the Scriptures, God, redemption, the Christian life, and the nature of the Church. The covenant evolved into an agreement among church members about formally constituting a church, how the church would be supported, how members would participate, and what the church's relationship to its community might be. As Separate Congregational churches in New England moved to become Baptists, the covenantal tradition was brought over into their new church life. Another affirmation of the covenanting process came from the desire, particularly of the Philadelphia Baptist Association, to start new churches. In fact, in the 1790s so many new congregations were started in the South and West that leaders called for a manual to make standard the practices of Baptist churches. Samuel Jones wrote such a book in 1798 in which he penned the first universal covenant, which rapidly achieved success in the churches.

Jones included in his covenant the principle of voluntary submission to the Lord and to one another and the specific duties expected of church members. In part, his list included a dozen concerns:

1. To be one body under one head
2. To act by the rules of the gospel

3. To do all that the Lord commands

4. To deny ourselves

5. Take up the Cross

6. Keep the faith

7. Assemble together

8. Love the brethren

9. Care for one another

10. Submit to one another in the Lord

11. Keep the unity of the Spirit in peace

12. Obey them who have rule over us.

Jones' version pointed the congregations in the direction of missionary endeavor (the advancement of the Redeemer's Kingdom) and he left the opportunity open for discipline of those who failed to honor their covenantal obligations.[32] With the publication of Jones' "official" covenant, the idea of covenant as a locally styled uniquely congregational compact was diminished.

Among the Freewill Baptists the tradition of church covenants was also important. Benjamin Randall,* founder of the Freewill Baptist Connexion, brought to the Baptists a strong sense of covenant from his Congregationalist roots. He recommended that each Freewill meeting be established by covenant. Randall himself met with the first covenanting families of the Freewills on 30 June 1780 to form a covenant "according to Scripture and necessary for the visible government of the Church of Christ." This first church at New Durham, New Hampshire, functioned on a simple and liberal theological basis, less specific than seventeenth-century models. His wider fellowship was based on monthly and quarterly meetings at which the covenants were recited and the larger intra-church relationships were affirmed and strengthened. Following the reading of the covenants, Freewill Baptists would proceed to celebrate the Lord's Supper and baptism if necessary. In a time of slackened growth in his Connexion, Randall lamented that morale was low and covenantal obligations were not being taken as seriously as they should have been.[33]

After the turn of the nineteenth century, Baptist Americans began to look for common patterns in covenantal expressions. With the publication of Samuel Jones's model covenant in 1796, the Philadelphia Association took the lead in providing an acceptable form. Jones assumed that the primary function of the covenant was to give written expression to the constitution of a congregation; he thus stressed promissory obligations. As later members were added, each one would publicly accept the covenantal obligations in the midst of the congregation. Unlike the earlier individual congregational covenants, Jones's standard form lacked the specificity needed for discipline of errant membership. Deacons, trustees, and prudential committees were thus left with a significant task in judicial interpretation.[34]

A secretary of the American Baptist Publication Society provided Baptists of all types with a standard covenant which is still in widespread use today. J. Newton Brown,* also the promoter of the New Hampshire Confession of Faith, added a covenantal statement to his *Baptist Church Manual* in 1853 and urged its adoption among the churches. Predictably, Brown focused his attention on the local congregation which he viewed as "one body in Christ." His intent was to provide a statement which would function as a vehicle of membership renewal and thus he called attention to the public and private spiritual life expected of church members and the need to maintain the "worship, ordinances, discipline and doctrines" of congregational life. Brown's covenant evinced some of the ultraism of the Second Great Awakening during the Finney revivals: "The sale and use of intoxicating drinks as a beverage" was forbidden. He also reflected the efforts of the Baptist benevolent empire in urging church members to contribute to the relief of the poor, the regular support of the ministry and global missionary endeavors. But all such work was to be ultimately scrutinized in the local church setting which Brown affirmed to the point of pledging "when we remove from this place, we will as soon as possible unite with some other Church, where we can carry out the spirit of this covenant and the principles of God's Word."[35] Due largely to its spirit of local church protectionism, Brown's "Church Covenant" achieved what few standard expressions have done among Baptists: It is broadly accepted and has outlived its author.

Strong membership participation is at the heart of the theology and polity of a vital Baptist congregation. This implies that persons with strong Christian commitments and an interest in the Church are accepted as members in the first place. Membership standards are initial and continuous, though it must be admitted that second and later generation Baptists have exhibited more flexibility and less intensity about church membership than the first generation. Part of this has been due to a decreasing propensity for disciplining errant members.

As stated elsewhere, a regenerate membership was essential to early Baptists. Those who were concerned "to walk in all His ways" defined specific marks of a believer. When candidates for membership were presented to the congregations, most important was an experimental declaration of the work of regeneration. In the seventeenth century, Baptist congregations were small enough to examine candidates for membership in the midst of the entire congregation. Later, this task was delegated to the deacons, who, when satisfied, presented the candidates for a voice vote and covenant ceremony. Unexpected pressure was applied to this process beginning in the eighteenth-century revivals where overt responses to emotive sermons were popularized and church membership came to be more closely linked to a public profession of faith and usually baptism. Baptist preachers on the western and southern frontiers in particular sought to build entire congregations and associations of churches around the "quick fires" of new conversions, in part because the preachers itinerated and could not remain long enough to follow more reflective procedures. As William Warren Sweet observed, ''Many a Baptist church on the frontier was first gathered and finally organized by licensed preachers''[36] rather than by fully ordained clergy.

In the mid–1800s, in part due to the impact of revivalism and partly to the crossover of many people from one Protestant group to another, Baptist polity evolved to allow for other means of accepting new members than by baptism. In many churches, a letter of membership transfer had always been acceptable for those who relocated geographically. The Landmarkers saw in this process a possible violation of the rights of a local church and warned that such a transfer of letter was not automatic. As James R. Graves put it, ''No church on earth is compelled to receive a person because he has a letter of credit from another sister church.'' Revivalism, in particular, promoted the higher priority of experience over sacrament and for Baptists this led to the widespread practice called ''statement of Christian faith.''[37] If a person was so moved by the Spirit in a given service to profess publicly his or her faith or a renewed commitment to Christ, and requested membership, the person could be quickly granted full membership. No questions were raised about former church relationships and sometimes not even about believer's baptism, though ''professors'' were urged to seek baptism in the new congregation. This procedure was especially helpful in renewing membership vows and encouraging backsliders. In the past century, most Baptists have encouraged public professions of faith and due to the forces of the church growth movement have readily provided membership on publicly experiential terms. A minority of more theologically Calvinistic congregations have maintained that members are to be scrutinized and then catechized prior to full membership.

Once membership is established, each covenanting believer is expected to provide a profile of ''discipleship.'' Members are ''not to forsake the assembling of themselves together''; each wage earner is to tithe or contribute at least 10 percent of income to the church treasury; and each person is to be ready to accept some responsibility in the fellowship commensurate with his or her gifts. Since the congregation, not a board of elders or the pastor, is the decision-making authority, it is essential that participation be high. Early and later, Baptists as a congregation decide upon matters relating to each other's welfare, the mission of the church, provision for a pastor, and what should be the social and perhaps political concerns of the church. With the voting decision comes the responsibility to provide the means to act. In general, no special office or responsibility in the church comes without membership and all members are expected to be active.[38]

Human behavior being what it is, Baptists have also had to deal with the reality of failure and uninterested members. From the earliest periods, Baptists have exercised discipline over each other and usually with the specific force of Scriptural injunctions. Typical of early (and later) membership problems were lack of support, drunkenness, gossip, and schismatic behavior. Early records are replete with reports of misbehavior and the efforts of congregational leaders to correct the problem. A first response would be admonition. The pastor would visit the individual and report the church's concern. Admonitions failing, the deacons would next visit and perhaps censure the person, probably depriving the individual the rights of membership for a stated period. The last resort was excommunication by vote of the congregation, which in many cases was counteracted, in a small community, by repentance and restoration. A classic case of church discipline in the early American context was that of Morgan Edwards,* erstwhile pastor at First Baptist Church, Philadelphia, who was dropped from the rolls of the church in 1785 ostensibly for drunkenness, but also certainly for his advocacy of the Loyalist cause during the Revolution and his misunderstood friendship with the Universalist Elhanan Winchester.* After several applications, Edwards was restored in 1788. Discipline could also come between family members as in 1916, when Augustus H. Strong* led the Prudential Committee of First Baptist Church, Rochester, New York, in the excommunication of his son, Charles Augustus Strong, for infidelity. In his diary, Strong later grieved over his action and rejoiced at John's restoration.[39]

Sadly for those who espouse a high quality of church membership, Baptists have lately experienced the same patterns of membership deficiencies that other Christian groups have. Typically, Sunday services do not exceed one-third of the membership roster and covenant responsibilities often go unheeded. Smaller churches have expressed anxiety over loss of members should harsh discipline be applied, while larger congregations, especially the "superchurches," almost seem to discourage much participation and watchcare because of the sheer numbers involved. The primary means of participation in such churches is by the financial offering; non-contributing members are the first candidates for removal.

LEADERSHIP PATTERNS AMONG THE CHURCHES

Most Baptists have held that the primary differentiation of leadership was between the membership and the "ministry." However, there has been much diversity as Baptists have identified deacons, elders, bishops, and executive ministers, not to speak of secretaries, presidents, missionaries, and moderators.

The earliest Baptists were convinced that one of the most vividly corrupt aspects of the Established Church was the ministry. Anglican ministers were ordained by a "corrupt" episcopacy and their personal lifestyles and dearth of pastoral concern ill fitted them to be true ministers of the Gospel. Presbyterian divines still operated on the basis of a parish system and, thought the Baptists, used political and social controls to maintain their hegemony. For the most part, the original Baptist ministry was built upon the Separatists and was influenced by the continental Anabaptists.

The purpose of the ministry, in the words of the First London Confession, was the "feeding, governing, serving and building up of Christ's Church . . . according to God's ordinance and not filthy lucre."[40] Particular Baptists recognized the propriety of pastors, teachers, elders, and deacons, while General

Baptists also added the offices of bishop and messenger, sometimes one and the same. The term "pastor" was used to denote the spiritual leader of a congregation who was elected, upon the basis of his or her call, by a local church and typically for life, until professional mobility increased in the nineteenth century.

In the Baptist tradition, ordination became the official blessing of a local church (and later an association) upon the gifts and fitness of candidates for the ministry. Ordination was itself controversial among early Baptists, some maintaining that "there is not one parish of ten [in the Church of England] that hath one of your ordained men that is able to preach Christ," and a goodly number of lay preachers canvassed the English countryside with no official certification except their effectiveness. By the 1650s, however, ordination as an investigation of qualifications, followed by the service of the laying on of hands, was commonly practiced by the General Baptists at the associational level and by the Particular Baptists within local congregations.[41]

In order to secure the liberty to preach during the Restoration, ordained Baptists were forced to secure licenses or certificates which attested to their approval by the Anglican authorities. Often these certificates were issued for "Presbyterians" or "Independents," which further irritated Baptists who still had no public recognition for their ministry. John Bunyan, for instance, more than once refused the certificate process as an infringement upon his rights and he continued to preach even while in prison.[42]

Baptists in early America were also forced to the ordination of clergy as a means of achieving a minimal public approbation of their status. In New England, to secure exemption from taxes, Baptist ministers were ordained by local churches and recognized by associations. During the mid to late eighteenth century in the middle colonies, the Philadelphia Association moved from a policy of reordination for each new pastoral assignment to issuing certificates that were valid as long as the ordinand did not violate Christian propriety or associational fellowship. One of the first persons to benefit from a certificate was David Thomas of Chester County, Pennsylvania, who relocated to Fauquier County, Virginia, in 1762, where he began a ministry as part of the up-country revival.[43]

Functionally, modern Baptists have tended to recognize only one order of ministry which they variously refer to as pastor, bishop, shepherd, or simply preacher. This is reflective of the continuing bias against a church hierarchy and clergy who are beyond the accountability of local congregations. The chief tasks of the pastor are to preach the word, administer the sacraments/ordinances and provide spiritual oversight for the congregation. Pastors are usually members of the churches they serve; however, they generally do not serve as moderators of the congregation. Pastors are assisted in their spiritual office by deacons and elders who are usually unordained. In the black Baptist tradition, the role of the pastor has an especially significant role from the slave period. It involved at times being the sole interpreter of Scripture, a community leader and father figure, and a prophet with unusual authority.[44] Something akin to this model may be seen in the Fundamentalist Baptist movement where pastors are highly authoritarian, creating the total program for the congregation and completely determining the theological and missional profile of a church.

Among contemporary Baptists, specialization of ministry and even ordination have been extended beyond the pastoral office. In the nineteenth century, the role of associate or assistant pastor was a recognized intern status. Later, however, in large congregations, permanent roles for educators, musicians, and visitation ministers emerged and the need for standard qualifications followed. By the 1920s Baptists started schools for Christian education and music and produced ministers of music and education, who among Baptists in America may be candidates for ordination.[45] Not infrequently, these specialized ministers also later seek recognition as pastors.

Unlike their Congregationalist brethren and sisters, Baptists did not long retain the title of teacher as a specialized ministry. Perhaps due to increasing opportunities to begin new churches with full pastoral tasks, the role of teacher was assumed by lay leadership. Deacons were elected from the congregation primarily to prepare the Lord's Supper and to care for the needs of the poor, as in the New Testament. Elders were sometimes elected to serve with pastors in the general oversight of congregations, though elected lay elders were not much in vogue by the eighteenth century. Records are clear that by the 1660s women were able to serve in all lay functions of the congregations and some, like Dorothy Hazzard of Bristol, actually helped to organize churches.[46]

General Baptists led in the development of an extra-parish function for ministers which has been variously called bishop, overseer, or messenger, and later association ministers or executive ministers. At first (probably not before 1650) a messenger was literally the outstretched hand of the congregations. Elected by associations or assemblies, these leaders had the right to preach outside local congregations, to strengthen weak churches and pastors and to defend the gospel against false teachers. Thomas Grantham,* the great exponent of General Baptist polity, wrote of these honored laborers that "we give them no more superintendency than Timothy and Titus had. . . . Their preeminence was only a degree of honor (not of power) in being greater Servants than others."[47]

While Particular Baptists did occasionally have association ministers, the idea did not progress until the 1770s in America. Five years before national independence, the Philadelphia Association elected evangelists to travel outside the Association to start new churches and collect statistical data on existing congregations. Two decades later the Shaftesbury, Vermont, and the Massachusetts associations commissioned domestic missionaries for much the same purpose.[48] The success of these labors led the Home Mission Society and later the state conventions to provide funds for permanent, full-time executive secretaries to supervise fundraising, assist in pastoral placement, strengthen feeble churches, and promote Baptist identity. In the twentieth century, several Baptist groups recognize the validity of "executive ministers" who perform all of the above functions and also serve as personnel officers, chief executive officers of mission organizations, and associate national secretaries.[49] Several black Baptist communions and overseas groups use the title "bishop" to designate these officers, while acknowledging that such folk have no theological or ecclesiological import beyond that of their own local church recognition and specifically defined associational tasks. It must be admitted that many Baptists still eschew the designation of political officers and extra-parish ministries, and this has been a major contributing factor in the advance of nonaligned or "independent" Baptist life.

While a definite sense of call from God plus the appropriate personal attributes and lifestyle have been chief determinants in the identification of a professional ministry, Baptists have more recently been concerned about education. In the seventeenth century, Baptists (and other Nonconformists) were barred from most avenues of higher education; hence the importance of Edward Terrill's trust in Bristol, England, which set up the first Baptist educational institution in 1679. In the American colonies only one school existed for the training of Baptist leaders until 1813, and few Baptists took advantage of other colleges. Ironically, even with the establishment of eighty colleges and seminaries by 1900, most Baptist ministers lacked much formal education. To no one's surprise, then, Baptist leaders of almost every type in the twentieth century have stressed the need for education.[50]

In the first Baptist academies in Britain and America, stress was laid primarily upon linguistic, historical, and theological studies. Graduates with baccalaureate degrees were considered quite competent until well into the 1800s. For several decades thereafter the Andover model of post-collegiate theological training competed with the four-year literary and theological institutions for still only a minority of Baptist clergy. One exception, missionaries, could be easily persuaded to obtain a sophisticated education in preparation for overseas translation and medical work.

Tragically, at about the time when Baptist congregations and ordination councils began to see the benefits of an educated clergy, controversy within the educational process itself broke out. In the 1890s, the University of Chicago's progressive curriculum was suspect for many Northern Baptists. Later Brown University and Crozer, Rochester, and Newton seminaries were scrutinized by conservative Baptist leaders and found wanting in their commitment to traditional Baptist ideas about Scripture and polity. In the wake of the investigations and schisms, a new educational tradition of Bible colleges and institutes arose to replace the traditional liberal arts–theological seminary model of an earlier era. For many anti-modernists, it was sufficient for a Baptist minister to attend a Bible college and accumulate as much English Bible content as possible.[51] History, theology, language, and the arts became almost forgotten to an increasing number of students.

To offset this challenging circumstance, Baptists in Great Britain and the United States sought to strengthen the ministry and denominational identity by tightening the standards for ordination. By 1960, most mainstream Baptists began to require four years of college education plus seminary work to achieve full ordination status in the associations. Those who were unable to meet this standard were given special consideration in tutelage programs and special diploma programs. And, because insufficient institutions were available within the Baptist family, over twenty-five new seminaries were opened in the past half-century. Still, it has been estimated that one third to one half of the primary pastors in Southern and Northern U.S. Baptist pastorates lacked a college degree or any seminary studies.[52] On the positive side this has allowed Baptists to maintain their historic mistrust of an overly institutional form of ministry and put in its place an often fresh and lively lay ministry. William Kiffin, the self-taught brewmaster-turned-pastor of the oldest Particular Baptist church of the seventeenth century, continues to be a role model for the Baptist ministry.

In the evolution of their new vision for the Church, Baptists set aside some longstanding notions about ecclesiology. More than cathedrals and social institutions, the church was a body of believers who voluntarily gathered for worship and mission. Unlike those in a covenantal tradition, Baptists argued that believer's baptism was the sign of the unity of the church. Members were expected to participate actively and directly in the life of the congregation; no parish system was recognized. And finally, in the identification of offices and persons to lead the church, Baptists looked to the New Testament for examples, rejecting a hierarchy or succession and even deciding that titles such as ''reverend'' were unwarranted in an egalitarian body of believers.[53] In providing a critique of existing Christianity, Baptists have often been harsh in their assessments, yet their urge to recover primitive patterns has also been fresh and provocative. As a non-Baptist has observed, ''The Baptists seem to prove that the Christian church can live and grow as a personal fellowship based on a directly shared experience, provided it is interpreted through a commonly accepted language of Scriptural symbols.''[54]

4
SACRAMENTS/ORDINANCES: SIGNS OF FAITH

Baptists chose to give the sacraments, or ordinances as many called them, a new interpretation in the life of the Church. Their sense of the importance of baptism and the Lord's Supper stemmed directly from their understanding of the believer's church and their attachment to literalistic readings of the key New Testament passages. Baptists agreed with the Reformers that the true Church was present "where the word was preached and the sacraments rightly administered," a definition that involved modes and forms as well as subjects. In their search to recover the primitive models, some Baptists were open to certain other practices as ordinances but did not consider them sacraments. The major Baptist contribution to modern Christian ecclesiology is without question an unwavering statement concerning the ordinances, particularly believer's baptism by immersion.

BAPTISM

Against charges of sacramentalism, Baptists are primarily differentiated by their view and practice of baptism. It is not merely an issue of timing, but a concern for the proper subjects, mode, and context. Baptism among Baptists is inextricably tied up with their doctrine of the Church, and it is the principal sign of their determination to imitate the New Testament churches. To use Morgan Edwards's* phrase, "Believer's baptism is our denominating article."[1]

The first Baptists thought that believer's baptism was an important point of departure for the reconstitution of the true and Apostolic Church. During the time when John Smyth* was a Separatist he continued to study the Scriptures and expressed unhappiness with his fellow Separatists' acceptance of baptism in the Church of England. About 1608, he was involved in a theological debate with other English Separatists in Amsterdam on the matter, and he proposed two arguments based on his understanding of Scripture: (1) Infants are not to be baptized; (2) Antichristians who are converted are to be admitted to the true

Church by baptism. Smyth thus made the radical leap of logic by suggesting that the sacramental tradition was invalid because the Church of England was a false church and he then created a door though which true believers could enter a new (and true) relationship. Smyth thus presumed that in the Anglican/Puritan/ Separatist tradition there was no true baptism and that a New Testament church could not be organized until New Testament terms of admission were met. To everyone's shock outside his small fellowship, he declared himself converted, disavowed the church's covenant, and he and the others stood as individual believers. To reconstitute the church upon solid footing, Smyth then baptized himself and his friends and the body was reorganized as baptized believers following repentance and profession of faith in Christ. What could be more logical, and yet absurd, in light of prevailing Christian practices? When his Separatist friends queried him about his right to commit such an act, he answered, "It was as sensible for a man to baptize himself as to administer the Lord's Supper to himself, which was enjoyed in the Prayer Book in harmony with unbroken custom."[2] So much for the role of the priest in the sacramental tradition!

How did the "self-baptizers" understand what they had done? First Smyth and his followers broke no rules of decorum; they were not immersionists. Historians familiar with the sources have demonstrated that Smyth used a basin of water and spread water on the forehead of the candidate, first of all, himself. Both Puritans and Mennonites followed this practice. Smyth also argued that he was not an "anabaptist." He was horrified at what he knew of Anabaptists in Muenster decades before, and he reasoned that since no one had been baptized in infancy upon his or her own profession of faith, there was no second personal baptism. Instead, to follow Smyth's reasoning, his baptism was the first and only true administration of the ordinance.

The reader of Smyth's work is confronted repeatedly with his use of the term "ordinance." Smyth was a careful student of Scripture and found many "ordinances" of Christ which applied to the true church, of which the Lord's Supper and baptism were two. Rather than stressing baptism as a means of grace (he sometimes used the word sacrament) he emphasized the signal aspects of outward forms with spiritual realities. Water baptism was important because it "witnessed and signified" the renewing of the Holy Ghost with "true, Heavenly, spiritual, living Water, cleansing the inward evil of the soul." The meaning of baptism did not end with the act, for Smyth admonished his congregation "not to hang only upon the outward but with holy prayer to mount upward, and to beg of Christ the good thing signified."[3]

Believer's baptism soon came to be adjectival for the Baptists of the seventeenth century. Both Generals and Particulars referred to themselves as "baptized believers," "antipedo-baptists," "Churches of the baptized way," or "baptized saints."[4] The opposition did not relent and forced Baptists to adopt a strong apologetic for their identity. At a famous public disputation held at Southwark, England in 1642, William Kiffin,* a leader among the Particular Baptists, stated their case succinctly: "We hold that the baptism of Infants cannot be proved lawful by the testimony of Scripture or by Apostolical Tradition; if you can therefore prove the same either way, we shall willingly submit to you."[5] No less than a hundred tracts and books came off the English presses in the seventeenth century to prove that "infant baptism was mere babism," to use Samuel Fisher's phrase.[6]

Baptists in the American colonies during the same century encountered the same accusations and responded with vehemence equal to that of the English. As a result of the persecutions which Obadiah Holmes* and other pioneer Baptists suffered in 1651, Henry Dunster,* first president of Harvard College, cogently defended the thesis, "Visible believers only should be baptized," against learned Congregational brethren and lost his presidency and home for his so doing. Similarly, Thomas Goold of Boston, although a friend of the governor of the colony, refused in 1655 to have his child baptized in the Charlestown church, because "we have no command in the Gospel, nor example for the baptizing of children."[7]

The debate over believer's baptism continued well into the eighteenth century with stiff opposition from Anglicans, Presbyterians, and Congregationalists, as a second generation of apologists arose. In England, the redoubtable John Gill* often caricatured pedo-baptists:

Now, infant baptism, with all the ceremonies attending it . . . makes a very considerable figure in Popish pageantry. Romanists administer the rite with circumstances of great pomp and show; such as the consecration of the water; the presence of the sponsors, who answer the interrogatories, and make the renunciation in the name of the child; exorcisms, exsufflations, crossings, the use of salt, spittle, and oil. Before the baptism the water is consecrated with much solemn parade. First, the priest makes an exorcism, breathing three times into the water in the figure of a cross, and saying, "I adjure thee, O creature of water!"[8]

Likewise in New Jersey in 1747, Abel Morgan, a Baptist preacher, found himself in a public debate with a Presbyterian minister who tried to make a case for infants who could not speak for themselves. Tongue in cheek, Morgan responded, "If Christ did not see meet to order the little children to be baptized, how comes it to pass that Mr. F. without His Command, or Example, orders they should be now? Is the servant wiser than the Master?"[9]

With the case for believer's rather than infant baptism being made, a second subject for debate arose over the correct mode or technique of baptism. About 1640 and after conversation with Dutch Mennonites and others, a church of English Particular Baptists adopted immersion as the only valid mode of baptism and this has been the common practice of Baptists ever since. In fact, the mode itself has enriched the Baptist theology of baptism so that no other technique adequately presents the desired statement.

A key word in the denominational understanding of baptism is "sign," by which seventeenth-century writers meant illustration. Just as most Baptists saw in the Lord's Supper a vivid reenactment of the Last Supper, baptism is an illustration of the essence of the gospel in Jesus Christ. Having established that linguistic evidence is on their side (*baptizo* means "to dip under water"), Baptists as early as 1644 saw illustrated in immersion three elements: a washing or regeneration of the soul; the death, burial, and resurrection of Jesus; and the promise of resurrection even as the candidate emerges from the water. The last point was especially telling since it was the practice of early Baptists to keep the candidate submerged long enough to cause anxiety! Later, the aspect of obedience was stressed as the candidate publicly agreed "to live and walk in newness of life." Little wonder that in the Second London Confession (1677) the writers stated explicitly, "immersion, or dipping the person in water, is necessary to the due administration of this ordinance."[10]

Because the obvious location for a baptismal service was a pond or river, the public perceived the Baptist character to be bound up in baptism by immersion. Early records abound of accounts of baptisms in "living waters" (running streams) as with Jesus: whole households, elderly persons, and the infirm. In cold climates, the service was maintained throughout the winter by breaking the ice. In some places like northern Wales, a particular spot was consecrated from baptism because a famous person like Vavasor Powell, the evangelist, was immersed in particular waters. Custom varied widely, though, as illustrated in the urban churches which often constructed "baptisterions" of stone with stairs which led to changing rooms for the candidates. Some wealthier meetinghouses even had spring-fed pools with brass plugs for the special occasion![11]

Many Baptists considered a baptismal service as a form of public witness and evangelism. In the Philadelphia region, Baptists would announce a service to the entire city and a large crowd would gather on the banks of the Schuylkill River to see the pastor stand on a stone in the water and immerse the candidates. Morgan Edwards recalled more than one thousand spectators at such a scene and Jacob Knapp* observed the President and several members of Congress present for the baptisms in Washington, DC, following his 1843 crusade. A hymn written for use in American colonial baptismal services read,

> Make this stream, like Jordan, blessed.
> Leprous Naamans enter in.
> Rise, saith Jesus, be baptized,
> And you wash away your sin,
> Be baptized, be baptized, be baptized,
> And wash away your sin.[12]

Of course, there have always been the critics. In the first decades of the seventeenth century, other Protestants argued that Baptists endangered lives by overexposure in weather and water (baths were not yet in vogue). Still others thought that so many human bodies in the water polluted the stream and, of course, scandalous rumors were purposely circulated that female modesty was violated, etc. More than anything else, opponents objected to the audacity, curiosity, and growing popularity. As one Presbyterian put it in 1642, "They practice their impieties openly. . . . They flock in great multitudes to their Jordans."[13] Decent, traditional Christianity required no such behavior.

There has always been a difference of opinion among Baptists about whether scriptural baptism should be a requirement for admission to the Lord's Supper or church membership. John Bunyan, for instance, won little support among Particular Baptists in England (and some historians) for his refusal to make baptism a bar to communion. As he saw it, "Baptism makes thee no Member of the Church, neither doth it make thee a visible Saint; it giveth thee, therefore, neither right to, nor being of membership at all."[14] To agree that believer's baptism by immersion was the true baptism was not to enforce it as a strict requirement of conscience.

In both the United States and Great Britain, some Baptists have taken quite a restrictive stance on baptismal requirements. Both Francis Wayland* and James R. Graves* held that Baptists who sincerely hold to the truth of believer's baptism could not and should not admit persons to communion or church membership where questions of a valid baptism existed. Each church could recognize the validity of another church's practices but was under no obligation to do so.[15] In the wake of such nineteenth-century protectionism, churches strengthened their terms of communion and often denied "alien immersions," that is, baptisms performed in another church or even meetinghouse. In order to deepen the baptismal experience in some of these congregations in an age of technology, present-day baptismal enthusiasts will transport water from the Jordan River in the Middle East for use in the baptistry or use special lighting and heating effects in the public ceremony.

In the spirit of John Bunyan, some progressive Baptists have recently entered into dialogues about the meaning of baptism and its relation to church membership in light of other Christian denominations. In the 1970s, Baptists in Great Britain and Ireland commenced a series of studies on the New Testament evidence concerning baptism and its overall biblical significance as an initiatory rite. Such studies have led to statements issued by the Baptist Union which point to an ecumenical understanding of the ordinance:

Baptism as a sacrament of mission for being united to Christ involves witnessing to the faith in the world. As we have suggested already, in such witness our unity is discovered. The unity of the Spirit is known in mission activity, and the wholeness of the baptismal understanding of unity requires the continued participation in mission.[16]

Other Baptists, including American and Southern delegates from the U.S., joined a discussion with the Lutheran churches in 1980–81 which made strides toward a reconciliation of Baptist and Reformation theologies. The joint statement on baptism read in part,

We both see baptism as embodying the whole gospel of God's grace and the response it calls forth. The importance of baptism is that which it signifies in relation to the gospel and the response it calls for. Baptism attests the redemptive work of God in Christ and the promise of salvation to believers, which is life in the kingdom of God. This promise must be appropriated by faith, but it is experienced in the community of the Spirit and of faith, where the gospel is proclaimed and people respond in faith. There baptism is seen as truly functioning in prospect of the day of final redemption.[17]

In an even broader context, several Baptists participated in the World Council of Churches consultation at Lima, Peru, in 1982, which concluded about the sacrament, "While the possibility that infant baptism was also practiced in the apostolic age cannot be excluded, baptism upon personal profession of faith is the most clearly attested pattern in the New Testament documents."[18] After almost four centuries of reflection, the Christian Church may now understand why John Smyth baptized himself in 1609.

THE LORD'S SUPPER

Of the sacraments or ordinances celebrated by Baptists, the Lord's Supper reflects the greatest degree of diversity in both theology and praxis. From the first two decades of the seventeenth century to the present there are differences of opinion on whether grace is imparted or a "mere memorial" meal is realized during the Supper. Baptists have also been concerned about those who are allowed to participate in the event; this issue depends upon one's view of the composition and rights of church membership. Finally, Baptists have expended much labor in defense of several positions on the matter of what beverage the cup should contain, usually wine or grape juice. Such practical issues, along with Baptist concerns over the proper mode of baptism, earned for the Baptists of the nineteenth century a reputation as unduly sacramentalist. That Baptists should be so specifically intrigued with questions related to form and mode is a further indication of their preoccupation with the practices of the New Testament churches.

We must assume that the first Baptists, Smyth, Helwys, and the rest, were part of the prevailing Puritan/Calvinistic theological tide of their day, which was itself a modification of Anglican and Roman Catholic sacramental theology. In 1265, Thomas Aquinas articulated for Roman Catholics the essence of the Eucharist as sacrament when he explained the traditional principle of *ex opere operato*, namely that in the act of breaking bread and passing the cup God imparts grace through the transformation of bread and wine into the body and blood of Jesus Christ. The elaborate liturgy of the Mass was conceived to guide the preparation of the communicant and invoke the necessary divine blessing upon the elements, thus ensuring the efficacy of the *sacramentum* or mysterious event.[19] In 1540, John Calvin, among others, modified the Roman position by arguing that while the bread and wine remain unchanged, the faithful communicant receives with them the power of the body and blood of Christ, thus avoiding "metaphysical explanations that baffle the intelligence." Calvin ultimately placed great stress upon the powerful activity of the Holy Spirit in the Supper.[20] Similar to his viewpoint was that of Thomas Cranmer, author of the Articles of 1553 and much of Elizabethan Christian thought. Cranmer rejected any corporeal presence of Christ in the elements and yet held firmly that "The body of Christ is given, taken, and eaten in the Supper only after an heavenly and spiritual manner."[21]

In the greater Genevan tradition, Puritan divines stressed the covenantal nature of sacraments and taught that the Supper is a sign of nourishment and preservation in the Church. To use the words of William Perkins, outward actions are

a second scale, set by the Lords owne hand unto his covenant. And they do give every receiver to understand, that as God doth blesse the bread and wine to preserve and strengthen the bodie of the receiver; so Christ apprehended and received by faith, shall nourish him, and preserve both bodie and soule unto eternall life.[22]

While the Puritans wished to maintain some of the liturgical elements of the Established Church, the Separatists moved a step further in the reformation of the sacrament to emphasize the method and drama of Jesus at the last supper as recorded in the New Testament. Simplicity and fidelity to the text were of utmost concern in the dramatic reenactment.

John Smyth, Cambridge graduate and Anglican priest-become-Separatist, was the first to consider the meaning of the sacrament of communion in a Baptist context. Eschewing what he thought to be the offensive language of Romanism and the Church of England, Smyth shifted the focus of the two sacraments he recognized from metaphysics to the "outward, visible supper" which he taught witnesses and signifies Christ's sacrifice and ministry to believers. By re-enactment of the Supper, Smyth believed Christians are challenged to deeper spirituality, to prayer, thankfulness, and love for one another. In his major work, *The Differences of the Churches of Separation* (1608) he emphasized commands and teachings of the New Testament, which he frequently calls "ordinances."[23] Smyth thus provided Baptists with a new generic term for those practices which they held to be urgent, visible, and educative.

The General Baptists in England appear to have continued in Smyth's tradition of simplicity for the celebration of the principal ordinances. Thomas Grantham* laid out a format for the Supper in his book, *Hear the Church: Or An Appeal to the Mother of Us All* (1687), in which the focus is upon the spiritual qualifications of the partakers and the "mystical signification" regarding the cross of Christ. If the Orthodox Creed of 1678 exemplified General Baptist thought on the subject of the Holy Communion, they joined their Particular Baptist co-religionists in urging obedience to Christ's call for union with each other and the view that primarily the Supper was primarily a "perpetual remembrance." Curiously, the General Baptists approached Calvin's view of the event as "a seal of their continuance in the covenant of grace" and they continued to call the Supper a "holy sacrament."[24] Against perceived Catholic and Lutheran influences, transubstantiation, consubstantiation, and the participation of children were prohibited, the latter on grounds that "they cannot examine themselves" and would partake unworthily.

Prior to the controversy over singing in the celebration of the Lord's Supper, which erupted in the 1670s, little is known of Particular Baptist practices. We may assume that the absence of any article on the matter in the first London Confession (1644) indicates basic Particular Baptist agreement with the Reformed/Separatist stress upon spiritual nourishment and the Last Supper. More detail comes to light in the Second London Confession (1677) where the Particular Baptists agreed that the Supper is "a bond and pledge of their communion with Christ and with each other" and they specifically rejected elevation of the elements, denial of lay participation, the doctrine of transubstantiation, and any theory of bodily presence of Christ.[25]

Significantly, the first mention of the terminology "only or mere memorial" occurs in the Second London Confession and only after 1677 did it become a distinction for Baptists in the theology of the Lord's Supper. This document, which was the product of leading Particular Baptists like Hanserd Knollys,* William Kiffin, and Benjamin Keach,* has a clear statement about the Supper and shows the distance which Baptists wished to create between themselves and others in the sacramental tradition. The operating principle of an ordinance— "That did Jesus command and teach"—is of primary relevance, as the Londoners confessed that "the Supper of the Lord Jesus was instituted by him . . . as a perpetual remembrance," by which they most likely meant *anamnesis* or simply making the past present. Instructions are given to ministers only about the blessing upon the elements and their distribution and the admonition that the "outward elements still remain truly and only Bread and Wine as they were before." Most telling is the function of spiritual renewal via recollection:

In this ordinance Christ is not offered up to His Father, nor any real sacrifice made at all, for remission of sins of the quick or dead; but only a memorial of that one offering up of Himself, by Himself, upon the cross, once for all.[26]

One can only speculate on the background influences upon the Particular Baptists at this point; whether Zwinglian—through Anabaptist—thought was involved, or an extreme desire to rid the Baptist congregations of all Popish influences (the language of the Confession) in a period of renewed Catholic influence in the 1670s, may never be known with certainty. To say, as some have, that Particular Baptists adopted a Zwinglian view would be inadequate, since Zwingli argued for the divine presence of Christ in the Supper, which the Baptists either rejected or did not comprehend.[27]

To sum up, there was consensus among both seventeenth-century Particular and General Baptists in England that essentially the Lord's Supper was to be understood as a memorial which Christ commanded to observe and that it was to be treated as a dramatic reenactment of the Last Supper. While the General Baptists preferred the term "sacrament," the increasingly numerous Particulars popularized the term "ordinance," by which they meant an act which Christ expressly commanded the Church to observe. The phraseology of the Second London Confession established the vividly symbolic meaning of the Supper, which by 1700 was the prevailing view of the denomination.

Baptists in America easily accepted the English Baptist understanding of the Supper as a memorial; the relevant question in the Colonies was over the terms of admission to the Lord's Table. As some writers have shown, this question is closely related to the issue of "closed" versus "open" membership, but they are distinct concerns. From the earliest period of Baptist development in England and America, the Baptist view of the true, visible church, composed only of believers who could testify to their Christian experience, posed problems for the allowance of non-church members to the Lord's Table. Baptists, like other Christians, considered the Supper to be an event of utmost significance in the commands of Christ and a means of establishing and nurturing fellowship of the congregation, or to use the contemporary phrase, "communion of the saints." Believer's baptism—and the profession of faith which accompanied it—was in the early years a prerequisite for admission to the Lord's Table. As Benjamin Cox put it in 1646, "We . . . do not admit any to the use of the Supper, nor communicate with any in the use of this ordinance, but disciples baptized."[28] To do otherwise was to "walk in a disorderly way," and this included pedobaptists and other professing Christian believers. British Baptist historians have shown that this "closed communion" position was maintained by most early Baptists, regardless of their General or Particular persuasion. The restriction was modified at the Particular Baptist Assembly in 1689 where some of the aged leadership recognized that strong differences of opinion existed on the matter and, while Kiffin, Knollys, and others urged closed communion, they also charitably recognized that "yet some others of us have a greater liberty and freedom in our spirits that way." In fact, among those who advocated open communion for "visible saints and Christians walking according to the Light with God" was the eminent John Bunyan of Bedford, who complained for over a decade that Baptists accused him of being too loose in his practice of Christian communion.[29] In the eighteenth century, it was the eminent Robert Hall of Arnsby who persuaded many English Baptists to adopt open communion.

The first churches in America generally desired theological consensus as a term of communion. Calvinistic Baptists usually did not have fellowship with Arminian churches nor did Sabbatarians mingle with first day congregations. While most Baptists of all kinds required believer's baptism as a requisite for admission to the Lord's Table, a few churches experimented with openness to professing Christians, and this caused questions to arise frequently at associational meetings. The Cohansey, New Jersey church, for instance, in 1740 queried the Philadelphia Association as to whether a "pious Pedo-Baptist" should be admitted to communion without believer's baptism. The delegates voted "no" and added the comment that such an action was a contradiction in terms![30]

Among the U.S. Baptist congregations, communion restrictions were laid down for a variety of purposes beyond the obvious concern for a membership of baptized believers. The Welsh Tract, Delaware, church, which practiced the laying on of hands as a gospel ordinance, refused communion at the Lord's Table with the Philadelphia and Pennepack congregations because the latter did not allow such practices.[31] In New England similar disputes caused strict closed communion rules of order, particularly between First and Seventh Day Baptists as in Newport, Rhode Island, where a schism occurred between these two factions in one church. An outstanding exception to this rule was the church at Swansea, Massachusetts, which provided for its communion to be open to Baptists and Pedo-Baptists alike, and others who were of the Puritan/Separatist theological tradition.

The first real breach of the wall of closed communion among Baptists came in 1780 with the establishment of the Freewill Baptist movement. Benjamin Randall,* a theological eclectic, saw closed communion as an undesirable and harsh manifestation of Calvinistic determinism among New England Baptists. For him, the Lord's Supper should be opened to all who have experienced saving grace, "by virtue of their Christian character." Unlike Thomas Baldwin* of Second Baptist Church in Boston, who posited baptism as a requirement for communion, the Freewillers proclaimed the Lord's Table open to all Christians, regardless of denomination. In an official statement on open communion in 1839, the leadership said, "Communion is a communion of saints and every true believer is rightfully a communionist."[32] Similar to the Freewill position was that of the Free Communion Baptists who built a theology of the church on the point:

We believe the church of Christ to be a spiritual school into which we enter for Divine instruction and teaching. . . . The door of this church is open night and day for all the children of the Kingdom. . . . To have liberty of conscience in meats and drinks . . . or other circumstantial points . . . steadfastly believing the term of external communion is to become a new creature.[33]

Such egalitarianism led the Free Communioners to merge with the Freewillers in 1841. A reaction soon came. During the Second Great Awakening and subsequent spiritual revivals in the nineteenth century, a blurring of denominational distinctives occurred, particularly on the frontier. Many Baptists churches found themselves closer to the ethos of Methodist and Presbyterian neighboring churches than to strict order associational life in the East. Often, Baptists shared meetinghouses with Methodists, Presbyterians, Congregationalists, and Universalists, especially in the Ohio Valley. This in turn caused deep concern for more "regular" Baptists and a resurgence of closed communion practice occurred in the mid to late nineteenth century. The chief architect of closed communion was James R. Graves, the Landmarkist who influenced vast numbers of churches in the South and West with his views. A local church protectionist, Graves wrote that it was the absolute right of a local church to control its own ordinances. Furthermore, he eschewed all forms of sacramentalism and declared that the one purpose of the Lord's Supper was "the commemoration of the sacrificial death of Christ—and not as a denominational ordinance, nor as an act expressive of our Christian or personal fellowship, and much less of courtesy towards others."[34] Graves's followers frequently would not allow persons who were not members of a given local church to participate in its celebration of the Lord's Supper, even if such persons were members of another duly constituted Baptist church. As James M. Pendleton, another Tennessee Landmarkist put it:

Disorderly members of other churches (Baptist churches, I mean) would claim seats at that table as a matter of right and the sacred feast would be contaminated by their presence. The truth is, no church can of right be required to invite to its communion those over whom it has no power of discipline.[35]

To many the Landmarkist position was rationally consistent and protective of perceived historic Baptist thought; this influence was felt in the northern churches, the Southern Baptist Convention, and in the western mission fields during the nineteenth century. Ultimately, the entry of the Northern Baptist Convention into the ecumenical movement after 1911, and the acceptance of many members from pedobaptist backgrounds on profession of Christian experience for membership, led to a greatly diminished concern for closed communion after the midtwentieth century. In contrast, many churches in the Southern Convention and the ethnically diverse and confessional Baptist bodies, retain closed communion, primarily because their theological understanding of the Church is restricted to the local congregation which guards jealously its membership qualifications and self-government.[36]

Ever concerned that practice replicate the New Testament model, Baptists, primarily in the United States, have also spent much time and effort debating the content of the cup in the Lord's Supper. In an era when pasteurization and food processing were virtually unknown, Baptists followed the rest of the Christian world in using wine for the Supper. We can deduce from John Smyth's writings that the first Baptists purchased bread and wine, for that was a legitimate reason for a collection. All of the confessions from the Second London (1677) to the New Hampshire (1833) prescribe bread and wine, and it is logical to assume that the alcoholic beverage was used in various vintages and types. In fact, some churches in New England frequently used beer and other alcoholic drinks when wine was not available.[37] However, partly in response to the temperance crusade which began in the 1820s, and partly thanks to the discovery of a chemically feasible means to produce grape juice, many Baptists rushed to substitute the use of the juice for wine.

Following the Civil War, arguments flared on both sides, complete with biblical exegesis and theological rationale. In defense of a "two wine theory," a medical doctor, Abraham Coles, reasoned before a learned society in 1878 that "the Greek word 'oinos,' translated wine, is generic, and includes unfermented grape juice, known as much, new wine, and sweet wine." The wine that Jesus made, Coles proposed, was unfermented and unintoxicating; the only remedy for the dreadful evils of intemperance is total abstinence.[38] Alvah Hovey,* president of the Newton Theological Institution, presented his view in a scholarly journal and declared that there was no biblical foundation for the two wine theory and that the terminology "fruit of the vine" most likely described wine mingled with water. Hovey warned his readers to study the scriptures on the questions, because "There is no body of Christians that is under more sacred obligations to ascertain and follow the law of Christ in the matter than the one to which we belong."[39] The vast majority of Baptists followed the advice of the temperance advocates and have used grape juice in the cup of the Lord's Supper.

Not unrelated to the application of applied science to theological issues was the transition from the common cup to individual glasses. Popular opinion in the early 1890s suggested that the spread of influenza and other maladies from cancer to diphtheria was due at least in part to the use of a common chalice in the communion service. In 1894, the Central Presbyterian Church in Rochester, New York, pioneered the use of specially crafted individual glass cups, and North Baptist Church in the same city followed suit quickly thereafter. Although Baptist congregations had taken pride in silver services for the Lord's Supper, which were frequently memorial gifts, churches adopted wholesale the use of individual cups and with them, the distribution of the elements to members seated in the pews. The benefits of the shift were many:

There is a sense of relief in using a clean, sanitary cup; devotion is promoted, the ceremony reverenced. Ministers say that individual cups are more convenient, and that there is less time occupied in serving them and without any confusion, than with common cups. . . . The number of church members who attend communion service has increased, and in some instances, greatly so.[40]

In some instances, Baptists were willing to sacrifice their dependence upon biblical procedures for the sake of improved sanitary habits.

In recent years, particularly among the American Baptist Churches, USA, and the British Baptists, there has been a restoration of some of the sacramental thrusts which Baptists in the seventeenth century set aside. The publication of the World Council of Churches statement, *Baptism, Eucharist and Ministry* (1982), has brought some Baptists to accept a fivefold sacramental meaning of the Eucharist as a proclamation of thanksgiving, a memorial of Christ, an invocation of the Spirit, a communion of the faithful, and a meal of the Kingdom.[41] Moreover, these same Baptists invite members of other Christian traditions to celebrate the Lord's Supper on special occasions and they freely engage in ecumenical studies about the nature of the sacraments. It must be noted, however, that most Baptists in the United States still practice closed communion with unfermented grape juice in individual cups and affirm only the memorial aspects of the ordinance.

OTHER ORDINANCES

While always a minority, quite a few Baptists over the years have called for the recognition of other gospel ordinances in addition to baptism and the Lord's Supper. These include the laying on of hands and footwashing that are seen as based on clear scriptural injunctions.

The act of imposition of hands was long recognized in the Church as a ritual which signified authority or delegation to an office; there is precedent in both the Old and New Testaments, and in the Reformation Era Anabaptist groups practiced it to confirm their ministers. The first Baptists followed suit and their early confessional statements each have articles describing the act as applied to the "setting apart" of leadership, whether bishops, elders, deacons, or others. Among the General Baptist churches a broader application of the imposition of hands occurs whereby following baptism, all Christian believers received the promise of the Holy Spirit by the act. For some, it thus became a general gospel ordinance, meaning that Christ taught it and the Church was obligated to recognize its value.[42]

Colonel Henry Danvers, a Particular Baptist polemicist, identified the origin of the laying on of hands for all believers in the teaching of Francis Cornwell, a General Baptist minister at White's Alley, Spitalfields. About 1646, Cornwell concluded from Epistle to the Hebrews 12:1–2, that imposition was necessary and "those who were not under laying on of hands were not babes in Christ, had not God, nor communion with God." Later, Cornwell refused communion with those who did not follow his teaching and he promulgated the idea widely through England and Wales.[43] During the 1650s, the issue caused great controversy and schism among churches throughout the kingdom, including both General and Particular Baptists. Many were willing to concede that imposition was a legitimate part of the ordination rite, perhaps even baptism, but as a term of communion it was not acceptable. In the seventeenth-century English context, the ablest defense of the laying on of hands was Thomas Grantham's *Christianismus Primitivus* (1678), which taught that it was surely a means of grace.[44]

General Baptists in America appear to have adopted the ordinance at a very early stage. Following Cornwell's teaching, laying on of hands became a "sixth principle" of gospel order, and the Arminians in the colonies soon became known as the General Six Principle Baptists. Richard Knight, the first historian of this tradition, in 1827 argued strongly that the first Baptist churches in America at Providence and Newport, Rhode Island, were Six Principle from their inception, though this is not likely in the case of Providence.[45] What is certain is that a controversy over imposition of hands occurred in both congregations during the 1660s and led to schism. The principle caught on in New England Baptist life and most of the churches by 1670 were General Six Principle. Elsewhere, in the Delaware Valley, several congregations practiced laying on of hands following baptism, but were not strictly Six Principle Baptists; the influence of Welsh Baptists may be seen there. In England, in 1698, Benjamin Keach published a book titled *Laying on of Hands upon Baptized Believers, as such Proved an Ordinance of Christ*, which no doubt supported his son Elias' practice of the rite in the Pennepack, Pennsylvania, congregation.

When the first edition of the Philadelphia Baptist Confession of Faith was issued in 1742, it differed little from the Second London Confession of 1677, except in the articles of singing and the laying on of hands, both of which are attributable to the Welsh tradition. In part, a new article read:

We believe that . . . laying on of hands (with prayer) upon baptized believers, as such, is an ordinance of Christ, and ought to be submitted unto by all such persons that are admitted to partake of the Lord's Supper.[46]

Philadelphia Baptists thus made formal their confidence that the rite signified the coming and gifts of the Spirit in the Church.

In England the ordinance of the laying on of hands declined in the early eighteenth century and when the New Connexion of General Baptists was organized in 1770, the practice was not adhered to. Among the Particular Baptists, there was never widespread acceptance, and, if John Gill's example is typical, most pastors disregarded imposition in the early eighteenth century. In America, the story was different. The Ketocton, Virginia, Association made the ordinance obligatory as late as 1790, as did the churches in North Carolina.[47] While the nineteenth-century historian David Benedict went so far as to say that in the period before 1800 most Baptist churches practiced the rite, Samuel Jones, pastor at Lower Dublin, Pennsylvania, believed that imposition was essentially an archaic Welsh Baptist influence and was limited to those churches and areas of Welsh background in eastern Pennsylvania and Virginia before 1790. In a much publicized handbill circulated about 1790, Jones denounced imposition as "unsupported by the work of God" and he urged those clergy who did not believe in its efficacy to desist from its practice. While the article on laying on of hands was never formally removed from the Philadelphia Confession, Jones won a major victory in 1797, when the Association adopted his *Treatise on Church Discipline*. He revised the salient points of the old confession and never once mentioned imposition in his discussion of the church, the ministry, and the terms of communion. Since this tract became authoritative in places as diverse as Charleston, South Carolina, and Lexington, Kentucky, we may assume that Samuel Jones was the chief catalyst in the demise of understanding the imposition of hands as a gospel ordinance.[48]

While most Baptists have retained imposition in the service of ordination for ministers and other church leaders, only a handful of surviving General Six

Principle Baptist Churches in New England and scattered General Baptists in the Southern states retain it as a requirement for new members. Baptists have also resisted the reintroduction of the laying on of hands as a recognition of the receipt of extraordinary gifts of the Spirit which modern Pentecostal groups practice.

Yet another practice which achieved the status of an ordinance among Baptists was footwashing. In Article 76 of John Smyth's "Propositions and Conclusions concerning True Christian Religion" (1612), Smyth described the ministry of deacons in his congregation as "to serve tables and wash the saints' feet." Most historians feel that Smyth acknowledged a practice which he observed among the Mennonite community in Amsterdam and wished to accommodate himself to it, in view of his desire to join his church to their fellowship. Whatever the source of his statement, General Baptists followed Smyth's advice and included footwashing among their ordinances, for "it is commanded and blest by Christ and when performed decently and in order it produced affections among the brethren."[49] From their extant literature, the General Baptists practiced the ritual as late as the eighteenth century, though it died out among British Baptists by the nineteenth century. In the United States, footwashing has been associated with smaller groups of Baptists and individual congregations, more than with any of the major traditions. Perhaps from the influence of Mennonites in Pennsylvania or General Baptist ties with Carolina Baptists during the colonial period, interest in footwashing emerged about 1810 in the Charleston, South Carolina, Association. In response to a query from a member church, the delegates reasoned:

It is not to be ranked with baptism or the Lord's Supper, as a church ordinance. For a variety of reasons it appears to us that the thing signified, rather than the bodily act is enjoined by the Redeemer; but should any think it their duty to perform that act as a religious rite, especially in a private manner, among friends, we think it may be done without just cause of offense to any.[50]

While there is no record of an association requiring the washing of feet as with other ordinances, several Baptist bodies encourage its practice and usually add it to their celebrations of the Lord's Supper. In the Southern States, the Freewill Baptists "wash the feet of the saints" as do the Separate Baptists in Indiana. The Church of God, followers of John Winebrenner, a quasi-Baptist group in Pennsylvania, practice footwashing as part of an evening Lord's Supper celebration which is conducted for participants in a sitting posture.[51]

While there have been some interesting and biblically defensible attempts to expand the sacraments or ordinances to include other practices such as the imposition of hands and footwashing, Baptists have joined other Protestants in adopting the two principal rites. For the most part, the group has understood baptism and the Lord's Supper in vividly symbolic terms with a secondary concern for the metaphysical meanings. From their intense preoccupation over textual details in the New Testament and a desire to re-create the primitive Church, Baptists have spent their energies on the techniques, styles, and fitness of candidates for participation in the sacraments, rather than the mystery of the divine-human relationships.

5
A NEW WAY: VOLUNTARY RELIGION

VOLUNTARISM PREDICATED UPON "SOUL COMPETENCE"

A voluntary spirit lies at the very heart of the Baptist self-understanding. A man or woman voluntarily seeks membership in a congregation; congregations voluntarily associate with each other for a variety of purposes; churches and individuals voluntarily join and contribute to benevolent enterprises in response to the call of the gospel and so on. Theologians of the seventeenth century, and historians ever since, have had a field day speculating on whether voluntarism was the result of prevenient grace or obedience to the commands of a sovereign God, while the indomitable Baptists have struck a chord for the independent, activistic spirit in Protestantism.

The foundation of the voluntary principle among Baptists is a presumed soul competence. The nineteenth-century Southern Baptist theologian, Edgar Y. Mullins,* has often been criticized for his affirmation of soul competence, but it appears he identified an important aspect of Baptist identity. As Mullins argued, "Human beings have no competence apart from God, but through evangelism whereby the human soul is set free from the power of sin, each individual has a right to approach God directly and transact with him in religion."[1] Whether Baptist theologians have ever satisfactorily solved the riddle of free will versus determinism they have assumed an enlightened axiom of soul competence in their ecclesial relationships, their sense of mission and their part in the Kingdom of God. Individually and collectively, Baptists have been intentional about the "good works" allowed in an early confession: thankfulness (stewardship), strengthening assurance (education), edifying the brethren (fellowship), adorning the profession of the Gospel (evangelism), stopping the mouths of adversaries (apologetics), and glorifying god (worship).[2]

Perhaps the first voluntary decision a Christian makes after repentance is to unite with a congregation. In contrast to inclusion in a church because of geographical proximity or as a followup to the act of infant baptism, Baptists maintain that church membership is to be initiated by the individual believer. What is perhaps the earliest Baptist church covenant written in America, the covenant of a small group of Christians in Kittery, Maine, begins, "We whose names are here underwritten . . . by His grace give up ourselves."[3] In the covenanting process Baptists may well be subject to more restrictions than those who are part of a more hierarchical church polity; the point is that the individual believer has chosen to limit his or her freedom. To underscore this decision, Samuel Jones, a leader in the Philadelphia Baptist Association, when asked to provide a model church covenant, wrote in 1798, "We, whose names are under written, being desirous to be constituted a church of Jesus Christ . . . do in the name of the Lord Jesus, voluntarily and freely give ourselves up to the Lord, and to one another." The obligations which followed in the agreement included faithful attendance, stewardship, watchcare for each other, and discipline, where needed.[4]

THE ASSOCIATIONAL PRINCIPLE

Not long after the first congregations were formed in England among the General Baptists, relations between churches developed. Between 1612 and 1625 four congregations joined Thomas Helwys's* original General Baptist congregation in a cluster around the city of London, constituting the first community of Baptists in history. They were united by common principles and a common sense of persecution. Apparently, these churches had more in common than style and persecution for a dispute arose in 1624 which indicated concerted action. John Murton and successors to Thomas Helwys in the Spitalfields church became disaffected with a splinter group of their own congregation, meeting at Southwark, and excommunicated the group on the basis of irregularities in the Lord's Supper. Both parties to the dispute sought the counsel and support of the Dutch Waterlander Mennonites (with whom John Smyth* had established relations over a decade earlier), indicating both the existence of an informal association and a desire to relate with other Christians of acceptable sentiments. The letter from the Tiverton church in 1630 speaks of a desire for union in 1626 with the Mennonites, who actually sent an Englishman to arbitrate the dispute. While the problems of 1624–30 among the General Baptists did not produce long-term relations with other Christians, or a sense of peace within the cluster, the circumstances did demonstrate that the earliest Baptists were associational. Ironically, then, the first evidence of an associational relationship came as the result of disagreements about the proper administration of the Lord's Supper.

Particular Baptists followed a similar pattern to that of the Generals. Seven congregations in and about London in 1644 met formally "all one in Communion, holding Jesus Christ to be our head and Lord" to draft the first London Confession of Faith. The purpose for the meeting and subsequent confessional statement (which was voluntarily signed and subscribed to), was to demonstrate that Baptists maintained a worthy doctrinal standard within the prevailing Calvinism of the era, and also to offset the calumny of their ardent critics. Significantly, article forty-seven advises that

> although the particular congregations be distinct and several Bodies, every one a compact and knit citie in itself; yet are they all to walk by one and the same Rule, and by all meanes convenient to have the counsell and help of another in all needful affairs of the church, as members of one body in the common faith under Christ their onely head.[5]

Therein was a positive explication of the associational principle that Particular Baptists were expected to acknowledge common theological and practical principles. By 1655 the term "association" was in common usage among the Particulars and there were at least five clusters of churches meeting for mutual advice and evangelistic purposes at mid-century.

Next, Baptists voluntarily sought to organize their work on a regional or national basis, and that accomplishment belongs first to the General Baptists in England. In 1651 General Baptist churches in the Midlands held a consultative assembly composed of twenty-eight church representatives. At that historic gathering (which may not have been the first of its kind), those present agreed to a wider fellowship which was organized in London in July 1654. The stated purposes of the brethren were to consider how and which way the affairs of the gospel of Christ might be promoted and divisions removed, to vindicate themselves from misstatements against them concerning the civil government, and to seek a door of greater opportunity to spread the gospel in the nations of the world. As the General Baptists held annual associational meetings, this national assembly met infrequently about every decade until the 1690s, when it began to meet annually into the eighteenth century. Among the accomplishments of the General Assembly of General Baptists were the agreement on a confession of faith (1660), home missions (1656), a permanent assembly structure (1689), and ministerial training (1700).

Voluntary association also characterized early Baptists in America. When there were but five Baptist congregations in all of the colonies, four of them (Providence, Newport, Swanzey, and North Kingstown, all General Baptist in sentiment) held the first yearly meeting in 1670. While no records exist of these meetings before 1700, it can be assumed that the General Baptist associational pattern in England, doctrinal differences with both Particular and Seventh Day Baptists, and relations with the state, provided a rationale. Even more significant was the formation of the Philadelphia Association in the Delaware Valley, where five congregations in what is now Pennsylvania, New Jersey, and Delaware, agreed "to choose particular brethren to meet yearly to consult about such things as were wanting in the churches, and to set them in order."[6] This body, which grew to forty churches by the American Revolution, dealt with practical matters such as supply preaching and membership qualifications, as well as a theological basis for association churches.

In 1746 issues relating to the history and purpose of the association were discussed and the representatives decided to ask Benjamin Griffith, pastor of the Montgomery, Pennsylvania, church to serve as a regular clerk and collect a history of the churches and the Association. Out of his research, Griffith produced in 1749 an essay which became the classic statement of the purpose of Baptist associations in America. Ever true to the voluntary principle, Griffith began his remarks with "an Association is not a superior judicature, having such superior power over the churches concerned." Of the cooperating churches he advised that they "may, and ought, . . . by their voluntary and free consent, to enter into an agreement and confederation."[7] Following a model that was popular in colonial political discussion, the term "confederation" more specifically defined what was meant by "association." As much as Griffith emphasized the functions of confederation, he also delineated the parameters of its relationships. As individuals choose to associate with a congregation, he reasoned, so congregations agree to associate or to break fellowship. Disorderly practice and unsound doctrine were causes for disfellowshipping churches, which was a matter for both the Association and the aggrieved church to consider. As it turned out, when the number of churches grew, some withdrew voluntarily to form new associations in the Carolinas, New England, New York, and Virginia. Such new directions were initiated by the churches, not decreed by the Association, though some of its leaders wanted to unite the new associations in a national organization of Baptists under the aegis of Philadelphia.

Once confederated, Baptists assumed the competence of the association itself. In matters of theology and ethics, associations passed resolutions on vital concerns. The Warren, Rhode Island, Association in 1785 defined the Christian family as a parallel with God's universal family, and the Mattapony, Virginia, Association in 1801 declared that "drunkenness is a sin and [Christians] are never to taste a drop of anything that can intoxicate." The Philadelphia Association in 1756 moved far beyond the concerns of any one church when delegates agreed to collect money to start a Latin grammar school under the tutelage of Isaac Eaton. Boldly, in 1771, this group also authorized the first extra-congregational evangelists and sent Morgan Edwards* and John Gano* to the South. In the midst of all this benevolent activity, the Shaftesbury, Vermont, Association was quick to remind its churches in 1791 that still the Baptist association was "no more than a number of churches in sister relation, mutually agreeing to meet by their delegates . . . for free conference on those matters that concern the general good of the churches."[8]

The self-prescribed limits upon the voluntary association among Baptists frustrated some leaders and created endless wrangling for others. Morgan Edwards, for instance, proposed in 1770 a union of associations to the Philadelphia Association "which must ever be central to the whole." He further suggested that the Association be incorporated, that each other association produce public declarations of its nature and that the only terms for associational membership should be the practice of believer's baptism. Many of the association leaders in the

South and New England thought their confederations to be of equal value and standing to that in Philadelphia and saw no need for such centralization. Baptists demurred on Edwards's recommendations and instead created 104 new associations between 1775 and 1815.

Perhaps the event that signalled a new beginning for organized voluntarism among Baptists was the disappointing response and cumbersome rules of procedure which William Carey* experienced following his invitation sermon at the Northamptonshire Baptist Association meeting on 31 May 1792. Having made an impassioned case for world evangelization ("Expect great things from God; attempt great things for God"), Carey expected his colleagues to respond enthusiastically. Instead, they agreed to support poor ministers and contribute to the antislavery crusade. Whatever discussion there was on world missions was deferred to the next session. However, with the assistance of his friend, Andrew Fuller,* a pastor at Kettering, Carey and eleven others circumvented the Association and formed on 2 October 1792 the Particular Baptist Society for the Propagation of the Gospel Among the Heathen. Essentially, twelve ministers agreed on a specific project and contributed a little over thirteen pounds sterling to its success, prayed several times, and the first voluntary society for missions was inaugurated.

SOCIETIES ORGANIZED FOR MISSION

The idea of a voluntary society was not new, not even among baptists. Other groups had formed in the last quarter of the eighteenth century to effect worthy goals such as antislavery and temperance. Some historians believe the concept originated among the joint stock ventures of the early colonial period or among the Inns of Court. Within the Baptist fold, the first example of a single purpose voluntary society was the Bristol Education Society formed in 1770 to promote the interests of ministerial education for the denomination. A small academy, operating out of Broadmead Baptist Church in Bristol from the resources of a deceased wealthy church member, had existed since 1679. Hugh and Caleb Evans, a father-son ministerial team at the Broadmead church decided that more funds were needed for their students and they wrote a letter to the Baptist churches of England and Wales. With the help of other local partners, the Evanses stressed a need for more adequately trained clergy and they reminded their colleagues of the utility of the Bristol Academy across the years. During the first year over £500 was raised for capital improvements and annual expenses. The Society that was formed broadened the support and accountability of what became Bristol Baptist College; it became the governing board of the school.

In their original forms, the Bristol and Kettering societies provided the ideal vehicle to accomplish their stated purposes. At Bristol the purpose was "to supply destitute churches with a succession of able and evangelical ministers," specifically to operate the Bristol academy. In Kettering, the general purpose was to propagate the gospel among the heathen, more specifically to outfit and maintain a foreign missionary program. Membership in the societies was limited to those who contributed, usually at least a guinea per year. From the membership a slate of officers was chosen, the most important of which were the treasurer and secretary who managed the accounts and kept the records. The annual meetings consisted of reports about the work, plans for the coming year, and an inspirational message which was designed to solicit funds.[9] The grand object of it all, in both cases, was the singular purpose adopted by the founders. Both the Bristol and Kettering experiments thrived and the objects for which they were founded—theological education and foreign missions—have survived almost two centuries.

Americans watched the developments at Kettering with real interest. The first response was an interdenominational missionary society formed by New York City churches in 1796. Its principal concern was the unchurched population in Western New York and the officers sent a Baptist minister, Elkanah Holmes,* to work with Indians on the Niagara frontier in 1800. Six years later a rift developed in the ecumenical venture when the Baptists claimed that they could not support pedobaptist practices even for the sake of mission, and a New York Baptist Missionary Society was founded. A second response occurred among evangelical Massachusetts Congregationalists in the founding of the Massachusetts Missionary Society in 1799, which seemed to be more concerned with a defense of the faith than with a full-fledged missionary outreach. One of those present at the first annual meeting of this society in 1800 was Mary Webb,* who was enraptured with the cause of missions. Later that year, Webb founded the Boston Female Society for Missionary Purposes which included both Congregationalists and Baptist women "desirous of aiding missions." In 1829 this pioneer U.S. Baptist voluntary society became solely a Baptist organization; it eventually merged with the Massachusetts Baptist State Convention. Its accomplishments far exceeded the cents it collected; the founder, Mary Webb, was the mastermind of a network of societies and women's missionary groups which stretched from Maine to Georgia. Her vision of missionary endeavor was truly comprehensive, including projects at home and overseas.

The Baptist voluntary societies which emerged in the United States in the wake of Mary Webb's "mother society" were of four basic types: single purpose–general, single purpose–local, single purpose–institutional, and auxiliary–regional. Examples of each are found in all sections of Baptist geography; taken together, they illustrate a unique type of denominational advance, which parallels in the Free Church tradition other more highly integrated systems. To the credit of a brimming voluntary spirit with genuine millennial expectations, Baptists made a disintegrative and often competitive network succeed.

An important example of a single purpose–general society was the American Baptist Home Mission Society (ABHMS). The organization was founded during an adjourned session of the 1832 Baptist Triennial Convention meeting in New York City. Those who elected to meet at Mulberry Street Baptist Church included prominent clergy such as Jonathan Going* of Worcester, Massachusetts, and

William Colgate* of New York City; each became a member by an annual gift of unspecified amount. The stated purpose was "to promote the preaching of the gospel to every creature in North America" and the directors included representatives from every state east of the Mississippi. The general nature of the ABHMS arose from its comprehensive task and its national support: All aspects of domestic missions, preaching, new church development and construction, foreign language ministry, and education, were under its administration, and all of the auxiliary societies and state organizations were to cooperate with and support its programs. Officially recognized auxiliary groups were entitled to at least one field missionary in their area as a reward for faithful support.

The New Hampshire Baptist Antislavery Society, formed in 1838, sheds light upon the local societies. This organization, which met annually after the state convention sessions, was brought into being as a result of a report by L. E. Caswell of Weare, New Hampshire, about the brutal treatment of slaves he witnessed while in Charleston, South Carolina. Enthusiastic hearers determined to start a single-purpose voluntary society "to use all Christian means for the immediate overthrow of oppression in the land." Officers were elected from fifteen members who presumably only had to acquiesce in the purpose. A modest offering was taken at each annual meeting to defray the expenses of what was essentially an educational campaign.[10]

Certain of the Baptist voluntary societies became support groups for institutions. This was the case with the Ohio Regular Baptist Education Society which was formed to launch a literary and theological institution in the region. At its first meeting in 1832, twenty members (who had paid one dollar each) elected six trustees for the Granville Literary and Theological Institution, which would "promote the welfare of a rapidly growing and free country where virtuous intelligence, industry, and enterprise are sure to meet a quick reward." As the Society members saw the situation, it was a matter of Baptist pride: "If we wish to see our denomination rise, and enlarge the sphere of its usefulness, let us come nobly to the work."[11]

Finally, the auxiliary societies formed the network of interest, accountability, and support for the larger general societies. No different in purpose from their general counterparts, there were auxiliaries for the foreign and home mission enterprises and for the Tract Society. Although Luther Rice* took credit for the U.S. Baptist system, the idea among Baptists was probably attributable to William Staughton, who witnessed it in England, as well as predecessor Congregationalist societies in the United States. Soon after the Kettering Particular Baptist Society was founded, arrangements were made in England for several regional auxiliaries. The relationship was a formal one, in which the state or local auxiliary would adopt a standard constitution that recognized the fundamental connection with the general society, elect officers, collect funds and usually provide an agent. The benefits were three-fold: More persons were involved in the enterprise, funds were increased, and the general societies were guaranteed widespread participation. Typical of this structure was the Connecticut Society Auxiliary to the Baptist Board of Foreign Missions, formed in 1814. At its birth the sole object was to transmit funds from voluntary contributors to the General Missionary Convention. In the nine years of its existence it aided the cause of foreign missions greatly while also promoting evangelism in Connecticut and sponsoring a Baptist newspaper, the *Christian Secretary.*[12]

Between 1796 and 1890 Baptists in the United States created well in excess of one hundred voluntary, single-purpose societies. During the first half of the nineteenth century, Baptists sensed an urgency in their task and were challenged by both religious and organizational advancement motives; as one observer put it, "The time has come for *action* and if we permit the present opportunity to pass away, we may never cease to regret it, nor our children to express their astonishment at our folly."[13] Bolstered by their own post-Revolutionary success and energized by the Second Great Awakening, Baptists found the voluntary society well suited to their ethos. Liberated by conversion, the soul, the congregation, the association, and now the voluntary society were "competent to bring about the Kingdom."

Mention must be made at this point of an alternative Baptist vehicle which was theologically more voluntaristic, but less so practically, than its mainstream or Regular Baptist counterpart. Faced with incredible odds against his success, including antagonism to his ideas from other Baptists and his own ignorance of contemporary trends in Baptist polity, Benjamin Randall* formed in 1781 the Freewill Baptist Connexion as a logical outgrowth of his revivalistic local church ministry in New Durham, New Hampshire. Essentially an evangelist at heart, Randall itinerated in New Hampshire and Maine and within three years he had started fourteen churches and was the key personality in their survival. His theology was a thoroughgoing Arminianism and thus appealed to "whosoever would"; however, he refused to allow the churches in his Connexion to stand independently, in part because he wanted each to retain the spirit of the Freewill tradition. An excellent organizer who witnessed a variety of church structures in his travels at sea and in the colonies, Randall designed a Quaker-like system of meetings—monthly, quarterly, and yearly—to unite his following. Monthly meetings were the scenes of celebration of the Lord's Supper, while the quarterly meeting was a kind of association in which Randall or some other traveling elder was a key figure. The members of the quarterlies were in fellowship with the New Durham church and met to conduct the business of the regional connection, ordination, disciplinary action and pastoral supply. When the entire system expanded beyond county clusters, a yearly meeting was established, generally according to state boundaries. Its purpose was to review the welfare of the entire Connexion and plan for greater missionary outreach. In 1826 the first general conference of the Freewill Baptists met in Tunbridge, Vermont, as delegates of each local church to utter the voice of the churches on moral and benevolent subjects of the day. In later years, the Freewill Baptists created their own benevolent societies as adjuncts to the General Conference and on behalf of the entire group.[14] Whether intentionally or not, as time went on, the Freewills developed an integration of structure and accountability that was similar to the Wesleyan model. At its peak in the 1830s, it combined the voluntary theology characteristic of other Baptists with a more sophisticated and efficient polity, the success of which was a function of the quality of its leaders. In the later nineteenth century, Regular Baptists accepted the Freewill theology but declined to adopt the unique structure.

THE EMERGENCE OF BAPTIST DENOMINATIONALISM

When the General Missionary Convention of the Baptist Denomination in the United States for Foreign Missions was formed in 1814, a new era in Baptist voluntary activity began. The Convention and its subordinate, the Baptist Board for Foreign Missions, were a visionary combination of democratic principles and the single-purpose–general-voluntary society. More importantly, the scheme was a blending of the differing perspectives and interests of Luther Rice, Richard Furman,* and William Staughton.* The result of their dreams and discussions broke new ground for Baptist ideas about the nature of the church in mission, and it instantly united a diverse and often contentious people.

Richard Furman, the eldest of the three, was a veteran of the War for Independence and had by the age of thirty developed a national reputation as a defender of liberty and American nationhood. As a Southerner he advocated strong central authority in government, in part because his state lacked the resources and advantages which the northern cities and states enjoyed. A Federalist politically, Furman foresaw the day when Baptists would aggregate their efforts regionally and nationally. His stirring oratory was a strong catalyst for unity, first in his association and later beyond. He was willing to concede the values of a society for foreign missions, but his own vision was focused on what he called "the more extended scale of a Convention in a delightful union." In his inaugural address at the first meeting of the General Missionary Convention, he urged the delegates to add to foreign missions, education, domestic concerns, and a sense of solidarity as Baptists in the United States. Furman also championed the incorporation of the Convention as a means of making permanent its identity and lending legal credibility to a "dissenter" organization.[15]

William Staughton brought to the project an ardent passion for missions and a penchant for order and detail. As a young man, he had witnessed the formation of the English society with its auxiliaries and its singular devotion to overseas effort. He recalled the intimacy of those strongly committed to world evangelization and the sacrifice their stewardship demanded. He also knew and respected Andrew Fuller, the corresponding secretary of the British society for eighteen years. Little wonder that in his first report to the Board in 1815, Staughton referred to Carey, Marshman, and Ward, Baptist missionaries in India, and to Fuller, Ryland, and Sutcliff at the home base in England. In providing a rationale for missionary stewardship, Staughton relied heavily upon William Carey's *Enquiry:* the benighted heathen of the earth, the financial resources of the churches, and the partnership of fellow-workers with God. Conceding the broader ideals of others, Staughton pointedly said, "A spirit for foreign missions has an excellent influence on those who are domestic. . . . Foreign missions are in reality only domestic missions extended."[16] For fourteen years Staughton was the ever-present agent of detail for both the Board and its missionary projects.

While much has been made of Luther Rice's claim to have designed the first structure of the American Baptist denomination and of his tireless efforts to advocate a larger agenda than Baptists could handle, Rice also brought much of his Congregationalist background to bear. In his immediate past was his own appointment as a missionary of the American Board of Commissioners for Foreign Missions. He had been one of the five young persons who had pressed the Congregational leadership in New England to form a missionary society and he later urged the format of the American Board on his Baptist colleagues. As Rice saw it, the Board was the locus of authority during most of the work, and to a group of commissioners (a name borrowed from the Congregationalists) who were delegates of the churches and associations should be given the direction of the program. Much of the terminology of the Baptist General Convention in its early years was transferred from the American Board, and the Baptist board had a decidedly Presbyterian style about it. Practically, Luther laid great stress on the accountability of the board to the regional Baptist bodies which he thought parallel to the Congregational and Presbyterian synods and associations.[17]

As its three parents conceived it, then, the Convention was a bold new venture in voluntarism for the Baptists. At its core was a fundamental shift from a society of individual contributors to a convention of selected delegates. In the new plan, a comprehensive organization was achieved through a representative process with much greater support and funding available. This indirect accountability to local churches presumed the competence of regional associations and mission societies, which the convention also promoted and involved in its work by the election of delegates according to gifts of at least one hundred dollars annually. Sensing the possible perception of a diminution of the local congregations, President Furman encouraged Baptists by asserting, "The independence of the churches, we trust will ever, among us, be steadfastly maintained." The expectation was that churches which had voluntarily associated would now elect delegates from the associations, and individuals who had joined local societies would also elect delegates to the general body. In a very egalitarian setting, the delegates "in convention" would debate issues and create policy for the board to interpret and the agents to execute. All in all, it was a harmonious dovetailing of egalitarianism and efficiency.

Unfortunately, some New Englanders disagreed, and so did local church protectionists. The Baptists of New England had been organized for missions beginning in 1800, and they had chosen the single-purpose voluntary society as their vehicle. Much had been accomplished in the name of foreign and domestic missions, Bible and tract distribution, temperance, and ministerial training, to mention their outstanding concerns. New England leaders had been watchful when what was supposed to have been a foreign mission enterprise in 1814, came to include a college and domestic missions by 1817. These objects conflicted with their own efforts or met regional needs other than those of New England. By 1821, when financial troubles hit the domestic missionary effort of the General Missionary Convention, it was the Massachusetts Baptist Missionary Society which rescued the western mission of John Mason Peck, a fact not lost in the debate of 1826. Predictably, when Luther Rice, Columbian College, and the entire program of the Convention came under review because of extreme financial difficulties in 1825–26, it was a New England coterie which led in the reduction of the General Missionary Convention to a single purpose foreign mission society and brought its offices to Boston.[18] Under the new management, the commissioners or Board of Managers were principally from Massachusetts and were also the associates in the Massachusetts Baptist Missionary Society, Brown University, and the Newton Theological Institution: Francis Wayland,* Lucius Bolles, Daniel Sharp, Herman Lincoln, Stephen Gano, Irah Chase, and David Benedict. This group reasoned that Southerners could control the Convention presidency as long as actual board business was managed in Boston. Owing to the general spirit of the era, a chorus of voices cried out in opposition to a perception of contrived voluntarism and the tendency toward centralization. The loudest spokesman in New England was president of Brown University and he questioned the whole convention principle. Francis Wayland wrote:

It is truly a violation of the independence of the churches, and the right of private judgment when several hundred brethren meet in some public convention, and manufacture public opinion, and adopt courses which their brethren are called upon to follow, on pain of the displeasure of the majority, as when they establish a formal representation, to whose decision all the constituency must submit.[19]

Still other, less erudite local church advocates met in northern Maryland in 1832 and contrasted the ''gospel order'' of missions with missions societies which can include the unregenerate as well as the people of God. Elsewhere in the Black Rock Resolutions, the antimissionists stated:

The missions community is so arranged that from the little Mite Society, on to the State Convention, and from then on to the Triennial Convention, and General Board, there is formed a general amalgamation, and a concentration of power in the hands of a dozen dignitaries, who with some exceptions have the control of all the funds . . . the authority to appoint females, and schoolmasters, and printers and farmers as such . . . as missionaries of the Cross, and to be supported from these funds.[20]

While the more radical spokesmen were always in the numerical minority, the trend after 1825 in the North and the West was to keep the authority and execution of conventions under severe restrictions.

In all sections, the convention principle did survive at one critical level. At the same time when the General Convention was being reduced in scope, state mission societies were being transformed into conventions and new state orga- nizations were started on that model. The older societies recognized the need to relate to churches rather than individuals, while others saw the value of "master associations." South Carolina led the way under Furman's leadership in 1821; their plan was to place religious education, missions, promotion, and "har- mony," under the watch care of association delegates and other appropriate representatives of Baptist bodies. Connecticut next followed with a vote to transform its auxilary society to the General Missionary Convention into a full- fledged convention of churches to prosecute vigorously the mission interests at home and abroad. In New York State a convention naturally evolved from the missionary labors of several societies and the "missionary convention" was formed in 1826.

The state conventions came to fill a need which guaranteed their survival. If associations were limited in scope and territory, the state bodies broadened both. Also, where the national General Convention was perceived as distant, the state conventions met annually and reflected the interests of a consistent and loyal body. Moreover, often the states and associations cooperated in joint missionary and educational projects of heightened value to local churches. Particularly in the American Baptist Home Mission Society (ABHMS), the national leadership realized the potential of the state conventions and urged its constituency in the trans-Appalachian region to form conventions as soon as possible after associ- ations. In Illinois, John Mason Peck was able to marshall the forces of antislavery and pro-missionary Baptists to form the convention in 1834, thus ensuring that the antimission forces would be kept in check. In the late nineteenth century, ABHMS leaders designed state convention bodies as the far western missionaries entered a region, and they used this pre-arranged pattern for the missionaries to develop new churches. Often such conventions were ill-conceived and burdened with educational institutions and other benevolent projects beyond their capa- bilities. Ironically, it was in the western context, where both Northern and Southern Baptists hoped to establish a foothold, that these Goliathan forces clashed over territorial rights before the local churches had the chance to express voluntarily their benevolent desires. Because the Southern Baptist Home Mission Board was often more aggressive than the northern Home Mission Society, the western state conventions were lured into the southern family despite comity agreements to the contrary. In the twentieth century, what began as a self- generated desire to unite churches within a state area has evolved into a second tier of denominational administration. Since the 1950s, Southern Baptists have moved north to create state conventions in most states or regions (New England) for new church development and promotion, despite neighboring churches af- filiated with the northern convention. The northern state conventions have been reduced in size and then in number, and a regional concept has emerged which combines several former state conventions and urban mission societies. These regions bear more of the marks of a national administrative pattern than the traditional voluntarism of the earlier conventions.

Despite the best efforts of local church protectionists, the concept of a national, general convention did survive the early nineteenth century. When the southern delegates to the General Missionary Convention departed in 1845 and left essentially a foreign missionary society in its place, the result in the South was a full committment to a national southern convention. In the great tradition of Richard Furman, William B. Johnson* presided over a plan to "elicit, combine, and direct the energies of the whole denomination in one sacred effort."[21] While in some ways the Southern Baptist Convention used precisely the same terminology of the earlier General Missionary Convention, the founders made some important improvements. Instead of a society approach limited to individual contributors, or the old Convention composition of delegates from associations, it was both and more. Southerners invited all churches which contributed at least one hundred dollars annually to have delegates, thus ensuring the opportunity for participation by churches directly and establishing an awesome accountability factor. The new triennial (later annual) convention was all-powerful in electing persons to boards, adopting a budget, and creating policy for all aspects of its work. Implementation of the work of the Convention was left to various mission boards or divisions and institutions which transact business only associated with their object and which are altogether accountable to the Convention. By design the Convention elects officers who reflect contemporary trends in the life of the constituency, and a salaried secretariat operates the routine affairs. State conventions, associations, and churches all have equal footing in the Convention delegations; thus a local congregation may be a member of the Charleston Association, the South Carolina Baptist State Convention, and the Southern Baptist Convention directly.

What the Southern delegates accomplished at Augusta, Georgia, in 1845 became a model for other Baptists in the United States. In 1886 black clergy organized the first national black Baptist convention composed of six hundred church delegates from seventeen states. In 1895, when several organizations coalesced as the National Baptist Convention, the membership was composed of "orthodox, missionary" churches, Sunday Schools, societies, associations, or state conventions which contributed five dollars per year. The boards were not as tightly controlled as in the SBC., but accountability through reports and elected officers was established with the Convention.[22]

After a half century of further experimentation with the society model, Baptists in the North returned to the convention plan about 1900. Just prior to the turn of the century, concern had arisen over the competitive nature of the societies' benevolent campaigns as well as the separate dates each year for the annual society meetings. The Chicago Baptist Association in 1906 requested the executives of all the mission societies to seek greater cooperation and to work for a permanent organization of the northern Baptist churches. As a result, in May

1907 the Northern Baptist Convention was organized at Washington, DC as an advisory, promotional, inspirational, and coordinating body for the churches. While the Convention itself had little direct responsibility, it provided the occasion for delegates of Baptist churches and cooperating state conventions, city societies, and associations to coordinate their interests with the general societies, which agreed to make a provision in their constitutions that all accredited delegates to each Convention meeting were annual members of the organization. The membership of these boards would continue to be selective; the Convention in 1911 voted to create a pension board and a general board of education. The number of delegates per church was to be determined by membership rather than contribution.[23]

The Northern Convention, unlike the Southern, has undergone several stages of reorganization which has created an increasing connectionalism. Early attempts were made to include regional personnel as officers and members of the Conventions' boards and agencies, and the Convention has, through its promotional officers, integrated its field staff with that of the city societies and state conventions. In a far-reaching reorganization in 1972, the convention created an overarching General Board which is composed of elected representatives from across the constituency, not directly on the basis of churches or associations, but by election districts within a state or region. The American Baptist Churches in the USA, as it is now called, continues to affirm the independence of local churches and the voluntary nature of all relationships, which relationships are realized in an elaborate system of formal covenants. One of the unique qualities of the Northern/American Convention, from its inception, has been its tendency to create cooperative relations with other Christian bodies, notably the Federal/National Council of Churches, the Home Missions Council, and other specific interchurch agencies. This irenic quality has served the Convention both well and poorly; in 1911 the Convention voted to merge with the Freewill Baptists, and on two later occasions in this century major schisms have occurred, in part over the ecumenical issue.

Other Baptist groups with a constituency not confined to one region and generally in either the Northern or Southern traditions have followed the convention model. The foreign language conferences whose voluntary affiliation was guaranteed by financial support of the northern societies, for the most part gradually severed relations with the Convention in the twentieth century and created independent conferences of churches. Like the "northern plan," the membership size of local churches determines the delegation to the annual convention, and the missionary organizations are administered by the executive committees of the conferences.[24]

Since the 1970s there has been a resurgence of local church protectionism growing out of the Fundamentalist movement and this has generally produced affiliations and coalitions of churches on more purely voluntary bases. In 1932 a reactionary group called the Baptist Bible Union, originally a theological coalition of northern, southern, and Canadian churches, reconstituted itself as the General Association of Regular Baptist Churches. Adopting a fondness for the freedom of the old association model, but with a desire to cooperate in missions and benevolence, this arrangement was predicated upon confessional agreement and the participation of pastors in inspirational and evangelistic meetings. Benevolent projects are mostly independent organizations which compete for the support of churches related to one or more of these coalitions. In each instance, care is taken not to use terms like "convention" or "society" and to safeguard practically the independence of each local congregation from structural entanglements.

Outside of the United States, Baptists have used the convention model to achieve fellowship and benevolent goals. Where the American missionary efforts have pioneered, a convention of Baptists in a given nation has been formed; where the English and European missionaries have been active, unions or federations have evolved. In each case, there are structural links with the parent traditions in which style and polity remain relatively constant. Usually, executive committees of the national Baptists coordinate programs and benevolence in conjunction with the missionary sending organizations and field personnel to achieve a functional partnership.

Since the days of Thomas Grantham, a seventeenth-century General Baptist in England, there have been advocates of an international Baptist federation, but typically the idea has suffered from sectarian biases and lack of any widespread voluntary support. Morgan Edwards, John Rippon, and William Carey all urged the idea but found it impossible to accomplish. However, in 1905, partly as a reaction to local church protectionism in the United States, and also partly due to the general cooperation achieved among other world Protestant fellowships, mainstream Baptists in England and America laid aside their differences to form a Baptist World Alliance (BWA). Russell H. Conwell,* a Philadelphia pastor, had urged greater unity and concerted witness, without legislation, to a scholarly precursor organization known as the Baptist Congress. In the South, William H. Whitsitt* espoused the idea at Southern Seminary, and James Rushbrooke and John Clifford* in England supported an alliance of a truly international type. When the Alliance was formed, its purpose was simply to encourage fellowship, study, and witness among the Baptists of the world on a voluntary basis. To its credit, the BWA has avoided interference in the affairs of its member bodies, while providing in its quinquennial congresses the forums for reconciliation and in its service programs a strong international voice for religious liberty, evangelism, education, and human rights.[25]

Over the years Baptists have savored the opportunity to involve themselves and their congregations in the work of the Kingdom of God. With every philosophical and theological support for independence and isolation, Baptists have volunteered to associate when they felt a sense of unity in the purpose for association. Only the unreconstructed Calvinists have refused to presume upon their souls' competence, and this has sharply diminished their identity in the Baptist family. The problem for most Baptists has, therefore, been to find a polity or structural style that allows for maximum achievement and maximum liberty to act as the spirit directs.

6
THE STRUGGLE FOR RELIGIOUS LIBERTY

ORIGINS OF AN IDEA

The Baptist passion for religious liberty was born out of specific circumstances and definite convictions about religious experience. As individuals, and later congregations, of the seventeenth century studied the Scriptures, arrived at tenable positions in matters of doctrine and practice, and announced their faith to their respective communities, opposition set in. Like any other persecuted sect, Baptists struggled for the freedom to behave religiously as they pleased; to win new converts to their ranks; to gather groups together for worship, study, and discipline, and to publish their views in printed form. Even more than the obvious, however, Baptists urged a principle which applied to persons of all faiths—or no faith—and this has been their genius in England, the United States, and elsewhere as their ranks have expanded. At their beginning, in the world of transition which England was in the seventeenth century, Baptists led other dissenters in championing the cause of religious liberty until the Toleration Act of 1689. Then the struggle shifted to new soils.

With the succession of King James VI of Scotland (James I of England) to the English throne in 1603, persons who could not conform to the traditions of the Church of England had real cause for concern. "Nonconformists" in the broadest sense included Puritans, Separatists, Presbyterians, Independents, Roman Catholics, Lutherans, Jews, infidels, and Anabaptists. The thirty-eight year old monarch announced in his first speech to a Puritan-dominated Parliament in 1604 that his overriding concerns were "peace and truth." He wished to assert his supremacy over the Puritans because "they are impatient of any authority" and over the Roman Catholics because of the ever-present menace of papal intrusion into English political and domestic affairs. In 1606 James announced the Oath of Allegiance, which simply required that allegiance to the King was supreme above all other spiritual or temporal decrees; the king was buttressed by a series of canons drawn up by the Church the same year, which repeated the doctrine of non-resistance to the Crown in all causes. While James held to his hereditary right to enforce the truth in God's Word, Anglican churchmen argued that Christ himself always submitted to the civil magistrate and counselled others to do likewise. It became fairly obvious rather quickly after the coronation of James I that the policy of the Crown was to establish peace through repression of diversity. Many Nonconformists struggled with this policy and eventually triumphed in the Revolution; others chose to follow the "command of Christ," that when they "persecute you or drive you out of one city, flee to another" (Matthew 10:23).

In view of growing royal intolerance at the Hampton Court Conference of 1604 and later events, Puritanism was sharpened for many in the adoption of Congregational or Independent principles of formal Nonconformity. Henry Jacob, an Independent pastor, proposed for instance that the true church was an independent, self-sufficient congregation covenanted together by free mutual consent. He argued that spiritual and temporal power are to be executed by the congregations and the magistrate respectively. Only five years after the Hampton Court Conference, Jacob fled to Holland where he joined other English Separatists in exile. Two other congregations of Separatists, one led by John Robinson of Scrooby Manor, the other by John Smyth* of Gainsborough, followed suit with other exiles and departed England in 1607, completely separating from the Church of England and calling for a magistrate who would defend the "Truth" against error. Robinson and his group eventually turned to the English colonies in America for a seedbed in which to grow their ideas; Smyth remained longer in Amsterdam where he became heavily influenced by the Mennonite community there. In 1610 Smyth concluded in his larger Confession that the magistracy is a permissive ordinance of God and that magistrates [kings] were "not to meddle with matters of conscience."[1] By 1610 Smyth was clearly a Baptist but had at least tempered his affection for Mennonite views to the extent that he allowed that Christians may be magistrates for the sake of civil concerns, if their powers had no bearing upon religion.

Since John Smyth died in 1612 in Amsterdam, the next logical steps would be taken by two of Smyth's followers, Thomas Helwys* and Leonard Busher, both of whom were recognized Baptists. Helwys took exception to the idea that it was legitimate to flee persecution and he returned in 1612 to commence with his following the first Baptist church on English soil. Helwys was no martyr; rather, he worked to create the first full-blown case for religious toleration in the English language. Helwys started with the dual premises that individuals, not churches, comprise the Kingdom of God and that individuals are accountable for attaining knowledge of God's truth. To forbid an individual from preaching or learning "is contrary to the liberty of the Gospel which is free for all men, at all times, in all places." For those Separatists and Independents who would argue for limited means of coercion by a Christian magistrate, Helwys answered, "No sword of justice may smite any for refusing Christ," and for those who would reject the gospel altogether, "Let them be heretics, Turks, Jews or what-soever it appertains not to the earthly power to punish them in the least."[2] Helwys' position could easily have been misunderstood as calling for religious anarchy, and no doubt his critics so accused him. He was careful, however, to state clearly that "Christians are not to resist by any way or means, although it were in their power, but rather to submit to give their lives as Christ and his apostles did, and yet keep their consciences to God." In a poignantly loyal "epistle dedicatory," Helwys pleads, "O King be not seduced by deceivers to sin so against God whom thou oughtest to obey, nor against thy poor subjects who ought and will obey thee in all things with body, life and goods or else let their lives be taken from the earth. God save the King!"[3]

Leonard Busher, like Helwys, also argued persuasively for toleration. Government "may please to permit all sorts of Christians; yea Jews, Turks, and Pagans, so long as they are peaceable and no malefactors." He went on to point out that persecution breeds hypocrisy and hypocrisy often breeds violence and plots against the king; further, as king and Parliament would not themselves be forced by the pope, so they ought to avoid forcing the consciences of others. In a very practical vein, Busher concluded that there should be complete liberty to publish religious writings so long as the proofs of the argumentation were based on the Word of God! Busher, a Baptist layman, was willing to allow the king to defend religious peace "but not the faith other than by the Word and the Spirit of God."[4] The individual conscience was ever in focus.

Although sophisticated notions of religious liberty flowered among the Baptists under James I, the sect as such did not make substantial progress toward toleration until after the Revolution began. The major reason for this discontinuity was that the earliest Baptists were Arminian in theology, which caused them much grief with Puritans, Independents, and Separatists, as well as with some Anglicans. A number of vicious attacks upon the Baptists were seen in the 1620s, which created a public perception that the group was associated with the fanatical continental Anabaptists. Indeed, some extant correspondence suggests that Helwys's successors did relate congenially to the Waterlander Mennonites to whom John Smyth had once enjoyed fellowship. For the most part, then, English Baptist leaders before 1650 were busy attempting to claim an orthodox identity for themselves among the increasingly powerful Puritan forces.

The Puritan Revolution did assist the Baptist case for religious liberty, but not as directly as the Baptists would have wished. Many General and Particular Baptists joined Cromwell's New Model Army in a united front against persecution by Charles I and Archbishop Laud. Their cause was religious liberty (along with a proliferation of other sects which by the 1630s included Seekers, Ranters, Levellers, Diggers, Quakers, and Fifth Monarchists). Once revolt against the King was declared, however, the dominant party in Parliament, the Presbyterians, sought to reorganize the Church of England along the Genevan model and suppress the sects. Starting in the 1640s, Baptists and Independents would not accept the Presbyterian takeover and called loudly for religious liberty.

Their answer came in the protectorate of Oliver Cromwell who between 1648 and 1653 did practice religious toleration as one of the precious fruits of the Revolution. It was not surprising, then, to learn from the Presbyterian controversialist, Daniel Featley, in 1646 that already Baptists

preach and print and practise their heretical impieties openly; they hold their conventicles weekly in our chief cities, and suburbs thereof.... They flock in great multitudes to their Jordans, and both sexes enter into the river and are dipt.... And as they defile our rivers with their impure washings and our pulpits with their false prophecies and fanatical enthusiasms, so the presses sweat and groan under the load of their blasphemies.[5]

At mid-century, it could be noted by friend and foe alike that Baptists had achieved religious liberty for themselves and a host of others. Their own numerical growth and the rich tradition of religious egalitarianism found in Helwys and Busher had opened the door.

The restoration of the English monarchy in 1660 found Baptists growing volatile in sentiment and greater in numbers. Essentially a lay movement, persons with Baptistic sentiment could be found in mercantile pursuits, government positions, the military, and the wealthy landowner class. To no one's surprise, reprisals broke out against those who had been sympathetic to the Commonwealth, and Baptists were not excluded. For Baptists the Restoration was the period when one of their outspoken adherents, John Bunyan,* was imprisoned for twelve years and a charitable ''Anabaptist'' woman in London named Elizabeth Gaunt* was the last woman to be executed for treason in English history. It is also to be remembered as a time when the Clarendon Code, a series of four Parliamentary acts designed to inhibit the practice of Presbyterianism, also prevented Baptists from preaching in public, holding public office, attending a Nonconformist worship service, and securing a university education.

In a veiled attempt to reestablish Catholicism in England, Charles II issued a Declaration of Indulgence in 1672 which allowed dissenters to worship in public and Catholics in private, so long as appropriate licenses were secured. Many Baptists openly opposed the matter of the licenses and still others joined forces again with Congregationalists and Presbyterians in composing the Orthodox Creed of 1677 which read in part:

The Lord Jesus Christ, who is king of kings and lord of all by purchase and is judge of quick and dead, is only Lord of Conscience; having a peculiar right so to be.... And therefore He would not have the consciences of men in bondage to or imposed upon, by any usurpation, tyranny or command whatsoever.... The obedience to any command, or decree, that is not revealed in, or consonant to His word in the holy oracles of Scripture is a betraying of the true liberty of conscience.[6]

Similar swings of the pendulum between utter intolerance of dissenters and declarations of indulgences occurred again under James II in the 1680s with similar unified responses from Baptists and other Protestants. The long struggle for religious liberty in England finally ended with the seal of William and Mary on the Act of Toleration in 1689. The Baptists could take no small credit for the force and breadth of that Act.

PERSECUTION CONTINUES IN AMERICA

As hinted earlier, the Baptist passion for religious liberty also spread to the English colonies in America. There, the shape of concern had an ironic twist and took longer to work aright. Moreover, Baptists in America gave new meaning to religious liberty and a legal sanction to its practice that had specifically religious influences and earmarks.

As some Englishmen understood it, America was supposed to afford the opportunity to escape religious bigotry and a corrupt establishment and build a "city on a hill"; twenty thousand of them thronged to America's shores from 1630–43. In fact, what eventuated in New England was a new form of Establishment with an old spirit of intolerance and ancillary persecutions. In the minds of its founders, New England was to have been a stronghold of Puritan orthodoxy; structurally it was a Congregational Way wherein there was little distinction between selectmen and ruling elders. From the beginning there was scant provision for diversity, particularly for Anabaptists.

Because the baptism of infants signalled membership in the covenanted community, Puritan leaders in Massachusetts were deadly serious about disciplining those who refused to comply. Their expectation was that once a part of the covenant, nurture and Christian experience would produce a community of visible saints, thus reforming the old "parish" of mixed religiosity. In reality, only two types of people offended the covenant at this point: the heathen who had little interest in godliness whatsoever (some of the commercial entrepreneurs were in this class), and those who refused by reason of conscience. Baptists fit into the latter category.

The first type of discipline applied to those who refused to have their children baptized was admonition and later censure by the local church pastor and elders. This usually worked, for if a person expected to remain in the community, the stigma of church censure and possible corporal punishment was more than most were willing to bear, so conformity came sooner or later. Not so for the "conscionists." Baptists and others continued to resist inclusion in the Puritan churches, and they met in their homes, practicing the ordinances as they believed the Bible established them.

When local measures proved insufficient against the Baptists, the General Court or legislative council of Massachusetts Bay Colony passed a comprehensive law to deal with refusal to follow the sacrament of infant baptism. This Law of 1644 sought to associate the offenders with the heresy of European Anabaptists "who have been the incendiaries of the commonwealths, infectors of persons, and troublers of churches in all places where they have been."[7] Specifically, anyone opposing or condemning the baptizing of infants, and doing so obstinately, was sentenced to banishment. Seemingly, the Puritan Establishment had an effective tool to deal directly with Baptists and there would be no further need to seek indirect action by defining the dissenters as "breakers of the peace" or insubordinate to civil or religious authority. Significantly, the issue at stake in the Law of 1644 was a theological one. Before and after 1644, though, there was another concern which was political with religious overtones. In the 1635 trial of Roger Williams,* Puritan leaders determined that religious dissent was also associated with the issue of the authority of the theocracy itself. The most important of the four counts of guilt levelled against Williams was his contention that "the civil magistrate's power extends only to the bodies, and goods, and outward state of men." Accepting fully the doctrine of the "two spheres," Williams put it far more eloquently nine years later in the first issue of his tract, *The Bloudy Tenent of Persecution*, "The spiritual peace, whether true or false, is of a higher and far different nature from the peace of the place or people, which is merely and essentially civil and human." Williams strictly delineated the boundaries of the civil state and power by describing a series of walls which separated various spheres of influence and by arguing that a false church cannot impair a state.[8]

The sources of Roger Williams' religious liberalism were his early disaffection with the Laudian policies in England, his subsequent ill treatment in Massachusetts, and his reading of earlier Baptist tracts on religious liberty. Originally in 1631 the young Anglican minister had left his country because he abhorred the corrupt ministry of the Church of England and the harsh treatment of the Puritan party by Archbishop William Laud. Arriving in Massachusetts, William expected to find a church free of defilement; instead he encountered Non-Separating Congregationalists who refused to speak ill of the old world parish system. Williams blatantly refused to join the Boston church; because of his abilities he was called to be the pastor at Salem. The General Court intervened and called upon the Salem elders to reject the young radical, whereupon he ventured to Plymouth and joined the Separatist community. In 1634 Williams returned to Salem as a teacher and drew the wrath of the magistracy by questioning the colonial patent, the value of oath-taking, and the authority of civil magistrates in spiritual matters. Underlying the actual charges, according to John Cotton, were Williams's obstinate attitude and unrepentant responses. In 1635 Williams was banished, and he sought refuge beyond the arm of Massachusetts law in the Narragansett Country.

Following Roger Williams's actual settlement at Providence and his shortlived relationship to the Baptists, he returned to England to secure a charter for his colony at Rhode Island. During this period he read widely in the classics of religious liberty, including that of a prisoner at Newgate who was probably the celebrated John Murton. Both the themes and argumentation of *The Bloudy Tenent* betray a dependence upon earlier materials, and this Williams freely admitted. From the wellspring of his own mind, he embellished the Baptist case for religious liberty with a careful history of strife over conformity in Old and

New England, and he followed Leonard Busher's notion that "it is the will and command of God that . . . a permission of the most Paganish, Jewish, Turkish or anti-Christian consciences and worships be granted to all men in all nations."[9] Therein was what the Standing Order feared the most: complete toleration and disintegration of the theocracy.

Rhode Island, with Roger Williams's liberal ideas at work, became a haven for the religiously persecuted, particularly the Baptists and Quakers. Williams's chief contribution to religious liberty as a Baptist was in providing a truly peaceful kingdom; to his discredit, few Baptists until Isaac Backus in the next century built upon the religious views of the "gentle radical," in part because Williams embarked upon an uncertain religious pilgrimage of his own. He had served to open "a wide door of liberty" which would ensure other Baptist thinkers the opportunity to carry the ideal to its next stages.[10]

CONTRIBUTIONS OF JOHN CLARKE

Though Williams is better known, it was John Clarke* who, for a longer time and with greater ultimate impact, made the clearest early exposition of the principle of religious freedom for the Baptists. Clarke's own spiritual pilgrimage forms much of the background for his ideas; he was also well-grounded in the political theory of his time, having trained in the law at Cambridge. His contemporaries knew him to have a fertile mind and he quickly won the widespread respect of not only the dissenters in New England, but the religious community in England as well.

Apparently, Clarke studied the Bible as a student at Cambridge and concluded that infant baptism was invalid. Probably rebaptized in England, he was a Separatist when he arrived in Massachusetts. His dissenter ideas created a stir in Portsmouth, New Hampshire, and he and his congregation removed to Aquidneck (later Newport), Rhode Island, perhaps as early as 1640. There he developed a reputation as a free thinker and Baptist, as John Winthrop's journal indicates. In 1651 he and two colleagues ventured to Lynn, Massachusetts, to visit William Witter for religious exercises. When the authorities determined the purpose of the visit, Clarke and his friends were imprisoned for ten days, being found guilty of several charges of contempt for the propriety and ordinances of the Church. Clarke interpreted this to be essentially a matter of liberty of conscience. The next year he published *Ill Newes from New England* which made his case for freedom of conscience.

Clarke hoped the English Parliament would react to his book by imposing a policy of toleration on New England. He retold his saga of his personal imprisonment on spurious charges and how the three Baptists had requested a public disputation and were denied it. Clarke carefully interlaced his narrative with theological and political insights and argumentation, including the propositions that Christ is the Lord of the Church in points of rule and order, that believer's baptism is a command of Christ, that believers should be allowed the freedom to work outside congregations, and that no one has any authority to force upon others any faith or order. Herein was the most cogent theory and defense of religious liberty presented in seventeenth-century America.

The legal acumen of John Clarke was evidenced in his careful recitation of the legal system and provisions in New England that had been used to suppress dissent and heteropraxy. Following his quotation of the Law of 1644 against Anabaptists, Clarke listed laws forbidding blasphemy, the gathering of unapproved churches, contemptuous behavior toward the Word of God, breach of the Sabbath, subversion of the Christian faith and gospel, and the disturbance of churches. Additionally, Clarke noted that the civil code required that "every inhabitant shall contribute to all charges both in Church and Commonwealth."

But it was Clarke, the theologian, who responded to such onerous pronouncements. His first conclusion was to make a strong biblical case for the supreme position and authority of Jesus Christ: "He is the only Lord and lawgiver of this spiritual building." Next he assaulted the sprinkling of children of the covenant as a valid baptism because, of baptism by immersion he stated, "Christ Jesus the Lord hath appointed it to disciples and to Believers and such only."[11] Not only were believers to be given the right to practice the ordinances as the Bible taught, but also to express themselves and work for the advancement of Christ's kingdom. When Clarke wrote that every servant of Christ had the duty "to improve that talent which his Lord had given to him," he fused the freedom to dissent with the liberty to propagate religious ideas, surely an unacceptable argument in the Puritan community. Finally, Clarke asserted that no one had the authority to use the "arm of flesh to constrain or refrain another's conscience . . . or worship of his God," which spoke to freedom from persecution. Clarke seems plainly to have relied on Roger Williams's thought at this point where he freely used the expression "human consciences" and he claimed that "outward forcing men in the worship of God is the ready way to make men dissemblers and hypocrites before God."[12] He also agreed with Williams that forced conscience cannot stand with the peace, prosperity, and safety of a place, commonwealth, or nation. This last emphasis of *Ill Newes* was to fall on productive soil within a decade.

John Clarke's greatest contribution came in his work to secure the charter for Rhode Island in 1663. In the petition process and the subsequent issuance of a royal charter, Clarke skillfully blended his political and theological premises. In his second petition to King Charles II on behalf of the residents of the colony, he wrote to the monarch, of Rhode Islanders, "They have it much on their hearts (if they may be permitted) to hold forth a lively experiment, that a flourishing civil state may stand . . . with a full liberty in religious concernments." To the credit of John Clarke, colonial agent, the Charter of 1663 incorporated his memorable phraseology and unequivocally stated,

We being willing to encourage the hopeful undertaking of our said loyal and loving subjects and to secure them in the free exercise and enjoyment of all their civil and religious rights . . . and to preserve unto them that liberty in the true Christian faith and worship of God which they have sought with so much travail, and with peaceable minds . . . and because some of the inhabitants of the same colony cannot in their private opinions conform to the public exercise of religion according to the liturgy, forms and ceremonies of the Church of England . . . our royal will and pleasure is that no person within the said colony at any time hereafter shall be in anywise molested, punished, disquieted or called in question, for any differences in opinion in matters of religion. . . . All and every person . . . freely and fully have and enjoy his own judgements and conscience in matters of religious concernments.[13]

If Roger Williams had created the "wider door of liberty" in establishing the colony in the first place, it was John Clarke, Baptist minister, physician, and political theorist, who finally brought the first legal sanction to religious liberty in America. How comprehensive was this liberty to be? In an early work, Clarke had called upon magistrates "to suffer the Tares,"[14] by which he meant erroneous, heretical, and anti-Christian persons professing the gospel. No statement could have been more encompassing or prove to create more anxiety in a Christian commonwealth.

Nineteen years after Charles II granted full religious freedom to the inhabitants of Rhode Island, the new Massachusetts Bay Colony charter proclaimed religious toleration and brought an end to persecution for dissent. Even the staunchest Puritan families, such as the Mathers, realized that Baptists, Quakers, and others were a permanent part of the social fabric. Indeed, the Reverend Cotton Mather recognized this reality when in 1718 he preached the ordination sermon for Elisha Callendar at First Baptist Church, Boston, the first Baptist minister to receive an education in America. But, outside of Rhode Island, religious liberty was still an embryonic idea. In Massachusetts, Baptists, like everyone else, were expected to pay taxes in support of the state church. In Connecticut, Governor Gurdon Saltonstall launched a concerted crusade to silence dissent (particularly the John Rogers family) by fines, imprisonment, and confiscation of lands. As Baptists refused to pay their taxes, lands were taken and stiff penalties executed. For thirty-eight years after toleration was granted in Massachusetts, Baptists and other noncomformists continued to pay—or resist—taxes for the support of clergy and churches other than their own.[15]

SEPARATION OF CHURCH AND STATE

During the early eighteenth century, the debate shifted from the question of individual liberties to worship, preach, and baptize, to the question of community obligation contrary to one's conscience. Protests and petitions were issued by dissenters to colonial legislatures and to the Privy Council in England for exemption from taxes. The Anglican community in New England was first exempted by the Massachusetts and Connecticut legislatures; soon afterwards the Quakers and Baptists were exempted. The landmark decision for these groups was made on 20 June 1728, when the Massachusetts General Court declared that those commonly called Anabaptists and Quakers "who allege a scruple of conscience as the reason of their refusal to pay any part or proportion of such taxes" were exempt from such taxes, provided that they attend meetings of their societies on the Lord's day and that they live within five miles of the place of meeting.[16] A similar act was passed in Connecticut in 1729. In the ensuing twenty years, these exemption acts expired and were, with great difficulty, renewed. In 1753 Massachusetts added the provision that exemption certificates could be issued only with the testimony of three other Anabaptist churches and in 1757 exemption was granted only to names on an official list. Locally, Baptists suffered ridicule from those who declared that "Baptists went to the rivers to wash away their taxes!"

Many Baptists continued the struggle for religious liberty, contending that no one had the right to evaluate another person's religious experience, even if it was for the purpose of greater religious freedom (exemption from taxes). On this foundation, recalcitrant preachers and laity refused to obtain certificates or to have their names placed on lists. Such a person was Elizabeth Backus, the mother of Isaac, illustrious pastor at Middleboro, Massachusetts through much of the eighteenth century. In 1752 she was imprisoned for ten days on charges that she refused to pay the religious tax or to seek exemption. Not everywhere did Baptists struggle as those in New England; after William Penn opened his new colony in 1681 and the English wrenched New Netherland from the Dutch in 1664, Baptists could and did move to a freer environment to live in peace. Illustrative of this trend was Thomas Dungan, who first settled at Newport, Rhode Island, and later at Cold Spring, Pennsylvania, where he founded the first Baptist church in that colony in 1684. Dungan's example attracted numerous co-religionists to the prosperous Delaware Valley in the first decades of the eighteenth century.

The Great Awakening provided the backdrop for the next stage of the fight for religious liberty. At about the time when Baptists in New England were achieving a better image, revival broke out among the Congregationalists which threatened the control by the Standing Order and deeply divided the religious community in New England and the South. The enthusiasm and demanding ethics of the New Lights or Separates so concerned the authorities in Connecticut, for example, that the Toleration Act was revoked in 1743 to provide legal means to determine what was legitimate dissent and what was not. While Old Baptists fared well for the most part, New Light Separates did not. Itinerant evangelists were billed as troublemakers and the Separate meetings were called illegal conventicles. Ministers and laity were fined and imprisoned as quickly as Baptists and Quakers had been a century before. In Virginia where Separates and early Baptists alike were often critical of the moral laxity and ineffectiveness of Establishment clergy, pro-Anglican county sheriffs arrested preachers and provided some of the most vivid scenes of torture in colonial America. As late as 1769 James Ireland was imprisoned for preaching in Culpeper County, Virginia, with further attempts to silence him by stoning, gunpowder explosions, smoke bombs of brimstone, and poisoning. Ireland, like Baptists elsewhere, continued to preach.

Out of this revivalistic fervor and antipathy to any form of restraint upon religious expression, Isaac Backus and John Leland* emerged to complete the case among Baptists for religious liberty. In these two exponents the concept of religious freedom was powerfully focused upon a full separation of church and state if the state attempted in any way to overstep its legal, moral, and spiritual bounds. Backus's concern evolved from tax exemption in Massachusetts, Leland's from a more general disinclination toward ecclesiastical structures and any form of establishment religion.

From the very beginning of Isaac Backus's ministry, he opposed interference in the affairs of the churches of Christ. In 1747, when he was to appear before a ministerial examination committee to establish his fitness for the pastorate at Titicut, Backus refused on grounds that only the bretheren of the church had a right to examine his qualifications. A few months later a major debate opened in Backus's town over a £5 tax levied on each inhabitant to pay for the construction of a meetinghouse. Backus again objected to the tax and with several members of his church refused to pay; he was nearly imprisoned for his obstinance. The state argued that both Non-Separate and Separate (Backus's party) were included in the parish and thus had a responsibility for the maintenance of public worship. It was also an attempt to deny the Separate faction a distinct place of worship and identity. In the end, Backus and his group split over the issue of baptism, and he organized a new Baptistic congregation that, for the time being, removed them from direct harassment within the parish.[17]

As a full-fledged Baptist, Isaac Backus forged ahead with a fuller explication of his view of the separation of church and state. Because Backus viewed the New England Congregationalists as essentially Presbyterian, he was naturally suspicious of any relationships external to the local congregations, including the Baptist association. Backus's church waited three years to join the Warren Association, even though Backus himself favored the formation of a New England Baptist association to press the case for religious liberty. In 1774 Backus was sent as agent for the Warren churches to present to the Continental Congress a petition seeking redress for the abuses his colleagues had suffered in New England. In part, the memorial read, "We claim and expect the liberty of worshiping God according to our consciences, not being obliged to support a ministry we cannot attend."[18] It is believed that Backus had a large part in the framing of the petition.

Unquestionably, Isaac Backus drew heavily upon the thought and expressions of Roger Williams. From the 1774 memorial of the Warren Association, it is evident that Backus built on the theory of the "two spheres" as he argued, "The kingdom of Christ is not of this world, and religion is a concern between God and the soul with which no human authority can intermeddle."[19] The previous year Backus had devoted an entire section to essential points of difference between civil and ecclesiastical government in his classic, *An Appeal to the Public for Religious Liberty* (1773). William G. McLoughlin has rightly identified Backus in the Williams tradition, pre-Lockean, theocentric, and typological, as both writers limit civil government to the function of maintaining civil peace until humanity is reconciled with the divine law. Indeed, Backus, in writing the first history of Baptists in New England in 1777, began his history of dissent with the saga of Roger Williams whom he described as "justly claiming the honor of having been the first legislator in the world in its latter ages that fully and effectually provided for and established a free, full and absolute liberty of conscience."[20] A Separate himself, Backus never raised the issue of Roger Williams's actual contemporaneous impact upon the Baptists.

Like John Clarke of Rhode Island, Backus had a significant influence upon the actual attainment of religious freedom in Massachusetts. During the Revolutionary era, Backus used the "taxation without representation" issue to keep alive the religious tax burden. In a statement to the Massachusetts legislature in 1774, Backus audaciously quipped, "All America are alarmed at the tea tax; though if they please they can avoid it by not buying the tea; but we have no such liberty. . . . These lines are to let you know, that we are determined not to pay either of them."[21] The Middleboro pastor had become so identified with the call for complete religious liberty in the state that in 1779 a delegate to the constitutional convention requested that Backus write his views for possible inclusion in the new state constitution. Backus responded with a draft bill of rights in which the second principle was

As God is the only worthy object of all religious worship and nothing can be true religion but a voluntary obedience unto His revealed will, of which each rational soul has an equal right to judge for itself, every person has an unalienable right to act in all religious affairs according to the full persuasion of his own mind. . . . And civil rulers are so far from having any right to empower any person or persons, to judge for others in such affairs, and to enforce their judgements with the sword.[22]

Significantly, while Backus's draft was not accepted in 1779, his principle was later incorporated into the state constitution in 1833.

Roughly a contemporary of Backus and born a Connecticut Yankee, John Leland also forcefully articulated the principle of religious liberty and is said to have influenced the thought of James Madison and Thomas Jefferson on the matter. Leland, like Isaac Backus, separated the domain of the civil from the spiritual, and he held a deep distrust of any form of ecclesiastical structure or hierarchy. Like his hero, Thomas Jefferson, Leland favored decentralized forms and "as far as church government on earth is the government of Christ, it is of democratical genius. Church government is congregational, not parochial, diocesan, nor national." For this reason Leland vehemently opposed national associations or societies as "unacquainted with the 'Galilean' society," and a potential danger to local churches just as the Establishment had been in colonial Virginia and New England.[23] Leland seriously questioned whether society or government could be Christian, and he worked energetically for disestablishment in both Connecticut (1818) and Massachusetts (1833).

Leland went beyond Backus in his understanding of the issues of church and state. It was not enough to argue that the state should not interfere with religion; religion should not, conversely, enjoy any special favors from the government. No one was to be exempt from taxation, military service, or any other duty associated with citizenship. Further, no preference should be given to religion or the lack thereof; in the libertarian tradition of seventeenth-century Baptists, Leland called for complete freedom whether there be "one God, three gods, no God, or twenty gods." The government should, moreover, "have the right to punish all unlawful acts, regardless of religious motivations." In the latter part of his career, Leland became involved in a host of functional questions relating to religious liberty and, as Edwin Gaustad has pointed out, he helped to define the practical meaning of the "wall of separation." For instance, he opposed paying chaplains from public funds and sabbatarian legislation, and he supported the right of the U.S. Post Office to remain open on Sundays.[24]

Leland may well have had a monumental impact upon the making of national public policy respecting religion. During his early ministry in Virginia, 1776–87, he provided effective leadership as an itinerant evangelist and organizer of the Baptists, as well as a political commentator whose views won widespread respect. When the news of a constitutional convention reached the Old Dominion, Leland expressed public opposition, reflecting the influence of Patrick Henry, and because he, himself, feared centralization of civil authority. In a letter to a friend, Leland listed ten reasons for his opposition, the final of which was that "it is very dangerous to leave religious liberty at the mercy of people whose manners are corrupted."[25] Apparently, James Madison was so concerned about the rising Baptist antifederalism in his home state that he returned to Virginia in March 1788 to survey the situation. Baptists tell the story that, in a legendary meeting, Leland dropped his opposition to the constitution in exchange for Madison's guarantee for a bill of rights, and one which particularly granted full religious freedom. Madison himself admitted later that "moderate amendments should be made in order to dissipate the doubts of honest opponents."[26] Thus it is quite possible that a Baptist preacher who had helped to tear down the Anglican Establishment in Virginia was a significant influence in prompting an Episcopalian politician to acknowledge the need for full religious liberty.

In 1791, at thirty-seven years old, John Leland returned to his native Connecticut, where he joined in a longer struggle for religious liberty. Obviously drawing upon his affection for the writings of Thomas Jefferson, he challenged the leaders of the Standing Order, "If government can answer for individuals at the day of judgement, let man be controlled by it in religious matters; otherwise, let man be free." He directly attacked the certificate laws as he itinerated among the churches, at one point reminding his audience that, since "dissenters" included Episcopalians, eminent Americans like George Washington would have to produce a certificate in Connecticut to avoid paying Congregational tithes!

Often phrasing his arguments in pithy lines, "Government has no more to do with the religious principles of men than it has with the principles of mathematics,"[27] in published works like *The Connecticut Dissenter's Strongbox* and *Van Tromp Lowering His Peak with a Broadside*, Leland was a consistent voice in favor of disestablishment in Connecticut. His objective was achieved in 1818, when a new constitution included a bill of rights which declared that "the exercise and and enjoyment of religious profession and worship, without discrimination, shall forever be free to all persons in this State."[28]

The relevance of the Backus/Leland contribution to the Baptist struggle for religious liberty lay in the focus of the concern upon specific church-state relationships. From concrete experiences, these two theocentric clergymen provided a cogent, functional definition of religious liberty and dared to press the state to concede not only toleration, but a "wall of separation." Part of their success was due to the context of the Revolutionary Era, in which issues of unfair taxation, despotic government, and individual freedoms were in the public mind. What both John Leland and Isaac Backus could not achieve was a full understanding of the implications of liberty in view of their own denomination's evangelical and missionary awakening in the new century.

Following ratification of the Bill of Rights and disestablishment in New England, the Baptist goal in calling for religious liberty was accomplished. The energies of the Baptist community soon shifted to the missionary enterprise, which brought with it a shift of venue and a dilemma for the chief architects of religious liberty.

EVANGELISM AND RELIGIOUS LIBERTY

When Baptists joined other American Protestants in the benevolent crusade of the early nineteenth century, they assumed a definite millennial value to their faith. Historians have long shown that the first two decades of the nineteenth century exemplified an unusual display of hope about the future of the nation and the faith. As Martin Marty has observed

The free individual in American republicanism paralleled the free Christian man of evangelical regeneration. The ideas of progress in the republic were reminiscent of millenarian Protestant hopes. The democratic faith and Protestantism alike called people to mission in the world. Both fed each other's sense of destiny.[29]

For Baptists, the spiritual kingdom came to supersede the civil kingdom and the command "to spread evangelic truth" overtook other considerations, historic and otherwise.

In this remaking of priorities, religious liberty was no longer the right of all persons to follow the dictates of individual consciences—the right to believe or not to believe. Nor was it a matter of the separation of church and state. With no sense of irony, the way for a change in perspective had been paved by one of the architects of eighteenth century religious liberty, Isaac Backus, who in 1804 asserted

Real Christians are the best subjects of civil government in the world, while they obey God rather than man. The apostles explained the prophets, and finished writing the book of God; and heaven and earth will rejoice to see his truth and justice glorified.[30]

Religious liberty became the freedom to create a Christian America, and other Christian nations as well, through the missionary enterprise. Jews, infidels, and barbarians were not to remain in their religious beliefs, but evangelized, and "set at liberty to follow their consciences and the leading of God's spirit." As the eighteenth century evolved to the nineteenth, the issues associated with religious liberty took on global dimensions for the Baptist community.

It was William Carey,* an English Baptist cobbler, who said in 1791 that Christians had an obligation to use every exertion to "introduce" the gospel, and his own denomination took up the challenge. By 1825 Baptist missionaries from England and America had penetrated every continent against the stiffest odds and government restrictions prohibiting evangelism. In many ways Adoniram Judson* and Ann Hasseltine (Judson)* exemplified this indomitable willpower when they began their missionary career by travelling halfway round the world to India, knowing that their residence was illegal; months afterwards they went to Burma on an equally tenuous basis. The Judsons painfully gained momentum for their efforts when in 1825 Adoniram was caught up in the political intrigues of the Burman Empire and captured, brutally tortured, and imprisoned. His resourceful wife, Ann, found ways to maintain his survival and managed to leak word of their plight to the western press. The accounts of "barbarous treatment" and personal deprivation suffered by the missionaries won the instant sympathy of Baptist Americans as they followed the serialization of the Judson predicament in religious periodicals. Poems and prayers were written in support of the missionaries, and significantly, financial support increased dramatically.[31]

The board of the General Missionary Convention was fully supportive of the British occupation of portions of the Burman Empire, in the confidence that "a grant of toleration in favor of the Christian religion might be secured."[32] Indeed, throughout the missionary mishaps in Burma the board and the field personnel had supported the British plan so as to gain a foothold for the faith in an otherwise hostile environment. For many, religious liberty had come to mean the right of the Baptists to propagate the faith in non-Christian cultures.

Among the European missions, also, Baptists kept alive the flame of religious liberty. Following his baptism in 1834 Johann Gerhard Oncken* penetrated central Europe as an appointee of British and American societies to start new churches of baptized believers. Oncken and his colleagues encountered inhuman treatment at the hands of both civil and ecclesiastical authorities:

Our beloved brethren in Oldenburg are also subjects of cruel persecution. Their infants taken by violence from them in order to be sprinkled and their religious meetings are prohibited under the severest fines so that they cannot visit one another.

The European missionaries were careful students of the political opposition and cautiously advised new converts to "obey conscience and the Savior without incurring the penalties of the civil law."[33] Oncken and his American constituency rejoiced greatly as each of the Germans and Habsburg states granted new degrees of liberty "to act in accordance with one's own conscience" which was an implicit toleration of Baptist missionaries to preach and organize new congregations according to Free Church principles.

Meanwhile, in the United States, racial and ethnic realities provided another frontier for the question of religious liberty in the nineteenth century. That great libertarian, John Leland, had introduced a resolution in 1789 to the General Committee of the United Baptist Churches of Virginia that called for the abolition of slavery, but four years later, after Leland left the state, the Committee rescinded its action for political considerations. Leland had dared to carry the issue of religious liberty beyond the color barrier to the slave community as well when he wrote, "Liberty of conscience, in matters of religion, is the right of slaves beyond contradiction; and yet many masters and overseers will whip and torture the poor creatures for going to meeting, even at night, when the labor of the day is over."[34]

While Baptists in the North, South, and West did support the abolition of slavery before the Civil War, there is little evidence that religious liberty was a central concern. In fact, the black population—slave and free—was an object of domestic missionary endeavor. When George Leile* formed the first African Baptist congregation in Georgia about 1778, he did so with the support of the white community; similarly, the First Baptist Church in Boston supported Thomas Paul when he created the first black congregation in New England and later, as a missionary to Haiti. Nationally, the General Missionary Convention instructed John Mason Peck* and James E. Welch in 1817 (the first domestic laborers) to work among the "negro" population of the Mississippi Valley, which Peck did with great energy. Collectively, it was the hope and expectation of the white church that Christian experience, morality, and behavior would provide Afro-Americans with the best chance of any form of integration into American society.

Baptists designed a similar outreach for immigrants to the United States which hardly affirmed total religious liberty. Four years after its founding in 1832 the American Baptist Home Mission Society (ABHMS) began its work with foreign populations among the Welsh and successively with Germans, Scandinavians, French Canadians, Mexicans, Chinese, Poles, Italians, Jews, Slavs, and Hindus. Partially to offset the Nativist movement which discriminated against non-English speaking Americans, Baptists sought to "Christianize" and "Americanize" the immigrants. Recognizing that few of these people were Baptist, missionaries were appointed to gather congregations, start schools, and design welfare programs to assimilate different cultural and social patterns into a sense of national unity. As late as 1919, a Baptist advocate of this "fusion approach" claimed,

We in America have the right, which we readily accord to every other nation, to enjoy the type of government and the social institutions which suit our taste. They may not be the best in the world, but if we like them, it is our privilege to enjoy them.[35]

Within the religious context, Roman Catholicism, Lutheranism, and non-English worship patterns were targeted for "Americanization." Eventually this approach backfired in the twentieth century as the German, Swedish, and Italian conferences evolved into separate denominational groups rather than remaining within the Northern Baptist family.

A similar, unpredicted reaction occurred among the black Baptist churches. During the Reconstruction Era the American Baptist Home Mission Society took a special interest in the needs of the recently freed slaves and sent missionaries south to start schools and churches in the black community. While many positive results eventuated from educational and evangelistic efforts, a separatist movement evolved among black leaders which called for discrete black organizations of churches and missionary endeavor. Part of the ethos of this movement concerned white educational literature for black congregations and the need to assert black leadership in an environment of continuing racism and segregation. By the time of the first Baptist World Congress in 1905, black Americans, for their own reasons, were among the loudest voices in support of religious freedom. As Elias C. Morris, a prominent black Baptist leader, put it at that meeting in London,"We hope to make it plain that the Negroes of the United States are the logical Christian leaders of the black people of the world."[36]

RELIGIOUS LIBERTY REDIVIVUS

One of the first projects of the Baptist World Alliance (BWA) constituency in the twentieth century was to survey the political realm for evidences of violations of religious liberty. In its earliest documentation the Alliance asserted its support for freedom:

The world must not be permitted to forget what the Baptist doctrine of soul liberty, broadening into the conception of personal liberty and finding expression in the ordinances of civil liberty, has wrought for the political emancipation of mankind.[37]

With scant financial resources, the Alliance Executive Committee authorized a British Baptist leader, Sir George MacAlpine, to head a delegation to Czarist Russia in 1911 to negotiate the freedom for Baptists to build churches and a college in which to train Baptist pastors. Sensing the opposition, this courageous group explained to the Czar's ministers that "the object of the Baptists everywhere is to make good and loyal citizens of the State and in their present enterprise, nothing but the welfare of Russia is sought"![38] The Russian leaders knew more about Baptists and religious freedom than the BWA delegation realized, and the petition was declined. Over the years, the Alliance has become an effective forum for the discussion of religious liberty apart from missionary implications, and the BWA Study Commissions on Religious Liberty have had a significant impact on the revival and encouragement of movements to strengthen and establish religious freedoms.

Among the Northern, Southern, and National Baptist groups, a significant revival of interest in religious liberty occurred during the New Deal era. Some Baptist leaders felt uneasy about how they perceived the philanthropic activities of the churches were being assumed by federal government programs like Social Security. In 1937 the Northern and Southern Baptist Conventions pressed the U.S. State Department to investigate charges of persecution of Christians in Romania, another evidence of violation of "a free church in a free state." Elsewhere in the world, invading Japanese troops seized the property of the University of Shanghai in China, which brought a loud protest from the American conventions which operated the school. Other potentially explosive issues were President Franklin Roosevelt's 1939 appointment of Myron C. Taylor as a representative to the Vatican, in the interest of world peace, and the use of public funds for graduate education in parochial institutions through the National Youth Administration. To many Baptists, the "wall of separation" had been breached in unhealthy ways and an effective form of redress had to be made.

In an unusually cooperative fashion, the three conventions organized first their own committees on public relations, which later became in 1941 a Joint Conference Committee on Public Relations. Issue by issue the associated committees and what became permanently the Baptist Joint Committee on Public Affairs in 1946, provided a "watchdog" surveillance on matters of church-state relations. Led by Rufus Weaver, pastor at First Baptist Church, Washington, DC, and later the executive secretary for the District of Columbia Baptist Convention, U.S. Baptists pressed through diplomatic channels and won freedom from persecution for Romanian Baptists as well as greater recognition of the Chinese situation due to the takeover of the University of Shanghai property. While President Roosevelt did not recall his ambassador to the Vatican and aid to church-related schools did continue, Baptists had proven that joint resolve was indeed an effective tool.

In the 1939 spring annual meetings of the Northern, National, and Southern Baptist Conventions, a joint pronouncement was approved and called the "American Baptist Bill of Rights." Noting the "sudden rise of European dictators," a trend toward paternalism and "special favors extended to certain ecclesiastical bodies," the writer (probably Rufus Weaver) asserted that "no issue in modern life is more urgent or more complicated than the relation of organized religion to organized society." The document rehearsed the historic Baptist contribution of Baptists to religious freedom and then condemned the union of church and state, concluding that "we stand for a civil state with full liberty in religious concernments,"[39] an obvious reference to John Clarke. The "Bill of Rights" reversed much of the trend of nineteenth-century discussion and restored the spirit of the seventeenth-century Baptist: "A Baptist must exercise himself to the utmost in the maintenance of absolute religious liberty for his Jewish neighbor, his Catholic neighbor, his Protestant neighbor, and for everybody else." This thoroughly egalitarian stance may well have been the background for President Roosevelt's espousal of the right "of every person to worship God in his own way—everywhere in the world," in his famous "Four Freedoms Speech" before Congress in January 1941, which brought cheer generally to the Baptist community.[40]

Since its founding in 1946 the Baptist Joint Committee has fostered research and public education on matters relating to religious liberty and the separation of church and state. The multi-Baptist denominational staff has reviewed the thousands of laws and legislation in the congressional arena as well as writing two dozen *amicus curiae* briefs for cases pending in the U.S. Supreme Court. Further, the position on separation of church and state that the Committee maintained has frequently caused consternation for many Baptists, as witnessed in the historic opposition to all forms of constitutional amendments promotive of prayers in public schools and opposition to all types of public assistance to parochial education.

Unaware of their basically liberal heritage in matters pertaining to religious liberty, many modern Baptists are not as concerned about freedom as with their task to create a cultural Christianity. Similarly, some Baptists make a strong case for their involvement in political affairs while eschewing altogether government intrusion into the affairs of the church. For instance, a large number of independent Baptist churches have started "Christian" day schools to provide elementary and secondary education for their own members and any others willing to pay the tuition and accept the social and intellectual regimen. Some of these schools have neglected state accreditation requirements; others have refused admission to non-white students. In both instances local governments have brought charges against the schools and/or churches, while the defense has argued for full religious liberty and no interference of the government in the right to operate a church-related school along specific socio-religious guidelines. The fundamentalist leaders of these institutions have watched with interest the quest of South Carolina–based Bob Jones University to maintain its tax exempt status while operating on racially segregationalist lines. To complicate matters, the American Baptist Churches and other mainstream Baptist groups have supported the Bob Jones University position on the grounds that "the beliefs held by the Petitioned are sincerely held and are protected by the First Amendment," noting also the opposition of the ABC to the racially discriminatory policies of Bob Jones University. Fundamentally, the Baptists question the right of the Internal Revenue Service to establish criteria for tax exemption as a religious organization.[41]

With equal but unpredictable vehemence, fundamentalist Baptists have also asserted their right to organize political action groups and affect public policy. In his book, *Listen America!* (1980), Baptist pastor Jerry Falwell of Lynchburg, Virginia, outlined his agenda for Christian responsibility against "abortion, homosexuality, pornography, humanism, and the fractured family." Falwell's colleague and Dean of the School of Religion at Liberty University, Edward Hindson, has observed that "for Christians to divorce themselves from the political process would be to divorce themselves from society itself." To no one's surprise, Falwell and his following organized the Moral Majority, Incorporated, in 1979, "to recapture America for God" and to defeat politically and philosophically what they called "secularists and humanists." Within this organization Baptists have mixed freely with Roman Catholics, Jews and other conservative forces to promote an agenda for a "Christian and moral America," true, they feel, to its founders' ideals.[42] Falwell also claims a wide following for his principles among other Baptists, as evidenced in the ministries of Ed McAteer (The Roundtable), Robert M. Grant (Christian Voice), James Robison (Day of Restoration), and Pat Robertson (700 Club), all of whom are Baptist clergymen. Southern Baptists, who have absorbed waves of fundamentalism for decades now, have among the ranks W. A. Criswell, Paige Patterson, Bailey Smith, and Charles Stanley (in 1985–86 the president of the Convention), all pastors of prominent urban Baptist churches. While these leaders have attempted to move the Convention (and the rest of conservative America) to accept their agenda, an equally vociferous part of Southern Baptist constituency behind leaders like James Wood of Baylor University, and Porter Routh, SBC executive secretary, have proclaimed that "it is unnecessary and wrong for any religious group or individual to seek to Christianize the government. . . . It is arrogant to assert that one's position on a political issue is 'Christian' and that all others are 'un-Christian.' "[43] In many ways the resurgence of religious conservatism has caused Baptists to choose once again between religious liberty and their vision of the Kingdom of God.

In the four centuries of their historical development, Baptists have for the most part maintained a steady concern for the principles of religious liberty. Out of circumstances hostile to their very survival, the first Baptists in England and America called for the freedom to worship as they desired and to propagate their faith without restriction. In the process of securing their own freedom, Baptists found themselves arguing for complete religious liberty for all persons, as an axiom of a valid religious experience.

In America, where new forms of government emerged in a frontier society, Baptists worked out new structures and guarantees to ensure the complete separation of church and state. During the nineteenth century, following significant achievements in the United States and Great Britain, Baptists developed a new concern for religious freedom overseas, as their missionaries encountered governmental restrictions and Establishment churches. Later, threatened by social welfare programs in the government sector and perceived special favors for some churches, Baptists again arose in defense of religious liberty in the early twentieth century. Even in the face of new voices in their own family who would ironically seek to establish a Christian Commonwealth not unlike the attempts of the seventeenth century, Baptists have continued to be "stubborn for liberty."

NOTES

INTRODUCTION

1. Quoted in Edward B. Underhill, ed., *Confessions of Faith and Other Public Documents Illustrative of the History of the Baptist Churches of England in the 17th Century* (London: Hanserd Knollys Society, 1854), p. 48.

CHAPTER 1

1. John Smyth, *The Character of the Beast or the False Constitution of the Church* (Amsterdam?: n.p., 1609), reprinted in William T. Whitley, editor, *The Works of John Smyth, Fellow of Christ's College 1594–98*, 2 vols. (Cambridge, England: Cambridge University Press, 1915), II, 660.

2. John Smyth, *Principles and Inferences Concerning the Visible Church* (1607), reprinted in Whitley, *Works of John Smyth*, I, lxii, 254.

3. John Smyth, *The Differences of the Churches of the Separation* (1608), reprinted in Whitley, *Works of John Smyth*, I, 308, 315.

4. A. C. Underwood, *A History of English Baptists* (London: Carey Kingsgate, 1947), pp. 46–47.

5. Adam Taylor, *The History of the English General Baptists*, 2 vols. (London: T. Bore, 1818), I, 463–80.

6. See B. R. White, "William Kiffin: Baptist Pioneer and Citizen of London," *Baptist History and Heritage*, 2 (July 1967), 91–126.

7. *Seventh Day Baptists in Europe and America*, 2 vols. (Providence, RI: Smith and Parmenter, 1927), I, pp. 37ff; and Louise F. Brown, *The Political Activities of the Baptists and the Fifth Monarchy Men in England During the Interregnum* (Washington, DC: American Historical Association, 1912).

8. Thomas Crosby, *History of the Baptists*, 4 vols. (London: 1738–1740) original emphasis.

9. William T. Whitley, *A History of British Baptists* (London: Charles Griffith, 1923), pp. 73–81.

10. B. R. White, *The English Baptists of the Seventeenth Century* (London: Baptist Historical Society, 1983), pp. 66–67.

11. Joseph Ivimey, *History of the English Baptists*, 4 vols. (London: Burdette, Buxton, Hamilton, 1811–1830).

12. Thomas Edwards, *Gangraena; or a Catalogue and Discovery of Many of the Errors, Heresies, Blasphemies and Pernicious Practices of the Sectaries of This Time* (London: R. Smith, 1646).

13. Winthrop S. Hudson, "The Associational Principle Among Baptists," *Foundations*, 1 (January 1958), 10–23.

14. C. C. Goen, *Revivalism and Separatism in New England 1740–1800: Strict Congregationalists and Separate Baptists in the Great Awakening* (New Haven, CT: Yale University Press, 1962), 302–27.

15. John Buzzell, *The Life of Benjamin Randall* (Limerick, ME: Hobbs, Woodman and Co., 1827) covers the successes and self-understanding of the movement.

16. George W. Paschal, *History of North Carolina Baptists*, 2 vols. (Raleigh, NC: State Convention Press, 1930), I, 132–57.

17. *Massachusetts Baptist Missionary Magazine*, 1 (September 1803), 5–6.

18. William H. Brackney, "Yankee Benevolence in Yorker Lands: Origins of the Baptist Home Missions Movement," *Foundations*, 24 (October 1981), 293–301.

19. Robert G. Torbet, *Venture of Faith: The Story of the American Baptist Foreign Mission Society, 1814–1954* (Philadelphia: Judson Press, 1955), pp. 90–115.

20. Of the antimission spirit compare John Taylor, *Thoughts on Missions* (Frankfurt, KY: n.p., 1820); with Francis Wayland, *Thoughts on the Missionary Organizations of the Baptist Denomination* (New York: Sheldon, Blakeman, 1859).

21. On state conventions see Norman H. Maring, *Baptists in New Jersey: A Study in Transition* (Valley Forge, PA: Judson Press, 1964), pp. 127–28; and Garnet Ryland, *The Baptists of Virginia, 1699–1926* (Richmond, VA: Board of Missions, 1955), pp. 204–22.

22. Robert A. Baker, *The Baptist Southern Convention and Its People 1607–1972* (Nashville, TN: Broadman Press, 1974), pp. 287–341.

23. Charles L. White, *A Century of Faith* (Philadelphia: Judson Press, 1932), pp. 125–63.

24. Leroy Fitts, *A History of Black Baptists* (Nashville, TN: Broadman Press, 1985), pp. 109–57.

25. A. H. Newman, *A Century of Achievement* (Philadelphia: American Baptist Publication Society, 1901), pp. 439–47.

26. Jeffrey H. Hadden and Charles E. Swann, "The New Denominationalism: Franchising the Electronic Church," *Foundations* 25 (April 1982), 198–204.

27. Samuel Wilson, ed., *Mission Handbook: North American Protestant Ministries Overseas* (Monrovia, CA: MARC, 1980).

CHAPTER 2

1. "Articles of Religion" in *The Book of Common Prayer and Administration of the Sacraments and Other Rites and Ceremonies of the Church* (Philadelphia: Female Protestant Episcopal Prayer Book Society, 1837), p. 489.

2. William T. Whitley, *The Works of John Smyth, Fellow of Christ's College 1594–98*, 2 vols. (Cambridge, England: Cambridge University Press, 1915), I, lxii.

3. *A Declaration of Faith of English People Remaining at Amsterdam in Holland* (Amsterdam: n.p., 1611), p. 9.

4. *The Faith and Practice of Thirty Congregations, Gathered According to the Primitive Pattern* (London: Larnar, 1651), p. 51; M. M. Knappen, *Tudor Puritanism* (Chicago: University of Chicago Press, 1939), pp. 355–57; *Confession of Faith Put Forth by the Elders and Brethren of Many Congregations* (London: 1677), 1.

5. Knappen, *Tudor Puritanism*, p. 357.

6. *Minutes of the Warren Baptist Association*, 1785, pp. 6–7; *Minutes of the Northamptonshire Baptist Association*, 1782–1792.

7. The positions of Richard Fuller and Francis Wayland are found in *Domestic Slavery Considered as a Scriptural Institution* (Boston: Gould, Kendall and Lincoln, 1845).

8. Thomas Helwys, *The Mystery of Iniquity* (London: Baptist Historical Society, 1935), introduction to the text.

9. Latta R. Thomas, *The Bible and the Black Experience*. (Valley Forge, PA: Judson Press, 1976), pp. 18–19.

10. William H. Wyckoff, ed., *Documentary History of the American Bible Union*, 3 vols. (New York: American Bible Union, 1857), I, 35.

11. Ibid., p. 43.

12. Thomas J. Conant, *The Meaning and Use of Baptizein Philogically and Historically Investigated* (London: Trubner, 1981), pp. 158–63.

13. For many the "Baptist Version" was symptomatic of an emerging sectarian spirit among Baptists, not unlike the Landmark Movement. Even many Baptists believed that the Scriptures were above such party spirits. Ibid.

14. *The Sword and Trowel*, 1887, pp. 122–26, 166–72.

15. The principal American Spurgeon enthusiast was Russell H. Conwell, pastor of Philadelphia Baptist Temple, one of the largest congregations in the denomination. See Conwell's biography of Spurgeon, *Life of Charles Haddon Spurgeon, The World's Great Preacher* (Philadelphia: Edgewood, 1892).

16. A fine survey of this transformation is Norman H. Maring, "Baptists and Changing Views of the Bible, 1865–1918," *Foundations*, 1 (July and October 1958), 52–76; 30–61.

17. Adoniram J. Gordon, *In Christ, Or the Believer's Union With His Lord* (New York: Revell, 1880), p. 54.

18. William N. Clarke, *The Use of the Scriptures in Theology* (New York: Scribner's, 1906), p. 15.

19. George D. Boardman, *The Kingdom: An Exegetical Study* (New York: Scribner's, 1899), pp. 62–63.

20. Shailer Mathews, *The Gospel and Modern Man* (New York: Macmillan, 1910), p. 235.

21. C. Allyn Russell, *Voices of Fundamentalism: Seven Biographical Studies* (Philadelphia: Westminster Press, 1976), pp. 22–25, 52–53, 96–97.

22. *A Confession of Faith* (Concord, NH: 1983), p. i; Robert G. Torbet, *History of the Baptists* (Valley Forge, PA: Judson, 1963), pp. 429–31; George Marsden, *Fundamentalism and American Culture: The Shaping of Twentieth Century Evangelicalism, 1870–1925* (New York: Oxford University Press, 1980), pp. 164–67.

23. W. H. P. Faunce to Frank M. Goodchild, 16 February 1921, in Archives, American Baptist Historical Society.

24. Compare the *Annual Reports for the Northern Baptist Board of Education 1940*,

and the same for 1955 for those schools which dropped from the denominational lists. In the mid–1980s a similar trend can be noticed among Southern Baptist universities like Wake Forest, Richmond, and Baylor, which have each redefined their church-related status.

25. Marsden, *Fundamentalism*, p. 171.

26. Ibid., p. 172; William H. Brackney, *Baptist Life and Thought, 1600–1980*. (Valley Forge, PA: Judson, 1983), p. 395–401, includes several of the primary documentation.

27. Henry C. Vedder, *The Fundamentals of Christianity: A Study of the Teaching of Jesus and Paul* (New York: Macmillan, 1922), pp. 215–16.

28. A very helpful account of this debate is James J. Thompson, *Tried as by Fire: Southern Baptists and the Religious Controversies of the 1920s*. (Atlanta, GA: Mercer University Press. 1982), p. 85.

29. See William L. Poteat. *Can A Man Be A Christian Today?* (New York: Oxford University Press, 1926); and Edward B. Pollard. "On Taking the Bible Literally," *Religious Herald* 71 (September 1919), 4–5.

30. Quoted in Thompson, *Tried as by Fire*, p. 85.

31. Ibid., pp. 137–65; this is also the position of Russell, *Voices of Fundamentalism*, pp. 26–27.

32. *The Baptist Faith and Message* (Nashville, TN: Sunday School Board, 1925); William H. Brackney, "Commonly, Through Falsely Called . . . Reflections on the Baptist Search for Identity," *Perspectives* 13 (Fall 1986): 67–83; critiques the 1925 statement.

33. *A Call to Arms*! (Toronto: Baptist Bible Union, 1924), pp. 20–27; see especially the paragraph, "Membership and the Millennial Question."

34. Ibid., p. 5.

35. Ibid., article II, p. 16.

36. Ibid., p. 18.

37. Thompson, *Tried as by Fire*, pp. 152–53. In 1923 Norris was expelled from the Baptist General Convention of Texas, but he continued until the 1940s to "maintain" his membership in the Southern Baptist Convention by demonstrating outside the meetings of each annual session and by contributing the minimal sum each year to the Cooperative Program.

38. Robert T. Ketcham, *Facts for Baptists to Face* (Rochester, NY: World's Christian Publications, 1936) misunderstood Beaven's emphasis upon "social Christianity" and responded out of "the Red Scare of Communism."

39. Elmer L. Towns, *The Ten Largest Sunday Schools and What Makes Them Grow* (Grand Rapids, MI: Baker, 1969), p. 11.

40. Harry E. Fosdick, *The Modern Use of the Bible* (New York: Macmillan, 1924), p. 24; I. M. Haldeman, *Dr. Harry Emerson Fosdick's Book The Modern Use of the Bible: A Review* (Chicago: Bible Institute Colportage Association, 1925), p. 107.

41. Frank H. Woyke, *Heritage and Ministry of the North American Baptist Conference* (Oakbrook, IL: Conference Press, 1979), pp. 360–63; Eric H. Ohlman, "The American Baptist Mission to German Americans: A Case Study of Attempted Assimilation" (Th.D. dissertation, Graduate Theological Union, 1973) presents an opposing perspective based on sociological factors.

42. Both incidents are detailed in Leon McBeth, "Fundamentalism in the Southern Baptist Convention in Recent Years," *Review and Expositor*, 79 (Winter 1982), 85–103.

43. Judson Press produced for the American Convention *An American Commentary on the New Testament*, 8 vols., (Valley Forge, PA: Judson, 1950–58); Broadman Press

published for the Southern Baptists, *The Broadman Bible Commentary*, 10 vols. (Nashville, TN: Broadman, 1969–73).

44. Helen B. Montgomery, trans. *A Centenary Translation of the New Testament* (Chicago: American Baptist Publication Society, 1924).

45. Carey's story is told in S. Pearce Carey, *William Carey* (New York: Doran Co., 1923).

46. *Works of John Smyth*, I, lxix.

47. Judson's most recent biographer has a chapter entitled, "Does the Bibliomania Rage at Tavoy?": Brumberg, *Mission for Life: The Dramatic Story of the Family of Adoniram Judson* (New York: Macmillan, 1980), pp. 44–78.

48. W. A. Criswell, *Why I Preach That the Bible is Literally True* (Nashville: Broadman Press, 1969), pp. 155–160.

49. William N. Clarke, *Sixty Years with the Bible* (New York: Scribners, 1909), p. 211.

CHAPTER 3

1. Henry C. Vedder, *A Short History of the Baptists* (Philadelphia: American Baptist Publication Society, 1907), p. 410.

2. Peter Riedemann, "Rechenschaft unserer Religion" in W. J. McGlothlin, *Baptist Confessions of Faith* (Philadelphia: American Baptist Publication Society, 1911), pp. 14–15.

3. "A Brief Confession of the Principal Articles of the Christian Faith" in William L. Lumpkin, *Baptist Confessions of Faith* (Valley Forge, PA: Judson, 1959), p. 57.

4. *A Declaration of Faith of English People* (1611) in McGlothlin, *Baptist Confessions*, art. 10, p. 88.

5. *The Confession of Faith* (London: Simmons, 1644), art. 33.

6. *Confession of Faith . . . of Many Congregations*, art. 26:6.

7. *A Declaration of Faith of English People Remaining at Amsterdam in Holland* (Amsterdam: n.p., 1611), p. 11.

8. *The Confession of Faith*, 1644, art. 26; *Confession of Faith*, 1677, art. 26:8.

9. *Confession of Faith*, 1677, art. 26:8.

10. Ivimey, *History of the English Baptists*, III, 488; Winthrop S. Hudson, ed., *Baptist Concepts of the Church* (Valley Forge, PA: Judson, 1959), pp. 57–60.

11. Andrew G. Fuller, *The Complete Works of the Rev. Andrew Fuller, with a Memoir of His Life* (London: n.p., 1862), p. 703; Hudson, *Baptist Concepts of the Church*, pp. 98–105.

12. Quoted in A. C. Underwood, *A History of the English Baptists* (London: Carey Kingsgate Press, 1947), p. 170.

13. A. D. Gillette, ed., *Minutes of the Philadelphia Baptist Association 1707–1807* (Philadelphia: American Baptist Publication Society, 1851), pp. 60–61.

14. William G. McLoughlin, ed., *The Diary of Isaac Backus*, 3 vols. (Providence, RI: Brown University Press, 1979), II, 671.

15. This was the reasoning of the Convention of Particular Baptists gathered at Black Rock, Maryland, in 1832. See *The Feast of Fat Things* (Middletown, NY: G. Beebe, 1984), p. 25.

16. Francis Wayland, *Notes on the Principles and Practices of Baptist Churches* (New York: Sheldon, 1867), pp. 177–78.

17. J. Newton Brown, *The Baptist Church Manual* (Philadelphia: American Baptist Publication Society, 1853), p. 16.

18. Robert G. Torbet, *History of the Baptists*, RAR, pp. 435–36; Robert A. Baker, *A Baptist Sourcebook, with Particular Reference to Southern Baptists* (Nashville, TN: Sunday School Board, 1966), pp. 200–5.

19. James R. Graves, *Old Landmarkism: What Is It?* (Memphis, TN: J. R. Graves, 1880), p. 38; J. M. Pendelton, *Distinctive Principles of Baptists* (Philadelphia: ABPS, 1882), p. 186.

20. Edgar Y. Mullins, *Baptist Beliefs* (Philadelphia: Judson, 1912), p. 64.

21. W. C. Bitting, ed., *A Manual of the Northern Baptist Convention, 1908–1918* (Philadelphia: American Baptist Publication Society, 1918), p. 20.

22. David Benedict, *Fifty Years among the Baptists* (Providence, RI: n.p., 1859), pp. 54–58.

23. Edward Judson, *The Institutional Church: A Primer in Pastoral Theology* (New York: Lentilhon and Co., 1899), pp. 29–31.

24. Joseph R. Carter, *The Acres of Diamonds Man: A Memorial Archive of Russell H. Conwell*, 3 vols. (Philadelphia: Temple University Press, 1981), II, 492–500.

25. Roger Hayden, ed., *Baptist Union Documents, 1948–1977*, (London: Baptist Historical Society, 1980), p. 6.

26. Melchior Hofmann, "Die Ordonnantie Godts," (1530) quoted in Champlin Burrage, *The Church Covenant Idea: Its Origin and Its Development* (Philadelphia: American Baptist Publication Society, 1904), pp. 19–20.

27. Burrage, *Church Covenant Idea*, pp. 45–61.

28. John Robinson, *Of Religious Communion, Private and Publique* (Amsterdam: n.p., 1614), p. 48.

29. Daniel Featley, *The Dipper's Dipt, or the Anabaptists Ducked and Plunged Over Head and Eares, at a Disputation at Southwark* (London: n.p., 1645), p. B2.

30. Quoted in Isaac Backus, *History of New England with Particular Reference to the Denomination of Christians called Baptists*, 2 vols. (Newton, MA: Backus Historical Society, 1871), I, 286.

31. Robert A. Baker and Paul J. Craven, *Adventure in Faith: History of the First Baptist Church, Charleston, South Carolina, 1682–1982* (Nashville, TN: Broadman Press, 1982), p. 61.

32. Samuel Jones, *A Treatise of Church Discipline and a Directory, Done by Appointment of the Philadelphia Baptist Association* (Philadelphia: S.C. Ustick, 1798), pp. 9–10.

33. John Buzzell, *The Life of Benjamin Randall*, pp. 131–34.

34. In early Baptist life, the entire congregation evaluated membership conduct and meted out discipline. By the eighteenth century, this was accomplished by the deacons; after 1820 frequently in the Northeast a "prudential" committee was charged with "looking after the conduct of members."

35. Brown, *Baptist Church Manual*, p. 24.

36. William Warren Sweet, *Religion on the American Frontier: The Baptists, 1783–1830* (New York: H. Holt, Co., 1931), p. 40.

37. See the discussion in Norman H. Maring and Winthrop S. Hudson, *A Baptist Manual of Polity and Practice* (Valley Forge, PA: Judson Press, 1963), p. 68.

38. Ibid., pp. 74–77, 87–124.

39. Thomas P. McKibbens, *The Life and Works of Morgan Edwards* (New York:

Arno Press, 1980), pp. 41–44; and Crerar Douglas, ed., *Autobiography of Augustus H. Strong* (Valley Forge, PA: Judson Press, 1981), p. 262.

40. *The Confessions of Faith . . . 1644*, art. 37.

41. Edmund Chillenden, *Preaching without Ordination* (London: George Wittington, 1647), pp. 2–3; E. B. Underhill, ed., *Records of the Church of Christ at Warboys* (London: Haddon Brothers, 1854), p. 272.

42. An example of the hated certificates is in William H. Brackney, ed., *Baptist Life and Thought, 1600–1980* (Valley Forge, PA: Judson Press, 1983), p. 77.

43. Ibid., pp. 127–128.

44. Floyd Massey, Jr., and Samuel B. McKinney, *Church Administration in the Black Perspective* (Valley Forge, PA: Judson Press, 1976), pp. 33–39.

45. Among Baptists in the North, Eastern Baptist Theological Seminary in Philadelphia pioneered religious education degrees in 1926; in the Southern Convention, Southwestern Baptist Theological Seminary began its programs in Christian Education in 1919 and in Church Music in 1922.

46. A. S. Clement, *Great Baptist Women* (London: Carey Kingsgate, 1955), pp. 9–16; and Roger Hayden, ed., *The Records of a Church of Christ in Bristol, 1640–1687* (Bristol, England: The Record Society, 1974), Book I.

47. Thomas Grantham, *The Successors of the Apostles or A Discourse of the Office of Messengers* (London: n.p., 1674), p. 18.

48. Gillette, *Minutes of the Philadelphia Association*, p. 130; William H. Brackney, "Yankee Benevolence in Yorker Lands," pp. 293–309.

49. "Role of an Executive Minister in the American Baptist Churches, USA," paper adopted by American Baptist Churches Regional Executive Ministers Council, December 1984.

50. Torbet, *History of the Baptists*, p. 546–49; Albert H. Newman, *A Century of Achievement* (Philadelphia: American Baptist Publication Society, 1901), pp. 322–54.

51. Compare the catalogue requirements of Baptist Bible College, Clark's Summit, PA (1970); Faith Baptist Bible College, Ankeny, Iowa (1981); and the Tennessee Temple Schools (1960).

52. Hugh Hartshorne and Milton C. Froyd, *Theological Education in the Northern Baptist Convention* (Philadelphia: Judson Press, 1945), pp. 99–105.

53. Brackney, *Baptist Life and Thought*, p. 127.

54. Daniel Day Williams, "The Mystery of the Baptists," *Foundations* 1 (1958), 9.

CHAPTER 4

1. Morgan Edwards, *Materials towards a History of the Baptists in Pennsylvania* (Philadelphia: Joseph Crukshank, 1770), pp. i–iv.

2. William T. Whitley, ed., *The Works of John Smyth, Fellow of Christ's College 1594–98*, 2 vols. (Cambridge, England: Cambridge University Press), I, xcviii.

3. John Smyth, *A Short Confession of Faith, 1610* in William J. McGlothlin, *Baptist Confessions of Faith* (Philadelphia: American Baptist Publication Society), article 30.

4. See, for instance, "A Short Confession of Faith, 1610," *The Confession of Faith . . .* (London: Simmons, 1644); *A Confession of the Faith of Several Churches of Christ in the County of Somerset* (London: Henry Hills, 1656); *Confession of Faith . . . of Many Congregations*; and "Records of the Philadelphia Baptist Association," Book I in Archives, American Baptist Historical Society.

5. Details of the debate are in William H. Brackney, "What Is a True Particular Visible Church?: The Great Debate at Southwark Rejoined" *Christian History Magazine* (June 1985), 10–12, 34.

6. Samuel Fisher, *Baby-baptism meer babism, or An Answer to Nobody in Five Words, To Everybody Who Finds Himself Concerned in It*. (London: Hills, 1650).

7. David Benedict, *A General History of the Baptist Denomination in America and Other Parts of the World*. (New York: Lewis Colby, 1848), p. 381.

8. John Gill, *Infant Baptism a Part and Pillar of Popery*. (London: n.p., 1766), pp. 51–52.

9. Abel Morgan, *Anti-PedoRantism or Samuel Finley's Charitable Plea for the Speechless Examined and Refuted: The Baptism of Believers Maintained and the Mode of It by Immersion Vindicated*. (Philadelphia: Benjamin Franklin, 1747), p. 109.

10. *Confession of Faith Put Forth by the Elders and Brethren of Many Congregations*, Chapter 29.

11. Thomas Crosby, *History of the English Baptists*, 4 vols. (London: John Robinson, 1738–1740), IV, 166–67.

12. Edwards, *Materials, Pennsylvania*, pp. 130–32.

13. Daniel Featley, *The Dippers Dipt*, p. B2.

14. John Bunyan, *Differences in Judgement About Water-Baptism, No Bar to Communion* (London: John Wilkins, 1673), pp. 3–4.

15. Wayland's views are presented in *Notes on the Principles and Practices of Baptist Churches* (New York: Sheldon, 1867), pp. 177–83; likewise, the Graves understanding is in *Old Landmarkism: What Is It?* (Memphis: Graves, 1880), pp. 53–63.

16. Roger Hayden, ed., *Baptist Union Documents, 1948–1977*. (London: Baptist Historical Society, 1980), p. 185.

17. George R. Beasley-Murray, "Baptism and the Theology of the Child," *American Baptist Quarterly*, (December 1982), 105–6.

18. *Baptism, Eucharist, and Ministry*. (Geneva: World Council of Churches, 1982), p. 4.

19. Horton Davies, *Worship and Theology in England: From Cranmer to Hooker, 1534–1603* (Princeton: Princeton University Press, 1970), pp. 80–81; also Edmund Bishop, *Liturgia Historica: Papers on the Liturgy and Religious Life of the Western Church* (Oxford: Oxford University Press, 1918), pp. 12–25.

20. John Calvin, *Institutes of the Christian Religion*, 2 vols., Henry Beveridge (Grand Rapids, MI: Eerdmans, 1966), II, 492: Davies, *Worship and Theology*, pp. 83–84.

21. Davies, *Worship and Theology*, p. 120; Geoffrey W. Bromiley, *Thomas Cranmer: Theologian* (New York: Oxford University Press, 1906), pp. 69–83, presents Cranmer's eucharistic views in detail.

22. William Perkins, *The Foundation of the Christian Religion, Gathered into Six Principles*. (London?: n.p., 1595), p. i.

23. Whitley, *Works of Smyth*, II, 558, 622, 638.

24. *An Orthodox Creed, or A Protestant Confession of Faith Being an Essay to Unite and Confirm All True Protestants* (London: n.p., 1679), pp. xxxiii.

25. *Second London Confession*, 1677, pp. xxx.

26. Ibid. See also the section in Benjamin Keach, *The Baptist Catechism or A Brief Instruction in the Principles of the Christian Religion* (London; n.p., n.d.), which provides a useful commentary on the Lord's Supper among English Baptists.

27. Zwingli distanced himself from those he called *syngrammateis* (Memorialists) and

he opted for a "universal" or spiritual presence. See H. Wayne Pipkin, trans. *Huldrych Zwingli Writings*, 2 vols. (Allison Park, PA: Pickwick Publications, 1984), II, 251–56.

28. Benjamin Cox, *God's Ordinance, The Saints Privelidge, in Two Treatises*. (London?: n.p., 1646).

29. Compare the appendix to the *Second London Confession* (1677) with the preface to John Bunyan, *Differences in Judgement.*

30. Records of the Philadelphia Baptist Association, 1740, in Archives, American Baptist Historical Society.

31. "Minutes of the Welsh Tract Baptist Meeting," *Papers of the Historical Society of Delaware* (1904), pp. 7–10.

32. Norman A. Baxter, *History of the Freewill Baptists: A Study in New England Separatism* (Rochester, NY: American Baptist Historical Society, 1957), p. 133.

33. Alvin D. Williams, *Memorials of the Free Communion Baptists* (Dover, NH: Freewill Press, 1873), pp. 40–41.

34. Graves, *Old Landmarkism*, p. 141.

35. James M. Pendleton, *Three Reasons Why I am a Baptist, With a Fourth Reason Added on Communion* (Memphis, TN: Graves, Jones, 1856), p. 208.

36. Adolf Olson, *A Centenary History, As Related to the Baptist General Conference of America* (Chicago: Conference Press, 1952), p. 580; Frank H. Woyke, *Heritage and Ministry of the North American Baptist Conference*, p. 91; Baker, *A Baptist Sourcebook*; p. 202.

37. See for instance the records of the First Baptist Church and the Charitable Baptist Society in Providence, Rhode Island. The originals are in the manuscript collections of the library of Brown University.

38. Abraham Coles, *Wine in the Word: An Inquiry Concerning the Wine Christ Made, The Wine of the Supper, Etc.* (New York: Nelson and Phillips, 1878), pp. 46–47.

39. Alvah Hovey, "What Was the 'Fruit of the Vine' Which Jesus Gave His Disciples at the Institution of the Supper?" *Baptist Quarterly Review*, 9 (1887), pp. 302–3.

40. "Report of the Committee on Individual Communion Cups" to Fifth Baptist Church, Philadelphia, in Archives, American Baptist Historical Society.

41. *Baptism, Eucharist and Ministry*, pp. 10–15.

42. See the *Orthodox Creed or A Protestant Confession of Faith, Being an Essay to Unite and Confirm All True Protestants* (London: 1679), p. xxxii.

43. Henry Danvers, *A Treatise of Laying on of Hands*. (London: n.d.).

44. Thomas Grantham, *Christianismus Primitivus, or the Ancient Christian Religion in Its Nature, Certainty, Excellence and Beauty*. (London: Francis Smith, 1678), pp. 35–47.

45. Richard Knight, *History of the General Six Principle Baptists in Europe and America* (Providence, RI: Smith and Parmenter, 1826).

46. *A Confession of Faith . . . Adopted by the Baptist Association Met at Philadelphia September 15, 1742* (Philadelphia: B. Franklin, 1743). Chapter 31.

47. *Minutes of the Ketocton, Virginia Baptist Association*, 1790.

48. The primacy of the Philadelphia Baptist Association was evident in the background of Jones's work. See Jones, *A Treatise on Church Discipline*. An edition was published in 1805 by the Charleston, South Carolina, Association.

49. "Propositions and Conclusions Concerning True Christian Religion" in William L. Lumpkin, *Baptist Confessions of Faith* (Valley Forge: Judson Press, 1959), p. 138;

A. C. Underwood, *A History of the English Baptists* (London: Carey Kingsgate, 1947), p. 123.

50. Adam Taylor, *The History of the English General Baptists*, 2 vols. (London: T. Bore, 1818), I, 451; *Minutes of the Charleston Baptist Association*, 1810, p. 3.

51. Benedict, *General History of the Baptists*, p. 914.

CHAPTER 5

1. Edgar Y. Mullins, *Axioms of Religion: A New Interpretation of the Baptist Faith* (Boston: Griffith and Rowland, 1908), p. 63.

2. *Confessions of Faith Put Forth by the Elders and Brethren of Many Congregations*, art. XVI, p. 2.

3. Quoted in Baker and Craven, *Adventure in Faith*; p. 61.

4. Samuel Jones, *A Treatise of Church Discipline*, pp. 9–10.

5. *The Confession of Faith of those Churches Which are Commonly (though falsely) Called Anabaptists* (London: Matthew Simmons, 1644), p. 17.

6. "Minutes of the Philadelphia Baptist Association," 1707 in Archives, American Baptist Historical Society.

7. The essay by Benjamin Griffith (1749) is reprinted in "Documents on the Association of Churches," *Foundations* 4 (October 1961), 335–37.

8. *Minutes of the Shaftsbury, Vermont Baptist Association*, 1791, p. 2; *Minutes of the Warren Baptist Association*, 1785, pp. 6–7; *Minutes of the Mattapony, Virginia Association*, 1801, pp. 12–14.

9. On Bristol, consult Norman S. Moon, *Education for Ministry: Bristol Baptist College, 1679–1979* (Bristol, England: The College, 1979); on Kettering see F. A. Cox, *History of the Baptist Missionary Society of England, 1791–1842*. (Boston: Damrel, 1843).

10. "Minutes of the New Hampshire Baptist Antislavery Society," 1838, in Archives, American Baptist Historical Society.

11. *Annual Report of the Meeting of the Ohio Baptist Education Society and the Trustees of the Granville Literary and Theological Institution*. 1832.

12. The original records of the Connecticut Auxilliary are in Archives, American Baptist Historical Society. A brief history is published in Philip S. Evans, *History of the Connecticut Baptist State Convention* (Hartford, CT: Convention Press, 1909).

13. *Annual Report, Ohio Baptist Education Society*, p. 23.

14. The Story of the Freewill societies is found in I. D. Stewart, *History of the Freewill Baptists* (Dover, NH: Freewill Press, 1861); and Norman Baxter, *History of the Freewill Baptists: A Study in New England Separatism* (Rochester, NY: American Baptist Historical Society, 1957), pp. 65–113.

15. *Proceedings of the General Missionary Convention of the Baptist Denomination in the United States* (Philadelphia: 1814), p. 42.

16. Ibid., 1815, p. 6.

17. William H. Brackney, ed., *Dispensations of Providence: The Journal and Selected Letters of Luther Rice* (Rochester, NY: American Baptist Historical Society, 1983), pp. 77–81.

18. The reduction of the Convention to a single-purpose society is covered in Winthrop S. Hudson, "Stumbling into Disorder," *Foundations*, (April 1958), 45–71; and William

H. Brackney, "Triumph of the National Spirit: The Baptist Triennial Conventions, 1814–1844," *American Baptist Quarterly*, 4 (Spring 1985), 165–72.

19. Francis Wayland, *Notes on the Principles and Practices of Baptist Churches* (New York: Sheldon, 1867), p. 143.

20. The "Black Rock Resolutions" are reprinted in *The Feast of Fat Things*, pp. 1–30.

21. *Proceedings of the Southern Baptist Convention, Held in Augusta, Georgia, May 8–12, 1845* (Richmond: Ellyson, 1845), pp. 1–5.

22. L. G. Jordan, *Negro Baptist History, U.S.A.* (Nashville, TN: Sunday School Publishing Board, 1930), pp. 114–19; *Minutes of the National Baptist Convention, U.S.A., 1895*; Leroy Fitts, *A History of Black Baptists*, pp. 49–84; James M. Washington, *Frustrated Fellowship: The Black Baptist Quest for Social Power* (Atlanta, GA: Mercer Press, 1986), pp. 159–87.

23. Documents and a contemporary account of the formation of the Northern Baptist Convention may be found in W. C. Bitting, ed., *A Manual of the Northern Baptist Convention, 1908–1918* (Philadelphia: American Baptist Publication Society, 1918).

24. See for instance, Woyke, *Heritage and Ministry of the North American Baptist Conference*, pp. 358, 432; and Adolf Olson, *A Centenary History*, pp. 406–444.

25. So far, no comprehensive essay on the history of the Baptist World Alliance exists. Two helpful works are Walter O. Lewis, *The First Fifty Years: Notes on the History of the Baptist World Alliance* (London: BWA, 1955); and Carl W. Tiller, *The Twentieth Century Baptist* (Valley Forge, PA: Judson Press, 1980).

CHAPTER 6

1. "Propositions and Conclusions Concerning True Christian Religion" in W. J. McGlothlin, *Baptist Confessions of Faith*, pp. 81–82.

2. Thomas Helwys, *The Mystery of Iniquity* (London: Baptist Historical Society, 1935), frontispiece.

3. Ibid.

4. Leonard Busher, *Religions Peace: Or a Plea for Liberty of Conscience*. (London: John Sweetling, 1646), pp. 41–42.

5. Daniel Featley, *The Dipper's Dipt*, p. B2.

6. *An Orthodox Creed*; art. 46.

7. *The Book of the General Laws and Libertyes Concerning the Inhabitants of the Massachusetts Bay Colony* (Cambridge, MA: Samuel Green, 1648), p. 1.

8. Roger Williams, *The Bloudy Tenent of Persecution, for the Cause of Conscience* (London: n.p., 1644), E. B. Underhill edition (London: 1848), pp. 246–47.

9. Ibid., p. 2.

10. Baptists had little interest in Williams until the next century because he left the Baptist community and became a "Seeker" and outlived most of his contemporaries. Other than John Clarke, a contemporary of Williams, there is no evidence of Baptist dependence upon Williams's thought in either England or America until 1760.

11. John Clarke, *Ill Newes from New England or a Narrative of New England's Persecutions* (London: n.p., 1652), p. 49.

12. Ibid., p. 53.

13. John R. Bartlett, ed., *Records of the Colony of Rhode Island and Providence Plantation in New England* (Providence, RI: A. C. Greene, 1856–1865), II, 3–21.

14. Clarke, *Ill Newes*, p.v.

15. William G. McLoughlin, *New England Dissent, 1630–1833* 2 vols. (Cambridge, MA: Harvard University Press, 1971), I, 149–224.

16. Ibid., p. 225.

17. Thomas B. Maston, *Isaac Backus: Pioneer of Religious Liberty* (Rochester, NY: American Baptist Historical Society, 1962), pp. 21–28.

18. Alvah Hovey, *A Memoir of the Life and Times of Rev. Isaac Backus* (Boston: Gould and Lincoln, 1858), p. 210.

19. A fuller treatment of the 1774 events is in McLoughlin, *New England Dissent*, I, p. 559.

20. William G. McLoughlin, ed., *Isaac Backus on Church, State and Calvinism: Pamphlets, 1754–1789* (Cambridge, MA: Belknap Press), pp. 17,44, Isaac Backus, *History of the Baptists*, 2 vols. (Newton, Mass., Backus Historical Society, 1871), pp. 75–76.

21. Quoted in McLoughlin, *New England Dissent*, I, 564.

22. McLoughlin, *Pamphlets*, p. 487.

23. L. F. Greene, ed., *The Writings of the Late Elder John Leland* (New York: Wood, 1845), p. 146.

24. Edwin S. Gaustad, "The Backus-Leland Tradition," *Foundations*, 2 (April 1959), p. 149.

25. Lyman H. Butterfield, *Elder John Leland: Jeffersonian Itinerant* (Worcester, MA: n.p. 1953), p. 188.

26. Ibid., p. 193.

27. Ibid., p. 199; Greene, *Writings of John Leland*, p. 184.

28. Albert B. Hart, ed., *Commonwealth History of Massachusetts*, 4 vols. (New York: Russell and Russell, 1966), IV, 13. The amendment was approved 11 May, 1833.

29. Martin E. Marty, *Righteous Empire: The Protestant Experience in America* (New York: Dial Press, 1970), p. 112.

30. Isaac Backus, *A Church History of New England* (Philadelphia: Baptist Tract Depository, 1839), p. 246.

31. *American Baptist Magazine*, 7 (March 1827), p. 74, 96. Brumberg, *Mission for Life*, pp. 63ff, surveys the popular response to the Judson saga.

32. Minutes of the Board of Managers, General Missionary Convention, 1814, in Archives, American Baptist Historical Society.

33. *American Baptist Magazine*, 24 (August 1844), p. 261.

34. Butterfield, *Elder John Leland*, p. 181.

35. Charles A. Brooks, *Christian Americanization: A Task for the Churches* (New York: n.p., 1919), p. 17.

36. Elias C. Morris, "The Negro Work for the Negro," *The Baptist World Alliance, Second Congress Record of Proceedings* (Philadelphia: Harper, 1911), pp. 286–90.

37. *Proceedings of the Baptist World Congress, 1905* (London: Baptist Publications Department, 1905), p. 76.

38. "Minutes of the Executive Committee, Baptist World Alliance," Book I, p. 133, in Archives, American Baptist Historical Society.

39. *The American Baptist Bill of Rights: A Pronouncement Upon Religious Liberty* (Washington, DC: Associated Committees on Public Relations, 1940), pp. 2–4.

40. For the "Four Freedoms Speech," see Stan L. Hastey, "A History of the Baptist Joint Committee on Public Affairs" (Unpublished Ph.D., Southern Seminary, 1978).

41. "ABC Files Brief Before Supreme Court Supporting Bob Jones University," in "Executive Special," *American Baptist News Service*, 11 December, 1981.

42. Edward E. Hindson, "Thunder in the Pulpit: The Socio-Political Involvement of the New Right," *Foundations*, 25 (April 1982), 147.

43. James E. Wood, Jr., "The New Religious Right and Its Implications for Southern Baptists," *Foundations*, 25 (April 1982), 161.

Appendix 1
CHRONOLOGY

1609   John Smyth,* an exile in Amsterdam, baptizes himself and others to form first English Baptist congregation.

1612   Thomas Helwys* returns to England and issues *The Mistery of Iniquity.*

1626   English General Baptists associate and seek advice from Dutch Mennonites.

1638   John Spilsbury and William Kiffin* organize first Particular Baptist church in England.

1638   Roger Williams* and Ezekiel Holliman organize first Baptist congregation in America.

1640   Dorothy Hazzard organizes the Broadmead Baptist Church, Bristol, England.

1641   English Particular Baptists stress baptism by immersion.

1642   Baptists participate in public theological disputation in Southwark, London.

1644   Association of London Baptists issue Confession of Faith.

1644   Massachusetts Bay Colony law banishes all convicted Baptists.

1651   First Seventh Day Baptist church organized in America.

1651   Obadiah Holmes* is publicly whipped in Boston for preaching.

1654   General Assembly of General Baptists holds first meeting in London.

1654   Henry Dunster,* first president of Harvard, is fired due to anti-pedobaptist views.

1660   John Bunyan begins his first prison sentence.

1663   Dr. John Clarke* writes and secures charter calling for full religious liberty in Rhode Island.

1665   Elizabeth Gaunt,* a Baptist, is last woman to be executed in England for treason.

1670   General Six Principle Baptists hold first association meeting in America.

1679   Edward Terrill, through his will, lays foundation for Bristol Baptist Academy.

1681	First congregation in American South formed at Charleston, South Carolina, by exile from Maine.
1689	Toleration achieved in England.
1689	Baptists issue the Second London Confession.
1707	Philadelphia Baptist Association is formed.
1718	Cotton Mather preaches the ordination sermon for Elisha Callendar at First Baptist, Boston.
1720	Rachel Scammon disseminates Baptist views throughout New Hampshire, planting the seed for later church growth.
1726	Hollis brothers of London establish chair in divinity and Baptist scholarships at Harvard College.
1742	Philadelphia Baptists publish first confession of faith in America.
1742	Thomas Crosby* completes first history of the Baptists.
1755	Great revival begins among Baptists in North Carolina under leadership of Shubal Stearns* and Daniel Marshall.
1755	Martha Stearns Marshall is a well-known preacher among the Separate Baptists.
1764	College of Rhode Island founded by American Baptists.
1769–70	John Gill* publishes *Body of Doctrinal and Practical Divinity.*
1769–70	New Connexion of General Baptists formed in England.
1774	Isaac Backus* presents a memorial for religious liberty to Continental Congress in Philadelphia.
1778	George Leile* gathers first black congregation in Georgia.
1781	Andrew Fuller* publishes *The Gospel Worthy of All Acceptation.*
	Benjamin Randall* of New Hampshire organizes the Freewill Baptist Connexion.
1783	Separate and Regular Baptists in Virginia unite.
1787	John Leland* persuades James Madison to support a Bill of Rights guaranteeing religious liberty.
1792	First missionary society formed in Kettering, England.
	William Carey* is appointed to India.
1795	Multidenominational New York Missionary Society appoints Elkanah Holmes* to work with Iroquois Indians.
1800	Mary Webb* of Boston forms the first Female Society for Missionary Purposes.
1800	Cheshire, Massachusetts, Baptists send President Jefferson a mammoth cheese and congratulations upon his election.
1802	Formation of Massachusetts Baptist Missionary Society.
1802	First issue of *Georgia Analytical Repository,* oldest Baptist periodical in the world.
1807	William Staughton* opens first Baptist theological school in his Philadelphia home.

1808	David Barrow of Kentucky publishes first abolitionist tract among Baptists.
1813	Luther Rice,* Adoniram Judson, and Ann Hasseltine (Judson)* convert to Baptist principles while on voyage to India.
1814	General Missionary Convention of the Baptist Denomination in the United States for Foreign Missions organized.
1817	John Mason Peck* and James E. Welch appointed missionaries to Mississippi Valley.
1821	First state convention organized in South Carolina.
1826	Daniel Parker* publishes his tract on the theory of the two seeds.
1826	Death of Ann Hasseltine Judson; the story of her life is a major influence upon the 19th-century missions movement.
1829	Baptists in Chautauqua, New York, vote to disfellowship Freemasons.
1832	Founding of American Baptist Home Mission Society.
1833	New Hampshire Confession of Faith emphasizes local churches.
1834	Johann G. Oncken* gathers first modern Baptist church in Europe.
1835	First black association formed in Ohio.
1838	Missionary Evan Jones and native preacher Jesse Bushyhead accompany the Cherokee Nation on the Trail of Tears from North Carolina to Arkansas.
1841	Free Communion Baptists merge with Freewill Connexion.
1843	First American Baptist hymnal published.
1844	Last meeting of the Triennial Convention.
1845	Southern Baptist Convention founded in Augusta, Georgia.
1845	Baptist Association in New York votes to exclude William Miller for adventist views.
1846	James R. Graves* issues first of "Landmark" editorials.
1847	Organization of the Freewill Baptist Female Missionary Society.
1850	American Bible Union formed to produce a Baptist version of the Bible.
1851	First meeting of the German Baptist Conference in United States.
1853	John Mason Peck founds American Baptist Historical Society.
1857	Formation of Swedish Conference in United States.
1861	Charleston, South Carolina, Association supports secession.
1865	Shaw University founded in Raleigh, North Carolina, for former Slaves.
1866	Augustus H. Strong of Rochester, New York, publishes first edition of *Systematic Theology*.
1871	Formation of the Woman's Baptist Foreign Missionary Society (Boston) and the Woman's Baptist Missionary Society of the West (Chicago).
1873	Organization of the Free Baptist Woman's Missionary Society.
1877	Formation of the Women's Baptist Home Mission Society (Chicago) and the Woman's American Baptist Home Mission Society (Boston).
1878	More than 9,000 people baptized as result of John Clough's work in India.

1879	Southern Baptist Seminary Board dismisses Crawford H. Toy* for heresy.
1880	Organization of National Baptist Convention, USA.
1881	The Baptist Missionary Training School, the first of its kind for any denomination, opens in Chicago to train women for the mission work.
1886	Walter Rauschenbusch* begins his pastoral ministry in "Hell's Kitchen."
1887	Charles H. Spurgeon* emphasizes opposition to liberalism in the Baptist Union; Down-Grade Controversy begins.
1888	Baptist Congress convenes to explore scholarly issues.
1888	Russell Conwell* delivers "Acres of Diamonds" speech for the first time. Organization of the Woman's Missionary Union, Southern Baptist Convention.
1891	First railroad chapel car "Evangel" is commissioned.
1894	U. S. Northern and Southern Baptists agree on geographical boundaries for mission work.
1896	Isabel Crawford* begins her work among the Kiowa Indians of Saddle Mountain, Oklahoma.
1905	Baptist World Alliance formed in London, England.
1907	Northern Baptist societies coalesce into Northern Baptist Convention.
1911	Freewill Baptists merge with Northern Baptists.
1913	Northern Baptists accept charter membership in Federal Council of Churches of Christ in USA.
1915	In rift with National Baptists, Richard H. Boyd* organizes National Baptist Convention of America.
1920	Baptist Bible Union of America founded; Curtis Lee Laws,* editor of *Watchman-Examiner,* coins term "Fundamentalist."
1921	Helen Barrett Montgomery* is the first woman to serve as president of the Northern Baptist Convention.
1925	Harry E. Fosdick called to Park Avenue, New York, church; policy of inclusive membership adopted.
1932	General Association of Regular Baptists founded.
1943	Baptist missionaries executed in Philippines.
1947	Conservative Baptist Association formed.
1949	Evangelist Billy Graham* holds first city-wide campaign at the Rose Bowl in Pasadena, California.
1955	Integration of the women's societies with the American Baptist Home Mission Society and the American Baptist Foreign Mission Society.
1961	Progressive National Baptist Convention formed.
1963	Martin Luther King, Jr.,* leads march on Birmingham, Alabama.
1964	Seven major U.S. Baptist groups join in Baptist Jubilee Advance.
1979	Jerry Falwell* of Lynchburg, Virginia, creates Moral Majority, Inc.

1984   General Council of Baptist World Alliance authorizes theological conversa-
            tions with Lutherans, Roman Catholics, and Mennonites.

1987   Southern Baptist Alliance, a coalition of theological moderates in the Southern
            Baptist Convention, is organized.

1988   Two hundred Baptists from over thirty countries convene at Sjovik, Sweden,
            as the first international gathering of a peace fellowship.

1991   The *American Baptist Magazine,* oldest religious periodical in North America
            in continuous print, ceases publication.

1992   Two Baptists, William Clinton and Albert Gore are elected, respectively,
            president and vice president, of the United States.

Appendix 2
THE INTERNATIONAL BAPTIST FAMILY

NORTH AMERICA

United States   # churches membership

	# churches	membership
American Baptist Association	1,705	250,000
American Baptist Churches in the USA	5,721	1,637,400
Baptist Bible Fellowship, International	3,449	1,405,900
Baptist General Conference	821	134,658
Baptist Missionary Assoc. of America	1,372	229,166
Conservative Baptist Assoc. of America	1,126	210,000
Duck River and Kindred Associations	85	8,632
Freewill Baptists	2,506	197,206
General Assoc., Regular Baptists	1,574	168,068
General Assoc., General Baptists	876	74,156
General Conference, Evangelical Baptists	31	2,200
General Six Principle Baptists	7	175
Liberty Baptist Fellowship	600	180,000
National Baptist Convention of America	12,400	3,500,000
National Baptist Convention, USA, Inc.	34,790	7,800,000
National Primitive Baptist Convention	616	250,000
North American Baptist Conference	385	61,389
Old German Baptist Brethren	55	5,439
Pentecostal Freewill Baptist Church	141	11,757
Primitive Baptists	1,000	72,000
Progressive National Baptist Convention	1,200	1,500,000
Reformed Baptists	150	10,000
Seventh Day Baptist General Conference	76	4,885
Southern Baptist Convention	38,458	15,365,486
Two Seed in the Spirit Predest. Baptists	16	200
World Baptist Fellowship	300	200,000
	109,460	33,278,717

Canada

	# churches	membership
Baptist General Conference	70	6,066
Canadian Baptist Federation	1,150	128,624
Canadian Convention of Southern Baptists	104	6,001
Fellowship Baptists	500	61,572
Freewill Baptists	19	2,225
North American Baptist Conference	105	15,825
Independent Baptist Churches	150	5,000
	2,098	225,313

130

Austria	15	942
Belgium	18	850
Bulgaria	30	2,500
Czechoslovakia	33	3,966
Denmark	45	5,805
Finland	31	2,262
France	93	5,600
Germany	591	86,956
Hungary	252	11,661
Italy	96	4,500
Netherlands	85	12,386
Norway	63	5,577
Poland	56	3,335
Portugal	59	4,000
Romania	1,422	84,043
Spain	64	7,752
Sweden	318	20,124
Russia	994	73,471
United Kingdom	2,831	200,814
Yugoslavia	62	3,500
	7,158	**540,044**

AFRICA

Angola	165	65,228
Burundi	87	32,000
Cameroon	866	124,986
Central African Republic	141	42,900
Ethiopia	51	8,009
Ghana	85	11,900
Kenya	2,000	107,000
Liberia	229	60,000
Malawi	1,585	140,394
Mozambique	7	4,000
Nigeria	3,170	768,046
Rwanda	36	33,625
Sierra Leone	40	4,500
South Africa	777	75,132
Tanzania	1,400	96,258
Togo	180	11,600
Uganda	400	15,000
Zaire	1,147	659,263
Zambia	445	40,200
Zimbabwe	524	119,996
	13,335	**2,420,037**

131

ASIA

Australia	785	64,560
Bangladesh	567	27,792
Myammar	3,528	497,711
Hong Kong	111	44,339
India	6,938	1,316,587
Indonesia	181	41,795
Israel	9	677
Japan	8,323	41,342
Jordan	9	500
Korea	1,548	323,750
Lebanon	28	1,000
Malaysia	83	7,000
New Zealand	211	24,064
Okinawa	38	3,092
Papua New Guinea	325	36,500
Philippines	3,425	194,055
Singapore	29	7,000
Sri Lanka	22	2,420
Taiwan	152	17,162
Thailand	217	23,100
	26,529	2,674,446

LATIN AMERICA

Antigua	2	200
Argentina	393	50,000
Bahamas	211	55,000
Barbados	4	421
Bermuda	4	336
Bolivia	143	14,575
Brazil	5,710	1,102,000
Chile	235	26,669
Colombia	106	12,600
Costa Rico	41	4,640
Cuba	251	16,471
Dominican Republic	14	1,150
Ecuador	100	9,312
El Salvador	61	5,402
Guatemala	140	13,900
Haita	407	63,726
Honduras	84	5,611
Jamaica	293	43,000
Mexico	791	65,398
Nicaragua	86	9,154
Panama	86	8 369
Paraguay	85	6,000
Peru	87	6,097
Trinidad and Tobago	23	3,460
Uruguay	46	3,200
Venezuela	172	16,900
	9,575	1,543,591

BIBLIOGRAPHIC ESSAY

GENERAL SCHOLARLY RESOURCES

Investigation of the Baptist saga must begin with the standard reference works available. The basic encyclopedias of Baptist life are William Cathcart, *The Baptist Encyclopedia* (Philadelphia: Everts, 1881); G. A. Burgess and J. T. Ward, *Free Baptist Cyclopedia* (Boston: Free Baptist Press, 1889); and Clifton J. Allen, Lynn E. May, Jr. eds., *The Encyclopedia of Southern Baptists,* 4 vols. (Nashville, TN: Broadman Press, 1958–82). Clues to research topics and scholarly concerns in the past three decades will be found in Edwin S. Gaustad, "Themes for Research in Baptist History," *Foundations* 6 (1963): 146-174; "Current Issues in Baptist Life: Historical Views," *Baptist History and Heritage* 16 (1981): 1–32; and William H. Brackney, "An Agenda for the Eighties," *American Baptist Quarterly* 1 (1982): 40–43.

Though not updated since 1975, an indispensable tool for published works is Edward C. Starr, *A Baptist Bibliography,* 25 vols. (Rochester, NY: ABHS, 1947–76); and its predecessor, W.T. Whitley, *A Baptist Bibliography, 1526–1776,* 2 vols. (London: Kingsgate Press, 1916).

Those interested in primary source materials should first consult William H. Brackney, *Baptist Life and Thought, 1600–1980: A Sourcebook* (Valley Forge, PA: Judson Press, 1983); Robert A. Baker, *A Baptist Sourcebook, With Particular Reference to Southern Baptists* (Nashville, TN: Broadman Press, 1966); and William L. Lumpkin, *Baptist Confessions of Faith* (Valley Forge, PA: Judson Press, 1963). Original manuscripts and rare book Baptistiana are the specialities of the American Baptist Historical Society library and archive centers at Rochester, New York, and Valley Forge, Pennsylvania; the Dargan-Carver Library of the Southern Baptist Historical Commission at Nashville, Tennessee; the Franklin Trask Library of Andover Newton Theological School, Newton Centre, Massachusetts; the Bethel Theological Seminary Archives (Swedish Baptist), St. Paul, Minnesota; the North American Baptist Seminary Archives (German Baptist) in Sioux Falls, South Dakota; and the Angus Library of Regents Park College, Oxford, for British materials.

The vast majority of periodical publication of scholarly research occurs in *American Baptist Quarterly, Baptist History and Heritage, Journal of Church and State, and Review and Expositor.* Predecessor journals now no longer active were *The Chronicle* (1938–58) and *Foundations: A Baptist Journal of History, Theology and Ministry* (1958–82).

HISTORIOGRAPHICAL LANDMARKS

A handful of books published within the past sixty years has dramatically reshaped the landscape of Baptist studies. The first among these was William Warren Sweet's *Religion on the American Frontier: the Baptists 1783–1830* (New York: H. Holt, 1931). Sweet challenged the prevailing eastern and New England myths, which held that Baptists were increasingly urban, middleclass, and mainstream, by arguing that Baptists were essentially a frontier people. In the spirit of Frederick Jackson Turner, Sweet saw Baptists as moving in harmony with the westward expansion of the American experience and contributing in no small way to the growth of frontier institutions and ideologies, particularly a fierce independence and an anti-centralization bias. The revivalistic, dissenting Baptists were preeminently egalitarians, and Sweet found evidences of this from Roger Williams* to the abolitionists. Sweet's interpretation caused a new generation of doctoral studies focusing on the Baptist social conscience, new expressions of American religious liberty, and the influence of Baptists on democratic processes.

The second watershed work was that of William Wright Barnes, the father of Southern Baptist historiography. In a revisionist article, "Why the Southern Baptist Convention Was Formed," *Review and Expositor* 16 (1944): 3–17, and later in his pioneering *The Southern Baptist Convention, 1845–1953* (Nashville, TN: Broadman Press, 1955), Barnes traced not only the differences between North and South over slavery, but also broader regional and ecclesiological issues that made Southern Baptists a distinct people with a discrete history. The need for a compact missionary organization and cultural ethos tending toward centralization were as important as any pro-slavery pronouncement of the early Convention, Barnes thought. His work spawned a new commitment to bifurcate for the long-term future, Baptist historiography and his heirs have affirmed his thesis in major books like Robert P. Baker, *Relations between Northern and Southern Baptists* (Fort Worth, TX: n.p., 1948); and Robert P. Baker, *The Southern Baptist Convention and Its People, 1607–1972* (Nashville, TN: Broadman Press, 1974); and most recently, H. Leon McBeth's weighty volume, *The Baptist Heritage: Four Centuries of Baptist Witness* (Nashville, TN: Broadman Press, 1986).

For those yet inclined to argue the Baptist persuasion from the issue of origins, B. R. White of Oxford, England, produced a seminal work in 1971 that has re-oriented the seventeenth century for Baptists. Even after the important discoveries of Champlin Burrage and others, twentieth-century Baptist historians such as Ernest Payne and William Estep have still embraced kinship with the Anabaptists, which has opened interesting discussions from time to time with modern Anabaptist groups. White, however, in his published doctoral thesis, *The English Separatist Tradition* (Oxford, England: Oxford University Press, 1971) laid a plausible case for Separatist views within Elizabethan Puritanism and left the onus of proof upon those who would continue to affirm a European Anabaptist influence. The extent of relationships and influences between Baptists and other English Protestant dissenters in Old and New England is now a major point of departure for seventeenth century studies such as Timothy George, *John Robinson and The English Separatist Tradition* (Macon, GA: Mercer University Press, 1982); and Joseph Ban, Paul Dekar, editors, *In the Great Tradition* (Valley Forge, PA: Judson Press, 1982).

No student of Baptist life and thought can neglect the significance of William G.

McLoughlin's masterpiece, *New England Dissent, 1630–1833: The Baptists and the Separation of Church and State,* 2 vols. (Cambridge, MA: Harvard University Press, 1971). McLoughlin exploded the myth that religious liberty was the sole province of Baptists, and he urged the thesis that a "pluralism of dissent was the best evidence of the many paths by which diversity designated the uniformity and conformity of the original Puritan ideal" (p.xvii). However, McLoughlin states, the classic doctrine of the separation of church and state has a historically contextual definition rather than a consistent dogma from Roger Williams to the constitution, as Isaac Backus* had earlier suggested. For him, the history of Baptists in America is a classic illustration of Ernst Troeltsch's theory of how sects evolve into churches, concomitant with social inferiority and ostracism. Because McLoughlin writes from outside the denomination, his ideas have sparked a lively debate over church-state issues and the meaning of his principal protagonist, Issac Backus.

Prior to the advance of Afro-American studies in general, most Baptist history was Caucasian in orientation, except to mention the establishment of the major black Baptist conventions. This attitude changed when Mechal Sobel published *Trabelin' On: The Slave Journey to an Afro-Baptist Faith* (Westport, CT: Greenwood Press, 1979). This book dredged up countless resources which evidenced the presence of a viable but often invisible Afro-American Baptist community, which began in 1758 and emerged well before Emancipation in the form of preachers, convenanting congregations, and associations. Within just a few years of the appearance of Sobel's work, major revisions to Baptist history were underway such as Edward Wheeler, *Uplifting the Race: The Black Minister in the New South* (Lanham, MD: University Press of America, 1986) and James M. Washington, *Frustrated Fellowship: The Black Baptist Quest for Social Power* (Macon, GA: Mercer University Press, 1986).

The final recent landmark in Baptist historiography was achieved when Joan J. Brumberg finished *Mission for Life: The Story of the Family of Adoniram Judson** (New York: Macmillan, 1980). Here for the first time was a feminist approach to Baptist missions and biography which carefully elucidated the role, struggles, and contributions of nineteenth-century Baptist women in America and on mission. Without detracting from America's first male overseas missionary, Brumberg demonstrates the degree to which the three Mrs. Judsons shaped Adoniram's image and the ideology of Baptists at home and abroad. Single women and the family unit in Baptist churches are now being scrutinized, as seen in Susan M. Eltscher, *"A Finer Sense of Moral Purity: The Role and Identity of Women in Baptist Life"* in *Discovering Our Baptist Heritage,* ed. William H. Brackney (Valley Forge, PA: ABHS, 1985), pp. 39–53.

THE GENERAL COURSE OF BAPTIST HISTORY

Historical writing about the Baptists began about a century and a half after the first churches emerged, and there has been a steady stream of attempts to properly identify the Baptists through their documented history as well as their theological kinship. The first solid work was of course Thomas Crosby's* four-volume *History of the English Baptists* (London: n.p., 1738–43), which was a continuation of Benjamin Stinton's collection of sources and essay. Crosby had originally hoped that Daniel Neal would make good use of the source materials with which Crosby supplied the author for his *History of the Puritans,* 4 vols. (London: Richard Hett, 1732); but in fact, Neal spent less than five pages in four volumes on the Baptists. The purpose of the first Baptist history was "to stop notorious falsehoods" and "to inform the honest and well-meaning Christian."

Unhappily for later critics, Crosby's own prejudices were too strong, and he deliberately blurred important distinctions such as the General and Particular groups. Following Crosby, Joseph Ivimey seventy years later sought to correct the errors and to establish the Baptists as the first Christians to understand the principle of religious liberty. His work, *A History of the English Baptists,* 5 vols. (London: T. Smith, 1811) was carefully researched and contained a number of new sources and lists of churches. At about the same time, Adam Taylor provided a comprehensive survey of the General Baptists in England, partly as an apologetic for the New Connexion.

An entirely new breed of historians emerged in the late nineteenth century to retell the English Baptist story. With the assistance of the Joseph Angus Trust and an extensive library of Baptist authors, which he helped to accumulate, William T. Whitley broke new ground with the publication of *The Witness of History to Baptist Principles* (London: Shepherd, 1897); critical editions of *General Assembly Minutes* (London: Kingsgate Press, 1909–10); *The Works of John Smyth* (Cambridge, England: Cambridge University Press, 1915); Histories of Worcestershire (1910): Yorkshire (1913); and finally, *A History of British Baptists* (London: C. Griffin, 1923). Whitley confirmed the thesis that English Baptists had emerged from English Puritanism and that associational life had grown up around the New Model Army. Whitley's outstanding student, H. Wheeler Robinson, lengthened his mentor's shadow and popularized the new data in *The Life and Faith of the Baptists* (London: Kingsgate Press, 1927). A good deal of historical research continued, sparked by American scholars interested in the question of origins and the Anabaptist links, necessitating a new and useful summary at mid-century in A. C. Underwood's *A History of the English Baptists* (London: Carey Kingsgate Press, 1947); and later Mervyn Himbury's *British Baptists: A Short History* (London: Carey Kingsgate Press, 1962), which stresses Welsh contributions and British Baptists in the larger world. In the present generation, the mantle of Whitley's scholarship has fallen on Barrington R. White, who has firmly established the lineage of English General and Particular Baptists in the Puritan-Separatist family in his works, *The English Separatist Tradition: From the Marian Martyrs to the Pilgrim Fathers* (Oxford: Oxford University Press, 1971); and *The English Baptists in the Seventeenth Century* (London: Baptist Historical Society, 1983). A recent unpublished dissertation which deserves attention for its coverage of Anglo-American relations is Hywel M. Davies, "Transatlantic Brethren: A Study of English, Welsh and American Baptists, with Particular Reference to Morgan John Rhys (1760–1804) and His Friends" (Ph.D. diss., University of Wales, 1984).

American Baptist historiography began at roughly the same time as Thomas Crosby's work and for roughly the same reasons. Isaac Backus, laboring under the burden of a New England Standing Order, intended his work, *A History of New England with Particular Reference to a Denomination of Christians Called Baptists,* 3 vols. (Boston: n.p., 1777–96) to be an exposure of the acts of oppression and intolerance perpetrated upon New England Dissenters. Backus made Roger Williams a Baptist hero and made John Clarke,* John Comer, Henry Dunster,* Thomas Goold, and Obadiah Holmes* a new panoply of American Baptist saints. In a more piecemeal fashion, Morgan Edwards* did for the middle colonies and the South what Backus did for New England. Edwards published in 1770 his first volume of a proposed twelve-part series on the history of Baptists, for which he had conducted extensive research while travelling as an evangelist for the Philadelphia Baptist Association: Morgan Edwards, *Materials Toward a History* *of Baptists in the United States* (Philadelphia: Cruikshank, 1770). Unfortunately, Edwards published only two volumes and never combined the works into a useful whole.

In the nineteenth century, David Benedict and Robert B. Semple led the way with major treatises on Baptist historical development. Benedict, in his first two-volume work of 1811, relied heavily upon Morgan Edwards (to the point of plagiarism) and later fully revised his work as *A General History of the Baptist Denomination in America*, 2 vols. (New York: Lewis Colby, 1848). The 1848 edition included a state-by-state history, tabulated data, and a lengthy theological/historical defense of believer's baptism. Semple was first to recount a unique story in *A History of the Rise and Progress of Baptists in Virginia* (Philadelphia: n.p., 1810). Much of Semple's material cannot be found elsewhere.

The effects of local church protectionism and Landmarkism in the mid-nineteenth century provoked an attempt by several Baptist historians to trace the family roots back to Jesus and the Apostles. This was the case, for instance, with James R. Graves,* who in 1855 republished George H. Orchard's *A Concise History of Foreign Baptists* (Nashville: Graves, Marks, 1855), boldly asserting that the New Testament Church was a Baptist Church and that a succession of similar churches had existed unbroken to the present. Baptist history became the rallying point for a new type of sectarianism. However, a more reasonable approach was found in Thomas Armitage, *A History of the Baptists* (New York: Bryan, Taylor, 1892), in which he asserted that "the unity of Christianity is not found by any visible tracing through one set of people" but "in the essence of their doctrines and practices by whomsoever enforced" (p. 1).

Henry C. Vedder of Crozer Theological Seminary and Champlin Burrage of Maine were among several U. S. Baptist scholars at the turn of the twentieth century who urged a more scientific approach to Baptist historical writing. Having studied for a time in Europe, Vedder wrote in *A Short History of the Baptists* (Philadelphia: ABPS, 1907) that "the history of Baptist churches cannot be carried by the scientific method, back farther than the year 1611" (p.4). Actually, since Vedder thought that the early General Baptists were really a branch of the Anabaptists, he held that the first "Baptists" emerged about 1640 as the Particular Baptists. Burrage went a step further in *The Early English Dissenters in the Light of Recent Research, 1550–1641* (New York: Russell and Russell, 1912) to suggest the linkage of the later General Baptists with John Smyth, Thomas Helwys, and others in the Puritan/Separatist evolutions.

Like A. C. Underwood in Great Britain, Robert Torbet replaced Vedder's work at mid-century with a comprehensive *History of the Baptists* (Philadelphia: Judson Press, 1950). Torbet's work pulled together countless monographs into a coherent story; he also paid serious attention to the growth of Baptists as a worldwide denominational family. This American Baptist's volume has become a standard reference tool for most Baptists, diminished only by a continuing need to update its later chronological coverage and statistical data.

Beyond the general surveys of Baptist history, several studies of institutional and organizational development are useful. For the story of Baptist missionary endeavor, there are F. A. Cox, *History of the Baptist Missionary Society of England, 1792–1842* (Boston: Gould & Lincoln, 1843) for the English side; and Robert G. Torbet, *Venture of Faith: The Story of the American Baptist Foreign Mission Society, 1814–1954* (Valley Forge, PA: Judson Press, 1955); and Baker J. Cauthen, *Advance: A History of Southern Baptist Foreign Missions* (Nashville, TN: Broadman Press, 1970) in the United States. For domestic and other types of missions consult Charles L. White, *A Century of Faith*

(Philadelphia: ABHMS, 1932); Lemuel C. Barnes, *Pioneers of Light* (Philadelphia: ABPS, 1924); Arthur B. Rutledge, *Mission To America: A Century and a Quarter of Southern Baptist Home Missions* (Nashville, TN: Broadman Press, 1969) and Wilbur Hopewell, *The Missionary Emphasis of the General Association of Regular Baptist Churches* (Chicago: GARBC Press, 1963).

The international story of Baptists has gained scholarly attention in recent years. Among the outstanding single nation or communion histories are T. M. Bassett, *The Welsh Baptists* (Swansea, Wales: Ilston House, 1981); and Alan C. Prior, *Some Fell on Good Ground: A History of the Baptist Church in New South Wales, Australia* (Sydney: Baptist Union Press, 1966). For Europe see also J.D. Franks, *European Baptists Today* (Zurich: n.p., 1950); Alexander de Chalandeau, *The History of the Baptist Movement in the French-Speaking Countries of Europe* (Chicago: n.p., 1950); and Margarete Jelten, *Unter Gottes Dachziegel: Anfange des Baptismus in Nordwest Deutschland* (Bremerhaven: n.p., 1984). G. Keith Parker, *Baptists in Europe: History and Confessions of Faith* (Nashville, TN: Broadman Press, 1982) presents some of the major theological documentation.

Within the Baptist family around the world there has been too little attention paid to the role and contributions of women. At present, but out of print, are A. S. Clement, *Great Baptist Women* (London: Carey Kingsgate Press, 1955), which is a series of biographies of British pioneers; and H. Leon McBeth, *Women in Baptist Life* (Nashville, TN: Broadman Press, 1979), which does about the same thing primarily for the American scene. Of more recent vintage is John Briggs, "She-Preachers, Widows and Other Women: The Feminine Dimension in Baptist Life Since 1600," *Baptist Quarterly* 31 (1986): 337–352, and *Baptist History and Heritage,* 22 (July 1987), which is entirely devoted to Southern Baptist women.

There are several major scholarly treatises that bear directly upon Baptist studies but that lie outside "denominational histories." Among those I would strongly recommend for the early English development are Geoffrey F. Nuttall, *The Beginnings of Noncon- formity* (London: 1964); Louise F. Brown, *The Political Activities of Baptists and Fifth Monarchy Men in England During the Interregnum* (Washington, DC: American His- torical Association, 1912); Antonia Fraser, *The Weaker Vessel: Women's Lot in Seven- teenth-Century England* (London: Methuen, 1984); and Evelyn D. Bebb, *Nonconformity and Social and Economic Life, 1660–1800* (Philadelphia: 1980). Similarly, for the Amer- ican scene, see Clarence C. Goen, *Revivalism and Separatism in New England, 1740– 1800* (New Haven, CT: Yale University Press, 1962); and his *Broken Churches, Broken Nation: Denominational Schisms and the Coming of the American Civil War* (Macon, GA: Mercer University Press, 1985); Robert G. Torbet, *A Social History of the Phila- delphia Baptist Association, 1707–1940* (Philadelphia: Westbrook, 1944); George A. Schultz, *An Indian Canaan: Isaac McCoy and the Vision of an Indian State* (Norman, OK: University of Oklahoma Press, 1972); William G. McLoughlin, *Cherokees and Missionaries, 1789–1839* (New Haven, CT: Yale University Press, 1984); Mary G. Putnum, *The Baptists and Slavery 1840–1845* (Ann Arbor, MI: G. Wahr, 1913); George M. Marsden, *Fundamentalism and American Culture: The Shaping of Twentieth Century Evangelicalism 1870–1925* (New York: Oxford University Press, 1980); and John L. Eighmy, *Churches in Cultural Captivity: A History of the Social Attitudes of Southern Baptists* (Knoxville, TN: University of Tennessee Press, 1972).

BAPTISTS AND THE BIBLE

In the early years of Baptist development there was no argument over the place or use of the Bible in congregational or individual life. This is best illustrated in the confessional statements from Smyth and Helwys to the major associational traditions. Both William J. McGlothlin, *Baptist Confessions of Faith* (Philadelphia: ABPS, 1911); and William L. Lumpkin, *Baptist Confessions of Faith* (Valley Forge, PA: Judson Press, 1963) have the relevant documents plus historical introductions. McGlothlin's edition contains more textually accurate editions in many instances. Barrington R. White, ed., *Associational Records of the Particular Baptists of England, Wales, and Ireland to 1660* (London: Baptist Historical Society, 1974); and A. D. Gillette, *Minutes of the Philadelphia Baptist Association, 1707–1807* (Philadelphia: ABPS, 1851) both demonstrate the functional significance of Scripture in corporate decisionmaking and advice to individual Christian inquiries. A fine example of how an early English congregation shaped its life around the Bible is G. B. Harrison, ed., *The Church Book of Bunyan Meeting, 1650–1821* (London: n.p., 1928).

The application of biblical content to social and political issues also provides interesting examples of Baptist biblicism. In the eighteenth century, for instance, compare the transcript of the trial of Obadiah Holmes in Edwin S. Gaustad, *Baptist Piety: Last Will and Testimony of Obadiah Holmes* (Grand Rapids, MI: Eerdmans, 1978); with David Barrow, *Involuntary, Unmerited, Perpetual, Absolute Hereditary Slavery Examined, On the Principles of Nature, Reason, Justice, Policy and Scripture* (Lexington, KY: D.&C. Bradford, 1808). Of course the most famous instance of clashing biblical interpretation is found in *Domestic Slavery Considered as a Scriptural Institution* (Boston: n.p., 1845).

Prior to the twentieth century, most published Baptist theological literature involved the scripture proof-text method, wherein doctrines were systematically arranged with accompanying lists of biblical texts to buttress the doctrines. John Gill, *A Body of Divinity* (London: n.p., 1770), for instance, followed the pattern set forth by the Anglican and Presbyterian divines of his era. Later, among Southern Baptists, J. L. Dagg's *Manual of Theology*, 2 vols. (Charleston, SC: Southern Baptist Publication Society, 1856) is a classic; as is John J. Butler, *Natural and Revealed Theology* (Dover, NH: Freewill Baptist Publishing House, 1861) for the Freewill Baptists. In the later nineteenth century, A. H. Strong's first edition of *Systematic Theology* (Rochester, NY: The Seminary, 1886) with its traditional approach, contrasts sharply with William Newton Clarke's *Sixty Years With the Bible* (New York: Scribner's, 1909), in which Clarke demonstrates autobiographically his liberation from proof-text methods.

The controversy over the translation of the Bible in the 1840s is best treated in William H. Wyckoff, ed., *Documentary History of the American Bible Union*, 3 vols. (New York: American Bible Union, 1857). To this should be added *The New Testament Translated by the American Bible Union* (New York: 1851) for the actual textual nuances; and Creighton Lacy, *The Word Carrying Giant: The Growth of the American Bible Society, 1816–1966* (Pasadena, CA: William Carey Library, 1971).

The nineteenth century witnessed great intellectual changes in attitude about biblical authority, and Baptists were not immune to the dialogues. The Chicago school is exemplified in William R. Harper, *The Trend in Higher Education* (Chicago: University of Chicago Press, 1905); and Charles A. Briggs, "The Scope of Theology," *American Journal of Theology 1* (1897): 51–54. David J. Hill of the University of Rochester explored "The Relative Authority of Scripture and Reason" in *Seminary Magazine* 7 (1894): 345–52; and sounded a note of alarm within the denomination. A year later, A. T. Robertson of Southern Seminary responded with "A Better Balanced Biblical Criticism" in *Seminary Magazine 8* (1895): 171–75; and the polarities emerged. A few writers like D. W. Faunce, *Inspiration as a Trend* (Philadelphia: ABPS, 1896) tried to moderate on the conservative side, while John Clifford, the venerable leader of the British Baptist Union, committed himself to the scientific method and recognized that all translations contain errors as he demonstrated in *The Inspiration and Authority of the Bible* (London: James Clarke, 1899). On the eve of the Fundamentalist battles, the major theologians were staking their claims: William N. Clarke identified his method in *The Use of the Scriptures in Theology* (New York: Scribner's, 1905); Clarence A. Barbour, *The Bible in the World of Today* (New York: Association Press, 1911); and Edwin C. Dargan assured his Southern Baptist constituency of a traditional approach in *The Bible, Our Heritage* (Nashville, TN: Broadman Press, 1924). Norman H. Maring accurately summarized these epochal transitions in "Baptists and Changing Views of the Bible," *Foundations* 1 (1958): 52–75. More recently, the history of biblical authority in the denomination is the subject of L. Russ Bush and Tom J. Nettles, *Baptists and the Bible: The Baptist Doctrine of Biblical Inspiration and Religious Authority in Historical Perspective* (Chicago: Moody Press, 1980).

Fundamentalism brought the issue of the Bible to the forefront of Baptist life. Even before the hard lines were drawn with the publication of *The Fundamentals* (Chicago: Testimony Publishing Co., 1912–1915), Baptist conservatives were urging a traditional posture. In England, Charles Spurgeon's monthly paper, *The Sword and Trowel,* set the pace and was read widely in the States as well. *The Watchman Examiner,* under the editorial leadership of Curtis Lee Laws, proclaimed a high value on Scriptural authority as a basic tenet of Baptists and kept the average pastor well informed of the issues. Once the battle for the Bible was announced, Baptists threw themselves into the conflict. As John Roach Straton denounced "modernism" in *Ragtime Religion: A Discussion of Sensationalism and Other Unscriptural Practices of the Modern Pulpit* (Louisville, KY: C.T. Dearing, 1923), Harry Emerson Fosdick issued his challenge, "Shall the Fundamentalists Win" (Sermon at First Presbyterian Church, New York: 5/21/1922). More scholarly was Henry C. Vedder's *The Fundamentals of Christianity: A Study of the Teaching of Jesus and Paul* (New York: Macmillan, 1922) as an antidote to the conservative claim on the "fundamentals of the faith." The confessional controversies are illustrated in Frank M. Goodchild, *The Faith and Purpose of Fundamentalism* (New York: General Committee on Fundamentalism, n.d.); Earle V. Pierce, "Why I Am a Fundamentalist" (Sermon in Sioux Falls, S.D., n.d.); and J. C. Massee, *Baptist Fundamentalism: An Authoritative Statement of Its Meaning and Mission* (New York: n.p., n.d.). Elmer J. Rollings, *The World Today in Light of Bible Prophecy* (Findlay, OH: Fundamental Truth Publishers, 1935) is typical of the apocalyptic approach; Chester E. Tulga, *The Doctrine of Separation in These Times* (Chicago: Conservative Baptist Fellowship, 1952) makes the case for Baptist sectarianism. John Marvin Dean, a founder of Northern Baptist Theological Seminary in Chicago, demonstrated the implications for Baptist polity of the debate over the Bible in "The Brougher and Dean Debate, July 13, 1926" (pamphlet in ABHS files) as he discussed his opposition to open membership. Two helpful contemporary reflections on the early and later stages of the movement are found in the *Watchman-Examiner:* "Has Fundamentalism Accomplished Anything" (1927) and "Interpreting Fundamentalism" (1953).

There are numerous works I have found useful in understanding Fundamentalism among Baptists, though none has exhausted the evidence, particularly as a possible series of interrelated regional movements. Among those books which should be consulted are: Stewart G. Cole, *The History of Fundamentalism* (New York: R.R. Smith, 1931): Norman F. Furniss, *The Fundamentalist Controversy 1918–1931* (New Haven, CT: Yale University Press, 1954); the sympathic George W. Dollar, *A History of Fundamentalism in*

America (Greenville, SC: Bob Jones University Press, 1973); David O. Beale, *In Pursuit of Purity: American Fundamentalism Since 1850* (Greenville, SC: Bob Jones University Press, 1986); and George Marsden, *Fundamentalism and American Culture: The Shaping of Twentieth Century Evangelicalism, 1870–1925* (New York: Oxford University Press, 1980). Four important dissertations not yet published are Carroll M. Harrington, "The Fundamentalist Movement in America 1870–1920" (University of California, 1959); Everett L. Perry, "The Role of Socio-Economic Factors in the Rise and Development of American Fundamentalism" (University of Chicago, 1950); Donald L. Tinder, "Fundamentalism among Baptists in the Northern and Western United States" (Yale University, 1969); and Walter E. Ellis, "Social and Religious Factors in the Fundamentalist-Modernist Schisms Among Baptists in North America, 1895–1934" (University of Pittsburgh, 1974).

For the more contemporary debate, compare Carl F. H. Henry, *Contemporary Evangelical Thought: Fundamentals of the Faith* (Grand Rapids, MI: Eerdmans, 1969) with Bernard L. Ramm, *After Fundamentalism: The Future of Evangelical Theology* (San Francisco: Harper & Row, 1982). Insightful interpretive essays focusing on the New Right among Baptists are Samuel S. Hill, *The New Religious-Political Right in America* (Nashville, TN: Abingdon Press, 1982); Samuel Southard, "The Moral Force of Fundamentalism" *Foundations* 8 (1965): 346–51, and the collective essays in *Foundations* 25 (1982): 116–227, and the *Review and Expositor* 79 (1982): 3–146. In the former, Richard Pierard provided a comprehensive bibliography of recent works on the New Right.

CHURCH AND MINISTRY

Baptist-generated discussions of the Church, congregational order and discipline, and the ministry are important in giving shape to the denominational ethos. A good introduction to these topics is in William T. Whitley, ed., *The Works of John Smyth, Fellow of Christ's College 1594–1598* (Cambridge, Eng.: Cambridge University Press, 1915), in which Smyth's views are placed in the context of the Church of England and Separatism. On the other hand, William Estep, *The Anabaptist Story* (Nashville, TN: Broadman Press, 1963) finds many historically Baptist principles among the Radical Reformers of the late sixteenth century. The many confessions of the seventeenth century help to define the doctrine of the church, its officers, and the nature of the ministry. Of particular relevance is the Second London Confession (1688), which points to a larger understanding of the Universal Church. McGlothlin, *Confessions* (1912) traces the evolution of the statements, while Lumpkin, *Confessions* (1963) points to the Mennonite influences of Smyth's doctrine of the Church. For an authoritative version of Anabaptist ecclesiology, see Franklin H. Littell, *The Anabaptist View of the Church* (Boston: Starr King Press, 1958). Littell's work was a watershed in Reformation studies.

Following the confessions, Baptist theologians developed the doctrine of the Church. Thomas Grantham, *Christianismus Primitivus or the Ancient Christian Religion* (London: Francis Smith, 1678) derived his definition from textual exegesis: "A Company of men called out of the world." John Gill, *A Body of Divinity* (London: n.p., 1770) placed his emphasis upon "a union of those mutually consenting and covenanting." After Gill died, Richard Hart, *Dr. Gill's Reasons for Separating from the Church of England* (Bristol: W. Bulgin, 1801) explained that Gill fundamentally rejected the principle of establishment and denied that the Church of England was "of a Scriptural Church order." In the late eighteenth century, Andrew Fuller offered a more evangelical basis for ecclesiology while holding fast to Calvinistic tradition. On Fuller, see A. H. Kirkby, "Andrew Fuller— Evangelical Calvinist," *Baptist Quarterly* (1954); Norman Maring, "Andrew Fuller" in *Baptists' Concepts of the Church* (Philadelphia: Judson Press, 1959), and Pope A. Duncan, "The Influence of Andrew Fuller on Calvinism" (Th.D. thesis, Southern Baptist Seminary, 1917).

During the nineteenth century, Baptist ecclesiology shifted to focus on the local church. In Lumpkin's *Confessions,* see the "New Hampshire Confession of Faith" and its revival in later conservative Baptist doctrinal statements. Francis Wayland, *Notes on Principles and Practices of Baptist Churches* (New York: Sheldon, 1867) presented the fullest defense of the local congregation as "entirely and absolutely independent." Of the Landmarkists, compare James M. Pendleton, *An Old Landmark Reset* (Nashville, TN: Graves & Marks, 1854), who later recanted, with James R. Graves, *Old Landmarkism: What Is it?* (Memphis, TN: Graves & Marks, 1880), who continued to uphold the marks of a "true gospel church." Three useful unpublished works are Eugene T. Moore, "Background of the Landmark Movement" (Th.M. Thesis, Southwestern Baptist Seminary, 1947); James E. Tull, "A Study of Southern Baptist Landmarkism in Light of Historical Baptist Ecclesiology" (Ph.D. Thesis, Columbia University, 1960); and Andrew H. Lanier, "The Relationship of the Ecclesiology of John Lightfoot Waller to Early Landmarkism" (Th.M. Thesis, Southwestern Baptist Seminary, 1963), the latter of which makes a connection with America's first "independent" Baptist in Virginia of the 1780s.

Aside from the theoretical concerns about the Church, Baptists have also written broadly about the life and work of local congregations. Most communions have a standard "manual" which defines membership matters; in 1798 Samuel Jones created a popular guide for the Philadelphia Association, *A Treatise of Church Discipline and a Directory* (Philadelphia: S. C. Ustick, 1798); to be followed by J. Newton Brown's *The Baptist Church Manual* (Philadelphia: ABPS, 1853); Francis Wayland's *Notes on the Principles and Practices of Baptist Churches* (New York: Sheldon, 1867); *A Freewill Baptist Church Member's Book* (Dover, NH: Freewill Baptist Publishing House, 1847); Edward T. Hiscox, *The Baptist Church Directory* (New York: Sheldon, 1859); W. R. McNutt, *Polity and Practice in Baptist Churches* (Philadelphia: Judson Press, 1935); and Norman H. Maring and Winthrop S. Hudson, *A Baptist Manual of Polity and Practice* (Valley Forge, PA: Judson Press, 1963). More reflective works worth attention are John Clifford, *The Relation of Baptism to Church Membership* (Milwaukee, WI: E.J. Lindsay, 1916) and Russell F. Aldwinkle, *Of Water and the Spirit: A Baptist View of Church Membership* (Brantford, Ontario: Baptist Union Press, 1964), which provides a Canadian perspective.

Baptists have joined others in the Puritan and Reformed tradition in utilizing the church covenant as a means of church discipline. The covenant is the subject of Champlin S. Burrage, *The Church Covenant Idea: Its Origin and Development* (Philadelphia: ABPS, 1904); Mitchell Bronk, "The Covenant, The New Hampshire Confession of Faith and J. Newton Brown," *Watchman-Examiner* (16 November 1939); and Charles W. Derweese, *A Community of Believers* (Valley Forge, PA: Judson Press, 1978). On discipline in general, compare Andrew Fuller, *The Discipline of the Primitive Churches* (Philadelphia: ABPS, 1824); with T. Dowley, "Baptists and Discipline in the Seventeenth Century" *Baptist Quarterly* 24 (1971): 157–165; and James R. Lynch, "English Baptist Church Discipline to 1740" *Foundations* 18 (1975): 121–35.

The nature and training of the ministry has been a concern for the denomination. In the early years, Edmund Chillenden, *Preaching Without Ordination* (London: G. Whittington, 1647) made the point that credentials were associated with the Establishment. Edward C. Starr, "The Story of Ordination Among the Baptists," *Colgate-Rochester Bulletin* 7 (1935): 218–27; traces the mainstream tradition; Jesse A. Hungate, *The Ordination of Women to the Pastorate in Baptist Churches* (Hamilton, NY: J. B. Grant, 1899) portrays an early openness to an inclusive ministry. The meaning of ordination is the subject of R. L. Child, "Baptists and Ordination," *Baptist Quarterly* 14 (1952): 243–51; Neville Clarke, "The Meaning and Practice of Ordination" *Baptist Quarterly* 17 (1958): 197–205; and Marjorie Warkentin, *Ordination: A Biblical Historical View* (Grand Rapids, MI: Eerdmans, 1982), the last of which stresses the importance of the laying on of hands. E. P. Y. Simpson, *Ordination and Christian Unity* (Valley Forge, Pa.: Judson Press, 1966) treats the topic as a dimension of the ecumenical dialogue. Of the many extant ordination sermons, my favorites are John Brine, *Diligence in Study Recommended to Ministers: A Sermon Preached at the Ordination of Mr. Richard Rist in Harlow, Essex, December 15, 1755* (London: John Ward, 1757); Robert Hall, *On the Discouragements and Supports of the Christian Minister: A Discourse Delivered To Rev. James Robertson at His Ordination* (London: Button, 1812); and Stephen Chapin, *The Proclamation of Christ Crucified, The Delight of God: A Sermon at the Ordination of Rev. Alonzo King* (Waterville, ME: William Hastings, 1826).

Several have championed the cause of ministerial education against such statements as Samuel How, *The Sufficiencies of the Spirits: Teaching without Human Learning* (London: n.p., 1640). See, for example, J. Newton Brown, "The Object and Importance of Ministerial Education," *Baptist Preacher* (1847); Alvah Hovey, *The Christian Pastor, His Work and Needful Preparation* (Boston: Gould & Lincoln, 1857); Frank Padelford, *The Relation of Baptists to an Educated Ministry* (New York: n.p., 1917); and Duke K. McCall, "Baptist Ministerial Education," *Review and Expositor* 64 (1967): 59–73. For the black Baptist community see also Mattie A. Robert, *Our Need of an Educated Colored Ministry* (n.p., 1878).

Ministerial offices have included the primary role of pastor plus deacons and messengers. An old standard on the pastor's office is Hezekiah Harvey, *The Pastor: His Qualifications and Duties* (Philadelphia: ABPS, 1879); it can be supplemented with Oren H. Baker, *A Profile of the American Baptist Pastor* (New York: Board of Education, 1963); Robert G. Torbet, "The Pastor and Power Structure of the Convention" (address at Chicago Baptist Association, 1967). Edward H. Pruden, for many years pastor in the nation's capital, comments on the political possibilities in "The Pastor's Role in Politics," *Review and Expositor* 65 (1968): 305–14. For the office of "messenger," see first Thomas Grantham, *The Successors of the Apostles, or a Discourse of the Office of Messengers* (London: n.p., 1674); then William Evershed, *The Messenger's Mission with the Foundation and Authority for Such an Order of Officers in the Christian Church Called Messengers* (London: Joseph Brown, 1783); with a contemporary analysis in J. F. V. Nicholson, "The Office of Messenger Amongst British Baptists in the Seventeenth and Eighteenth Centuries," *Baptist Quarterly* 16 (1958). In the Baptist tradition, the deaconship is a lay office, as defined in Thomas Armitage, *The Office and Qualifications of a Deacon in the Church* (New York: n.p., 1852); and the classic R. B. C. Howell, *The Deaconship: Its Nature, Qualifications, Relations and Duties* (Philadelphia: ABPS, 1846). Ernest Payne added an historical note in "The Appointment of Deacons: Notes from the Southwark Minute Book, 1719–1802," *Baptist Quarterly* 17 (1957); and George Beasley-Murray, *The Diaconate in Baptist Churches* (Geneva: n.p., 1965) demonstrated interest in the role as understood by other Christian groups.

Baptists have not been disinterested in the physical shape of church structures and interiors. J. O. Aldeman, "A Study in Church Architecture," *Seminary Magazine* (1891) called for Baptist worship contributions; John D. Kern, "Should We Discard Our Pulpit-Centered Churches?" *Watchman-Examiner* (September 5, 1940) questioned the split chancel concept as a reduction of the centrality of Scriptural proclamation in the Baptist tradition. John G. Davies, *The Architectural Setting of Baptism* (London: Barrie and Rockliff, 1962) is the only major study of indoor provisions for fonts and baptisteries and is fascinating.

Finally, there are legion numbers of histories of local Baptist churches. In my opinion, the most reliable are the archival reprints: Roger Hayden, ed., *The Records of a Church of Christ in Bristol, 1640–1687* (Bristol: The Record Society, 1974); William T. Whitley, ed., *The Church Books of Ford, or Cuddington and Amersham in the County of Bucks* (London: Baptist Historical Society, 1912); G. B. Harrison, ed., *The Church Book of Bunyan Meeting, 1650–1821* (London: n.p., 1928); Nathan E. Wood, *History of the First Baptist Church of Boston* (Philadelphia: ABPS, 1899). Among the best documented secondary sources, see Robert A. Baker and Paul J. Craven, *Adventure in Faith: History of the First Baptist Church, Charleston, S.C., 1682–1982* (Nashville, TN: Broadman Press, 1982); James Simms, *The First Colored Baptist Church in North America* (Philadelphia: Lippincott, 1888); and William W. Keen, *The Bicentennial of the Founding of the First Baptist Church, Philadelphia* (Philadelphia: ABPS, 1899).

SIGNS OF THE FAITH

More Baptist literature has been produced on the subject of the sacraments/ordinances than any other subject. Since baptism is a key to Baptist ecclesiology, it is the most prominent of sacramental topics.

Baptist apologists are fond of pointing out how ancient are their positions on believer's baptism and immersion. In the introduction to his *History of the Baptists* (New York: Lewis Colby, 1848), David Benedict spent three hundred pages detailing the passages from the Novatians through the Waldensians, to Peter DeBruys the Dutchman, in affirmation of believer's baptism or at least anti-pedobaptism. Fifty years later, the eminent professor Albert H. Newman traced the same path in his *History of Antipaedobaptism* (Philadelphia: ABPS, 1897), which focused upon opposition to child baptism from the third century through the establishment of the first Baptist congregation in 1609.

Of the important seventeenth and eighteenth century British Baptist polemical literature, the following are the major works: Edward Barber, *A Treatise of Baptism* (London: n.p., 1641); Henry Denne, *The Foundation of Children's Baptist Discovered and Razed* (London: n.p., 1645); Samuel Richardson, *A Reply to Dr. Featley's Work Against the Baptists* (London: n.p., 1646); Hanserd Knollys, *An Answer to Mr. Sattmarsh* (London: n.p., 1646); Francis Cornwell, *The Vindication of the Royal Commission of King Jesus* (London: n.p., 1643); Samuel Fisher, *Baby Baptism Mere Babyism* (London: H. Hills, 1650); Christopher Blackwood, *Apostolical Baptism* (London: n.p., 1652); Jeremiah Ives, *Infant Baptism Disproved and Believer's Baptism Proved* (London: n.p., 1655); John Tombes, *Antipaedobaptism* (London: H. Hills, 1652); John Norcott, *Baptism Discovered Plainly and Faithfully According to the Word of God* (London: n.p., 1672): Henry D'Anvers, *A Treatise of Baptism* (London: F. Smith, 1674); Benjamin Keach, *The Ax Laid At the Root* (London: n.p., 1693); Thomas Grantham, *An Apology for the Baptized Believers* (London: n.p., 1678); Joseph Stennett, *Infant Baptism not Proved by the Scripture nor the Early*

Fathers (London: n.p., 1704); John Gale, *Reflections on Dr. Wall's History of Infant Baptism* (London: J. Darby, 1711); Thomas Davye, *The Baptist of Adult Believers only Asserted and Vindicated* (London: J. Darby, 1719); John Gill, *Infant Baptism a Part and Pillar of Popery* (London: n.p., 1766); Abraham Booth, *An Apology for the Baptist* (London: C. Dilly, 1778); Robert Robinson, *History of Baptism* (London: Couchman and Fry, 1790); and Alexander Carson, *The Mode and Subjects of Baptism* (Edinburgh: Waugh & Innes, 1836). Of these books, Gill became the most useful apologetic over time, Robinson provided the most extensive survey of baptisteries and customs, and Carson wrote the best explanation of biblical texts and the meaning of the term *baptizo*.

Of course the other side of the debate in Britain was ably represented by Francis Johnson, *A Christian Plea* (London: n.p. 1617); Richard Baxter, *Plain Scripture Proof of Infant Church Membership and Baptism* (London: Robert White, 1649); Daniel Featley, *The Dippers Dipt* (London: n.p., 1645); William Wall, *History of Infant Baptism* (London: n.p., 1705); and James Peirce, *An Essay in Favor of the Ancient Practice of Giving the Eucharist to Children* (London: n.p., 1718). Baxter's works were so severe and frequent that he earned the title of the "great maul" of anabaptists, according to David Benedict.

In America, the British writers were available and popular, with homebred supplements after 1740 such as Abel Morgan, *Antipedorantism* (Philadelphia: Benjamin Franklin, 1747); Isaac Backus, *A Letter to Rev. Benjamin Lord* (Providence: Wm. Goddard, 1764); Thomas Baldwin, *The Baptism of Believers Only* (Boston: Manning & Loring, 1794); Stephen Chapin, *Letters on Baptism* (Boston: Lincoln & Edmands, 1819); Henry J. Ripley, *Christian Baptism* (Boston: Lincoln and Edmands, 1833); A. Bronson, *Christian Baptism* (Providence: H. H. Brown, 1835); Barnas Sears, *A Review of a Series of Discourses on the Mode and Subjects of Baptism* (Boston: n.p., 1838); Isaac Hinton, *A History of Baptism* (Philadelphia: ABPS, 1840). Controversies over baptism in America led to memorable debates such as John Clarke versus John Cotton in Massachusetts, in 1651, Abel Morgan versus Samuel Finley at Cape May, New Jersey, in 1740, and Alexander Campbell et al. versus N. L. Rice at Lexington, Kentucky, in 1843.

For more modern treatments of baptism see George R. Beasley-Murray, *Baptism in the New Testament* (London: St. Martin's Press, 1962); George R. Beasley-Murray, *Baptism Today and Tomorrow* (New York: Macmillan, 1966); F. C. Bryan, ed., *Concerning Believer's Baptism* (London: Kingsgate Press, 1943); John D. Fisher, *Christian Initiation: Baptism in the Medieval West: A Study in the Disintegration of the Primitive Rite of Initiation* (London: Society for Promoting Christian Knowledge, 1965); Alec Gilmore, *Christian Baptism: A Fresh Attempt to Understand the Rite in Terms of Scripture, History and Theology* (Chicago: Judson Press, 1959); Julius R. Mantey, *Should Baptists Abandon Baptism?* (Cleveland, OH: Roger Williams Press, n.d.); Rollin S. Armour, *Anabaptist Baptism: A Representative Study* (Scottdale, PA: Herald Press, 1966); Dale Moody, *Baptism: Foundation for Christian Unity* (Philadelphia: Westminister Press, 1967); and Genna R. MacNeil, *A Study Guide for Baptism, Eucharist and Ministry* (Valley Forge, PA: Judson Press, 1986). The proceedings of two major intra-confessional meetings pool several good papers: *Consultation on Believer's Baptism* (Louisville, KY: n.p., 1979) and *Conference on the Concept of the Believer's Church,* ed. Merle D. Strege (Grand Rapids, MI: Sagamore Books, 1986).

The early confessions supported by the actual practices of the local congregations, as revealed in their records, demonstrate the diversity and mixed theologies of the Lord's Supper. Some of the confessions speak of a sacrament (e.g., *The Orthodox Creed,* London: n.p., 1679) while most churches practice "holy ordinances." See E. B. Underhill, ed.,

Records of a Church of Christ Gathered at Fenstanton, Warboys and Hexham, 1644–1720 (London: Baptist Historical Society, 1854). Curiously, one church is reputed to have served lamb at the Supper; see C. Marius D'Asigny, *Mystery of Anabaptism Unmasked* (London: S. Butler, 1709). It is difficult to discern what theological dependence is present; the likely influences were Calvin and Zwingli, according to Horton Davies, *Worship and Theology in England*, vol. 1 (Princeton, NJ: Princeton University Press, 1961), which is the authoritative source.

On the debate over believer's baptism as a prerequisite to communion, the classic statements are found in John Bunyan, *Differences in Judgement about Water Baptism, No Bar to Communion* (London: n.p., 1673); two centuries later, James R. Graves, *Intercommunion: Inconsistent, Unscriptural, and Productive of Evil* (Memphis, TN: Graves, Marks, 1881). More moderate views are expressed in John T. Christian, *Close Communion, or Baptism As a Prerequisite to the Lord's Supper* (Louisville, KY: Baptist Book Concern, 1892); and the seminal Robert Hall, *On Terms of Communion: With a Particular View to the Case of the Baptists and Paedobaptists* (Boston: Wells & Lilly, 1816). Hall argued successfully among British and later U.S. Baptists that "paedo-baptists are a part of the true Church" and that "we are expressly commanded to tolerate in the Church those diversities of opinion not inconsistent with salvation." John J. Butler, a Freewill Baptist, presented the most thorough exposition of open communion in *The Free Communionist* (Dover, NH: W. Burr, 1841).

The smaller Baptist groups on the contemporary scene seem convinced that closed communion is defensible and place much evidence upon nineteenth-century works like Edward T. Hiscox, *The Baptist Church Directory* (New York: Sheldon Co., 1859). In contrast, Norman Maring presents a perspective typical of mainline thought in *A Baptist Manual of Polity and Practice* (Valley Forge, PA: Judson Press, 1963); and ecumenically-inclined Baptists have received with enthusiasm the statements in *Baptism, Eucharist and Ministry* (Geneva: World Council of Churches, 1982), which reflects worldwide Christian study and opinion.

There has been little discussion of the imposition of hands except at the ordination of ministers, since the early nineteenth century. On footwashing, see J. L. Dagg, *Manual of Theology* (Charleston, SC: Southern Baptist Publication Society, 1858) and a lone article in the British tradition, "Original Sin, Feetwashing and the New Connexion," *Transactions of the Baptist Historical Society* 1 (1909): 129–41.

VOLUNTARY RELIGION

Voluntarism is a popular theme in general English and American religious historiography. As early as the 1820s scholars began to analyze the phenomenon. See for example, Charles Stovel, *Hints on the Regulation of Christian Churches, To Which are Added, Remarks on the Voluntary System* (London: n.p., 1835); Baron Stow,* *Voluntary Associations—Their Use and Abuse* (Boston: Gould, Kendell & Lincoln, 1837); and Nathaniel Haycroft, *The Voluntary Principle: A Lecture at Bristol* (Bristol: n.p., 1860).

On voluntary associations in general, see James D. Hunt, "Voluntary Associations as a Key to History" in *Voluntary Associations: A Study of Groups in Free Societies*, ed. D. B. Robertson (Richmond: 1966), R. T. Anderson, "More On Voluntary Associations in History," *American Anthropologist* 75 (1973): 904; and Paul M. Harrison, "Weber's Categories of Authority and Voluntary Associations," *American Sociological Review*, 25 (1960): 232–37. The impact of structured voluntarism in England is the theme of

Eugene C. Black, *The Association: British Extraparliamentary Political Organization, 1769–1793* (Cambridge, England: Cambridge University Press, 1963).

Numerous American scholars have treated the subject as part of the cultural milieu. See, for instance, Sidney E. Mead, *The Lively Experiment: The Shaping of Christianity in America* (New York: Harper & Row, 1963); Winthrop S. Hudson, *The Great Tradition of the American Churches* (New York: Harper & Row, 1953); and Martin Marty, *Righteous Empire: The Protestant Experience In America* (New York: Dial Press, 1960). In contrast to the others, Franklin H. Littell, *The Anabaptist View of the Church* (Philadelphia: American Society of Church History, 1952) lays a theological foundation in Europe of the Radical Reformation; Milton Powell, ed., *The Voluntary Church: American Religious Life Seen Through the Eyes of European Visitors* (New York: Macmillan, 1967) provides primary observations by Europeans in the eighteenth and nineteenth centuries.

There are several good studies of the associational principle among Baptists. The ablest early defenses were John Sutcliff, *The Nature, Design and Advantages of Associations* (Northampton, England: n.p., 1812); and John G. Stearns, *The Primitive Church: Its Organization and Government* (Utica, NY: Bennett and Bright, 1832). Later, after the nineteenth century growth of state conventions, Lemuel Barnes laid a romanticized foundation in *A Baptist Association and the Kingdom of Heaven on Earth* (New York: ABHMS, n.d.); Judson C. Barber linked associations to the conventions in "The Relation of the Association to the State Convention," *Minutes of the Oneida, N.Y. Association* (1904). Frank Padelford saw the mosaic of a denomination in *The Commonwealths and the Kingdom* (Philadelphia: A.B.P.S., 1913). More recent essays of value are Lynn E. May, *The Work of the Baptist Association* (Atlanta, GA: Home Mission Board, 1969); William W. Barnes, "Churches and Associations Among Baptists," *Review and Expositor* 52 (1955): 199–205; Winthrop S. Hudson, "The Associational Principle Among Baptists," *Foundations* 1 (1958): 10–23; and John P. Gates, "The Association as It Affected Baptist Polity in Colonial America," *The Chronicle* 6 (1943): 19–31. Two useful works on the English associations are William T. Whitley, "Associational Life Till 1815," *Baptist Quarterly* 5 (1916): 19–34; and R. Dwayne Connor, "Early English Baptist Associations: Their Meaning for Connectional Life Today," *Foundations* 15 (1963): 163–186.

To discover the British foundations of structural voluntarism in the Baptist tradition, begin with Norman S. Moon, *Education for Ministry: Bristol Baptist College, 1679–1979* (Bristol, England: n.p., 1979) and the rise of the Particular Baptist Fund. In the missionary context, Andrew Fuller, *A Brief Narrative of the Baptist Mission Society* (London: n.p., 1805); and F.A. Cox, *History of the Baptist Missionary Society, 1792–1842* (London: n.p., 1842) are still good resources.

For the followthrough of organized Baptist voluntarism in the United States, see Robert G. Jones, ed., *Voluntary Associations in a Free Society* (Washington: George Washington University, 1983) for essays by Clarence Goen, "Evangelizing to Beat the Devil: Voluntary Religion in Post-Revolutionary America" (pp. 1–11), which lays the evangelical/ mission imperative as a base; and William H. Brackney, "Dissenter Religion, Voluntary Associations, and the National Vision: Private Education in the Early Republic" (pp. 31–52), which delineates the limits of effective associations as single purpose societies. Robert G. Torbet, *Venture of Faith: The Story of the American Baptist Foreign Mission Society 1814–1954* (Philadelphia: A.B.F.M.S., 1955) is the best account of the founding of the first national society for foreign missions. W.H. Eaton, *Historical Sketch of the Massachusetts Baptist Missionary Society, 1802–1902* (Boston: n.p., 1902) holds the same distinction for domestic endeavor. A small but relevant study is Albert L. Vail,

Mary Webb and the Mother Society (Philadelphia: ABPS, 1914), which traces the formation of the first women's missionary organization among Baptists in the United States. Other single society histories are *The Missionary Jubilee With Commemorative Papers and Discourses* (New York: n.p., 1865); *Baptist Home Missions in North America, 1832–1932* (New York: ABHMS, 1883), Charles L. White, *A Century of Faith* (Philadelphia: ABHMS, 1932); and Daniel G. Stevens, *The First Hundred Years of the American Baptist Publication Society* (Philadelphia: ABPS, 1925).

There are several informative works on specific Baptist associations. A good guide is Walter Shurden, "The Development of Baptist Associations in America, 1707–1814," *Baptist History and Heritage* 4 (1969): 31–39. Of the early local associations, A. D. Gillette, ed., *Minutes of the Philadelphia Baptist Association, 1707–1807* (Philadelphia: ABPS, 1851) is the place to begin. Also useful are George Purefoy, *A History of the Sandy Creek Baptist Association, 1758–1858* (New York: Sheldon, 1859); Lemuel Burkitt and Jesse Read, *A Concise History of the Kehukee Baptist Association* (Philadelphia: A. Hodge, 1850); and Robert G. Torbet, *A Social History of the Philadelphia Baptist Association* (Philadelphia: Westbrook, 1945).

Stronger treatments of the ever-broadening circle of associations are available for state conventions. A good general study is Ellwood L. Goss, "A Survey of the Development of American Baptist State Conventions" (Th.D. thesis, Central Baptist Seminary, 1951). For specific states, the best books are Norman H. Maring, *Baptists in New Jersey: A Study in Transition* (Valley Forge, PA: Judson Press, 1964), Garnet Ryland, *The Baptists of Virginia, 1699–1926* (Richmond: State Convention, 1955); and Albert W. Wardin, *Baptists in Oregon* (Portland, OR: Judson Baptist College, 1969).

For the national bodies, the following are standard: Robert A. Baker, *The Southern Baptist Convention and Its People, 1607–1972* (Nashville, TN: Broadman Press, 1972); Frank H. Woyke, *Heritage and Ministry of the North American Baptist Conference* (Oakbrook Terrace: Conference Press, 1979); Adolf Olson, *A Centenary History* (Chicago: Conference Press, 1952); Peder Stianson, *History of the Norwegian Baptists in America* (Philadelphia: ABPS, 1939); John I. Fredmund, *Seventy-Five Years of Danish Baptist Missionary Work in America* (Philadelphia: ABPS, 1931); and Joseph H. Jackson, *A Story of Christian Activism: History of the National Baptist Convention U.S.A.* (Nashville, TN: Townshend Press, 1980) all treat the basic "convention" model. Different organizational nuances include Norman A. Baxter, *History of the Freewill Baptists: A Study in New England Separatism* (Rochester, NY: ABHS, 1957); to be used with Stephen Marini, *Radical Sects in Revolutionary New England* (Cambridge, MA: Harvard University Press, 1982); James Bailey, *History of the Seventh Day Baptist General Conference, 1802–1865* (Toledo, OH: The Conference, 1866); A.D. Williams, *Memorial of the Free Communion Baptist* (Dover, NH: Morning Star Press, 1873); and John B. Rogers, *The Rogerenes: Some Hitherto Unpublished Journals Belonging to the Colonial History of Connecticut* (Boston: n.p., 1904). The Northern (American) Baptist Convention as a conglomerate of original societies is the subject of W. C. Bitting, ed., *Manual of the Northern Baptist Convention* (New York: n.p., 1918); it is ably analyzed in Robert T. Handy, "American Baptist Polity: What's Happening and Why?" *Baptist History and Heritage* 14 (1979): 12–22; and Paul M. Harrison, *Authority and Power in the Free Church Tradition* (Princeton, NJ: Princeton University Press, 1959). Finally, an international association, the Baptist World Alliance, is chronicled in Carl W. Tiller, *The Twentieth Century Baptist* (Valley Forge, PA: Judson Press, 1980); and Walter Shurden, ed., *The Life of the Baptists in the Life of the World: 80 Years of the Baptist World Alliance* (Nashville, TN: Broadman Press, 1985).

Against the prevailing tide of associationalism among Baptists stood antimissionism and local church protectionism. Primary sources for this tradition include John Taylor, *Thoughts on Missions* (Lexington, KY: n.p., 1819); Cushing B. Hassell, *History of the Church of God from Creation to A. D. 1885* (Middletown, NY: Beebe & Sons, 1886); James R. Graves, *Old Landmarkism: What is It?* (Memphis, TN: Graves, Marks, 1880); and strangely enough, Francis Wayland, *Thoughts on the Missionary Organizations of the Baptist Denomination* (New York: Sheldon, 1859). Among the more penetrating analyses by modern historians are Winthrop S. Hudson, "Stumbling Into Disorder," *Foundations* 1 (1958): 45–72; and Robert T. Handy, "Biblical Primitivism in the American Baptist Tradition" (Paper delivered at Abilene Christian University September, 1985). Doctoral theses worth consulting are Byron C. Lambert, "Rise of the Anti-mission Baptists: Sources and Leaders 1800–1840" (Univ. of Chicago, 1957); C. Bezerra, "Sources and History of the Antimissionary Controversy in the United States 1814–40" (Southern Seminary, 1956). Also see the published essays, Harry I. Poe, "The History of Antimissionary Baptists," *The Chronicle* 2 (1939): 51–64; and Ira Hudgins, "The Antimissionary Controversy Among Baptists," *The Chronicle* 14 (1951): 147–164.

RELIGIOUS LIBERTY

The literature on religious liberty is among the most extensive of any area of Protestant and dissenter studies. Since the Baptist struggle for liberty is part of a larger course of events, it is best to begin with general sources. E. B. Underhill, *An Historical Survey of Controversies Pertaining to the Rights of Conscience from the English Reformation to the Settlement of New England* (New York: Hanserd Knollys Society, 1851) is a good summary of the major events in Elizabethan and Stuart England, if one allows for a broader use of the term "baptist" than would be the case today. Underhill's companion volume, *Tracts on Liberty of Conscience* (London: Hanserd Knollys Society, 1846) lays great stress on Roger Williams's contribution. A more modern work that explains the foundation for toleration in the sixteenth century and that summarizes all the literature is W. K. Jordan, *The Development of Religious Toleration in England,* 4 vols. (Cambridge, MA: Harvard University Press, 1932); Benjamin Brook, *The History of Religious Liberty from the First Propagation of Christianity in Britain to the Death of George III* (London: n.p., n.d.) emphasizes the eighteenth century and contains a plea for toleration. There is a helpful section entitled "Arminian Baptists" that discusses John Smyth and Thomas Helwys in T. Lyon, *The Theory of Religious Liberty in England 1603–39* (Cambridge, England: Cambridge University Press, 1937); as does Stephen B. Nutter, *The Story of the Cambridge Baptists and the Struggle for Religious Liberty* (Cambridge, England: Cambridge University Press, 1912). The best treatment of liberal theory is Russell Smith, *Religious Liberty under Charles II and James II* (Cambridge, England: Cambridge University Press, 1911).

Of course, it is important to consult the actual English literature on the subject. Two guides are H. Leon McBeth, "English Baptist Literature on Religious Liberty to 1689" (Unpublished Th. D. thesis, Southwestern Baptist Seminary, 1961); and A. D. Lindsay, ed., *Puritanism and Liberty; Being the Army Debates 1647–49 from the Clarke Manuscript* (Chicago: University of Chicago Press, 1951). The major Baptist tracts are: Thomas Helwys, *The Mystery of Iniquity* (n.p., 1612); Leonard Busher, *Religions Peace or a*

Plea for Liberty of Conscience (n.p., 1614); Christopher Blackwood, *The Storming of Antichrist* (n.p., 1644); John Murton, *A Most Humble Supplication* (n.p., 1620); William Dell, *The Way of True Peace and Unity Among the Faithful and Churches of Christ* (n.p., 1649); Samuel Richardson, *The Necessity of Toleration in Matters of Religion* (n.p., 1647); Samuel Richardson, *Liberty of Conscience Asserted* (n.p., 1649); Thomas Collier, *The Decision and Clearing of the Great Point Now in Controversy* (n.p., 1659); Henry Danvers, *Certain Quaeries* (n.p., 1649).

On the American scene, the classic, Anson P. Stokes, 3 vols., *Church and State in the United States* (New York: Harper & Row, 1950) still contains more helpful documentation than any other source. Stokes distinguishes between "separation," "liberty," and "toleration" and presents the relevant letters, laws, and representative documents. On a regional basis, M. Louise Greene, *The Development of Religious Liberty in Connecticut* (Boston: n.p., 1905); and Charles F. James, *Documentary History of the Struggle for Religious Liberty in Virginia* (Lynchburg, VA: n.p., 1900) are well-framed. As noted earlier, William G. McLoughlin, *New England Dissent, 1630–1833,* 2 vols. (Cambridge, MA: Harvard University Press, 1971) presents a telling case for the "pluralism of dissent" of which Baptists, Quakers, Rogerenes, and sabbatarians were all parts.

Baptists are proud of their contribution to religious freedom and have written extensively on the subject. In the seventeenth century, John Clarke's *Ill Newes from New England* (London: n.p., 1652) was powerful; the following century, Isaac Backus, *An Appeal to the Public for Religious Liberty Against the Oppressions of the Present Day* (Boston: John Boyle, 1773) was likewise. In the nineteenth century, John Dowling, *Soul Liberty* (Boston: Lewis Colby, 1853) kept the case alive, followed by a more reflective Sewall S. Cutting, *Baptists and Religious Liberty* (New York: Randolph & Co., 1876) in the Centennial era; and the scholarly Albert H. Newman, *Liberty of Conscience: A Fundamental Baptist Principle* (Toronto: n.p., 1883).

More recently, the leadership of the Baptist Joint Committee on Public Affairs has produced Joseph M. Dawson, *America's Way in Church, State, and Society* (New York: Macmillan, 1953); and *Baptists and the American Republic* (Nashville, TN: Broadman Press, 1956); plus a Bicentennial compendium, James E. Wood, *Baptists and the American Experience* (Valley Forge, PA: Judson Press, 1976); which contains essays by Baptist leaders across confessional lines.

The historical community has found interest in religious liberty for well over a century. Early examples include George C. Lorimer, *The Great Conflict: A Discourse Concerning Baptists and Religious Liberty* (Boston: Lee & Shepherd, 1877); Henry S. Burrage, "The Contest for Religious Liberty in Massachusetts," *Church History* (1894). In the last generation, Lewis P. Little, *Imprisoned Preachers and Religious Liberty in Va.* (Lynchburg, VA: J.P. Bell, 1938) introduced new characters to the saga of persecution. Winthrop S. Hudson reexamined "The Theological Basis for Religious Freedom," *Journal of Church and State* 3 (1961), pp. 130–136; while Robert T. Handy produced *The American Tradition of Religious Freedom: An Historical Analysis* (New York: National Conference of Christians and Jews, 1965) and Glenn T. Miller wrote for the Bicentennial, *Religious Liberty in America: History and Prospects* (Philadelphia: Westminister Press, 1976). William G. McLoughlin showed just how far Baptists were willing to go in "Massive Civil Disobedience as a Baptist Tactic in 1773," *American Quarterly* 21 (1969): 710–28; as Franklin Littell examined "Religious Liberty and Missions," *Journal of Church and State* 7 (1965): 374–87; an important contribution, considering the Baptist proclivity toward foreign missions. Miner S. Bates, *Religious Liberty: An Inquiry* (London: n.p.,

1945) surveyed for the International Missionary Council just how the issue shaped up on a global basis at the end of World War II.

No treatment of Baptists and liberty is adequate without a large consideration of Roger Williams, John Clarke, and Isaac Backus. Samuel H. Brockunier, *Roger Williams, The Irrepressible Democrat* (New York: Ronald Press, 1940) called Williams the "father of democracy and foremost egalitatian"; Perry Miller, *Roger Williams: His Contribution to the American Tradition* (Indianapolis: Bobbs Merrill, 1953) limits Williams to a church-dominated world. Likewise, Cyclone Covey, *The Gentle Radical: A Biography of Roger Williams* (New York: Macmillan, 1966) suggests the importance of Puritan influences; James E. Ernst, *The Political Thought of Roger Williams* (Seattle: University of Washington Press, 1966), argues for the context of medieval corporation law in his theories of church and state. Rounding out this portrait of Williams are Edwin Gaustad's "separating the saint from worldliness" as the basis of separation of church and state, in "Roger Williams and the Principle of Separation," *Foundations* 1 (1958): 55–64; and Leroy Moore's challenge of Backus's view of Williams, by asserting that Williams actually had little impact on American revolutionary ideology in "Religious Liberty: Roger Williams and the Revolutionary Era" *Church History* 34 (1965): 57–76. A seven volume set, *The Complete Writings of Roger Williams* (New York: Macmillan, 1963) contains the original pagination of all the relevant primary sources.

Rhode Island's other libertarian is less well treated. Wilbur Nelson, *The Hero of Aquidneck* (New York: Fleming H. Revell, 1938) has too long claimed Clarke as a source for Thomas Jefferson; William G. McLoughlin, *New England Dissent* (Cambridge, MA: Harvard University Press), sees Clarke as arrogant and blunt. Somewhere between these poles of opinion are George Selement, "John Clarke and the Struggle for Separation of Church and State" *Foundations* 15 (1972): 111–26, in which Clarke called for "a government which would foster religious sincerity"; and Bryant R. Nobles, "John Clarke's Political Theory," *Foundations* 13 (1970): 221–37, who calls Clarke the "pre-eminent liberal" who opposed all forms of tradition and the status quo.

Isaac Backus has seen a resurrection among the historians. In the oldest biography, Alvah Hovey, *Memoir of the Rev. Isaac Backus* (Boston: Gould & Lincoln, 1858) Backus is the leading champion of religious liberty. Years later, T. B. Maston in *Isaac Backus* (Rochester, N.Y.: ABHS, 1962) found that Backus was more keenly a Congregationalist than a Baptist, thanks to his view of the Christian state. William G. McLoughlin, *Isaac Backus and the American Pietistic Tradition* (Chicago: University of Chicago Press, 1969), saw the preacher as the embodiment of radical pietism and evangelicalism, for whom religious liberty was the natural conclusion for individual, voluntary religion. Recently, Stanley Grenz, *Isaac Backus: Puritan and Baptist* (Macon, GA: Mercer University Press, 1983) controverts both Maston and McLoughlin as too conservative on Backus and sees Backus as a comprehensive Protestant, Puritan, then Baptist, and among the most progressive thinkers of his era. Backus's voluminous and articulate papers were edited by William G. McLoughlin, *Diary of Isaac Backus,* 3 vols. (Providence, RI: Brown University Press, 1979).

RECENT STUDIES

In addition to the categories listed above, within the last five years a wide variety of scholars has made major advances in Baptist studies. New surveys of Baptist groups include Nancy T. Ammerman, *Southern Baptists Observed: Multiple Perspectives on a*

Changing Denomination (Knoxville: University of Tennessee Press, 1993); Don A. Sanford, *A Choosing People: A History of Seventh Day Baptists* (Nashville: Broadman Press, 1992); Paul N. Tassell, *Quest for Faithfulness: The Account of a Unique Fellowship of Churches* (Chicago: Regular Baptist Press, 1991). R. Paul Drummond, *A Portion for the Singers: A History of Music Among Primitive Baptists Since 1800* (Atwood, TN: Christian Baptist Publications, 1989) exploits the ethos of the difficulty to document tradition. George A. Rawlyk, *Champions of the Truth: Fundamentalism, Modernism, and the Maritime Baptists* (Montreal: McGill-Queens University Press, 1990) provides a different perspective on Baptist fundamentalism in Canada. Helpful to students of Canadian Baptist history is J. K. Zeman et al., eds., *Baptists in Canada: 1760–1990: A Bibliography of Selected Printed Resources in English* (Hantsport: Lancelot Press, 1989).

Important themes have been traced. A volume of good general use for theology and polity is Charles W. Derweese, *Baptist Church Covenants* (Nashville: Broadman Press, 1990). Likewise, a reference tool, specifically focused, is Paul R. Dekar, *For the Healing of the Nations: Baptist Peacemakers* (Macon, GA: Smith and Helwys, 1993). On the church-state theme, Robert T. Handy has surveyed the issue at the turn of the century in *Undermined Establishment: Church-State Relations in America 1880–1920* (Princeton: Princeton University Press, 1991) and William Estep has analyzed the U.S. constitution in *Revolution Within the Revolution: The First Amendment in Historical Context* (Grand Rapids: Eerdmans, 1990). A thematically related biography of excellence is Edwin S. Gaustad, *Liberty of Conscience: Roger Williams in America* (Grand Rapids: Eerdmans, 1990). An interesting sidelight on Baptist patriotism in the United States is John W. Baer, *The Pledge of Allegiance: A Centennial History 1892–1992* (Annapolis, MD: private printing, 1992).

The black Baptist tradition has been substantially enriched with Clayborne Carson, ed., *The Papers of Martin Luther King, Jr., Vol. I, Called to Serve, 1929–1951* (Berkeley: University of California Press, 1991), Peter J. Paris, *Black Religious Leaders: Conflict in Unity* (Louisville: Westminster/John Knox Press, 1991), Wyatt T. Walker, *Spirits That Dwell in Deep Woods III: The Prayer and Praise Hymns of the Black Religious Experience* (New York: Martin Luther King Fellows Press, 1991), Walter F. Pitts, *Old Ship of Zion: The Afro-Baptist Ritual in the African Diaspora* (New York: Oxford University Press, 1993), J. M. Gaskin, *Black Baptists in Oklahoma* (Oklahoma City: Messenger Press, 1992), and Evelyn B. Higginbotham, *Righteous Discontent: The Women's Movement in the Black Baptist Church, 1880–1920* (Cambridge: Harvard University Press, 1993). Two popular biographical works on black Baptists are: E. B. Hicks, *I Couldn't Quit: Autobiography* (Kansas City: Jesus Loves You Publishing Co., 1992) and Grant Gordon, *From Slavery to Freedom: The Life of David George, Pioneer Black Baptist Minister* (Hantsport: Lancelot Press, 1992).

Four books focus on early Baptist development. For primary sources, consult S. L. Copson, *Association Life of the Particular Baptists of Northern England, 1699–1732* (London: Baptist Historical Society, 1991), and *Church Book: St. Andrews Street Baptist Church, Cambridge, 1720–1832* (London: Baptist Historical Society, 1991). Stephen Brachlow's doctoral dissertation is now available as *The Communion of Saints: Radical Puritan and Separatist Ecclesiology, 1570–1625* (New York: Oxford University Press, 1988); on the seventeenth-century period, Particular Baptist leadership is the subject of B. A. Ramsbottom, *The Life of William Kiffin* (Harpenden: Gospel Standard Trust Publications, 1989).

Studies that go beyond North America and worth noting are David Lagergren, *Am-*

biguous Advance: History of the Baptist Union of Sweden (Orebro: Libris Media, 1989); Kornel Gyori, *Let Us Investigate Our Ways: A History of Hungarian Baptists During the Stalinist Era* (Budapest: Bekhnirnok Press, 1990); Sunil Chatterjee, *Felix Carey: A Tiger Tamed* (Hoogly: 1991); Richard K. Moore, editor, *Baptists of Western Australia: The First Ninety Years* (Bentley: Baptist Historical Society, 1992); F. Calvin Parker, *The Southern Baptist Mission in Japan, 1889–1989* (Lanham: University Press of America, 1990); George H. Kircher, *Punching Holes in the Darkness: 50 Year History of Baptist Mid-Missions in Brazil* (Cleveland: Baptist Mid-Missions, 1991); and Warren P. Mild, *Howard Malcolm and the Great Mission Advance* (Valley Forge: American Baptist Churches, 1988) on American Baptist overseas mission strategies in the nineteenth century. Lynn E. May, *A Bibliography of Histories of BWA Member Bodies Other Than USA* (Nashville: Historical Commission, 1991) is a good guide to international Baptist organizations.

Finally, the bicentennial of the first Baptist missionary society is the thrust of Brian Stanley, *The History of the Baptist Missionary Society, 1792–1992* (Edinburgh: T & T Clark, 1992); a focus on the longer heritage of the BMS are in William H. Brackney, "The Baptist Missionary Society in Proper Context: Some Reflections on the Larger Voluntary Religious Tradition" in *Baptist Quarterly* XXXIV:8 (October, 1992), 364–378. T. Bassett's *The Baptists in Wales and the Baptist Missionary Society* (Ilston: Baptist Union, 1991) and James R. Beck, *Dorothy Carey: The Tragic and Untold Story of Mrs. William Carey* (Grand Rapids: Baker Book House, 1992) round out a spate of popular literature on Carey, Baptists, and missions.

INDEX

About the Author

WILLIAM H. BRACKNEY is Principal and Professor of Historical Theology at McMaster Divinity College in Hamilton, Ontario. The author of four books and contributor to numerous scholarly publications in Baptist and North American religious history, Dr. Brackney is Chairman of the Division of Study and Research of the Baptist World Alliance. His education includes degrees from the University of Maryland, Eastern Baptist Theological Seminary, and Temple University, where he received his doctorate in history and religion.